April 2000

Nextarchitects maakt een jongensdroo[m]

'an onze verslaggever
{EN MAANDAG

ROTTERDAM – Het idee ontstond tijdens wat loze lunchuurtjes, toen ze [a]e Technische Universiteit] n Delft met z'n vieren een [a]telier volgden. Ach, iedereen heeft wel eens van die gesprekken. Beetje dagdromen, beetje filosoferen over onalledaagse projecten en dan vervolgens weer met beide benen op de grond. Het gespreksonderwerp van toen: wat is nou eens iets echt fantastisch om te doen? Wat begon met een reisplannetje voor Brazilië groeide uit tot een omvangrijke wereldreis.

De eerste ingeving van de vier jonge architecten was: op naar Brazilië. Daar gebeurt nogal wat op het gebied van architectuur. Groot land, grote steden. Echt een bestemming om als je jong, aanstormend architect inspiratie op te doen, onderzoek te verrichten, de praktijk van de grootstedelijke problematiek aan den lijve te ondervinden.

Maar Brazilië alléén geeft natuurlijk geen compleet beeld van stedelijkheid en hedendaagse metropolitane ontwikkelingen. Daarvoor zou je eigenlijk ook in andere steden moeten kijken. Niet alleen in Zuid-Amerika, maar ook in Europa, Azië, en als we dan toch bezig zijn, Afrika, Noord-Amerika. Zo ontstond langzamerhand een plan.

Tijdschema
Met als lichtend voorbeeld Phineas Fogg, de wereldreiziger die in de fantasie van Jules

Bart Reuser, architect
John van de Water, architect
Marijn Schenk, architect
Michel Schreinemachers, architect

□ Nextarchitects voor de nieuwbouw in Amsterdam. V.l.n.r. Bart Reuser, Michel Schreinemachers, John van de Water en Marijn Schenk.
Foto GPD/Emiel van

Wereldreis van 125 dagen mondt uit in 12.500 foto's voor expositie

mee. De meest draagkrac[htige] gen vertrekken uit de sta[d, de] negatieve kanten blijven [...]. De scheidslijnen worden [...] hard.

In Johannesburg zie je al de wolkenkrabbers in be[ton] zijn genomen door de ha[ve-] nots, de kampvuren bran[den] er achter het spiegelglas [...]

March 2001

JvdW

October 2004

Zhou Huan, architect

Mr Xia, architect

JvdW

October 2004

Professor Deng

Mr Xia, architect

November 2004

Mr Chen, architect
Mr Jiang, architect
JvdW
Mrs Hu, CEO

March 2005

Mr Yang, director
Mr Ding, director
Mrs Hu, CEO
JvdW
Mr Chen, architect

May 2005
Building site of Shangdi International Plaza, Beijing

August 2005
Marijn Schenk, architect
Mr Xie, architect
Mr Lu, architect
Michel Schreinemachers, architect

February 2006

Mr Jiang, architect

JvdW

November 2006

Michel van Tilborg, architect

Laz Çilingir, architect

Donna Riedel, architect

Wopke Schaafstal, architect

Thijs Klinkhamer, architect

March 2007

Mr Zheng, feng shui expert

May 2007

Mr Ma, model maker

Model of IBM China R&D head office

November 2007

Ms Song, architect
Mr Zhen, architect
Ms Liu, graphics
Ms Tu, assistant
Mr Lu, architect
Mr Guo, architect
Ms Wang, graphics
Mr Yang, architect
Ms He, marketing
Ms Yu, graphics
Ms Su, graphics
Mr Li, architect
JvdW
Mr Chen, architect
Mr Jiang, architect
Wopke Schaafstal, architect
Ms Lu, assistant
Bob de Graaf, architect

March 2008

Ms Jia, project assistant

JvdW

Mr Liu, project manager for contractor

April 2008

Mr Liang, project manager for client

Mr Ma, project manager of curtain wall company

Elevation mockup 1:5

December 2007
Building site of IBM China R&D head office, Beijing

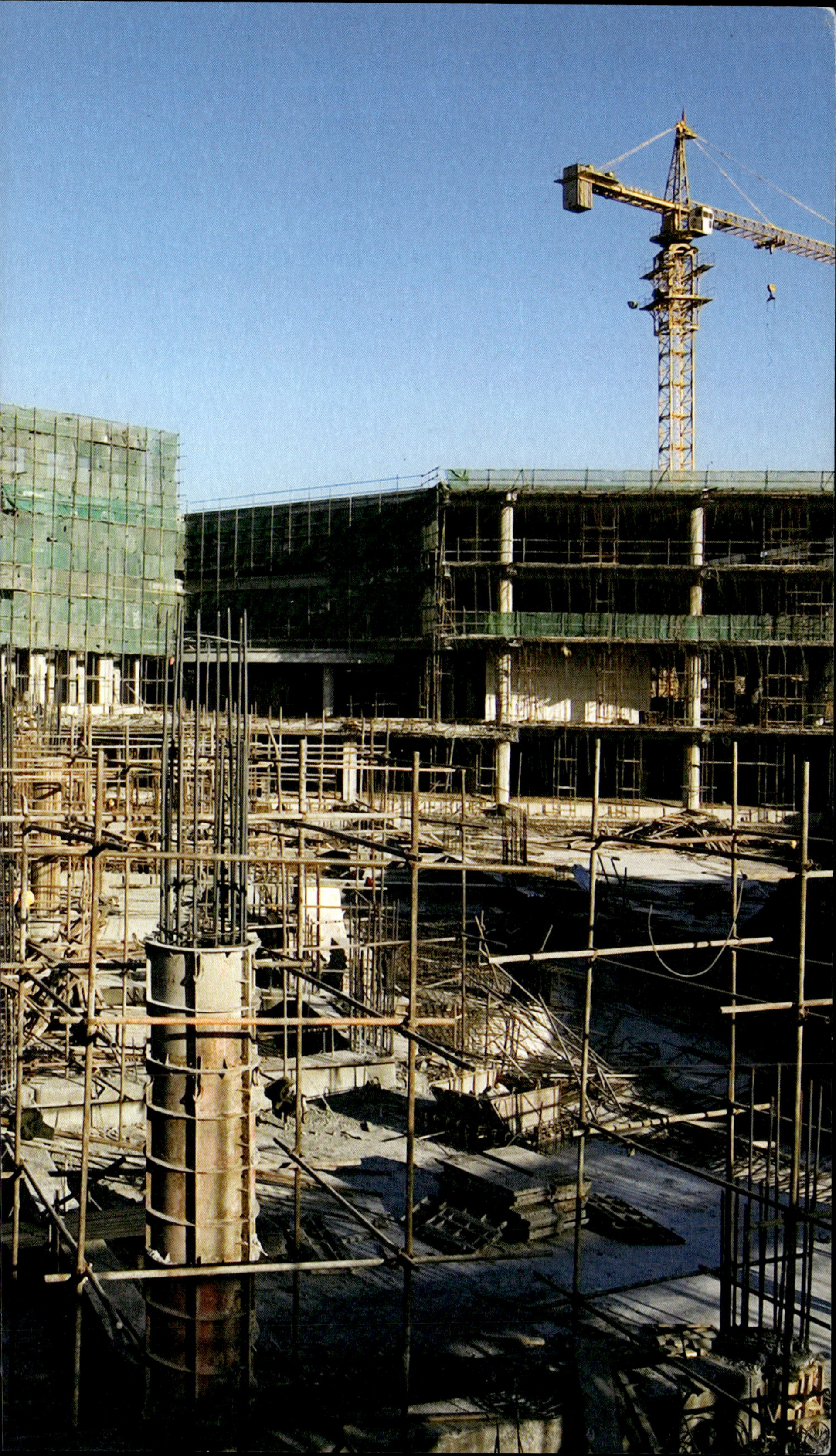

September 2008

Mrs Ye, project manager for client

JvdW

Mr Zhao, architect

October 2008

Mr Ma, vice-general manager for client

JvdW

Mrs Jiang, entrepreneur

Mr Zhang, director of Design Institute

May 2009

JvdW

Ms Xia, Chinese teacher

September 2009

Mr Guo, client

Mr Wu, contractor

Mr Wen, project assistant for contractor

Mr Chen, architect

Mr Zhu, project manager for client

October 2008

Mr Wen, engineer
Mr Tao, intern
Ms Wang, graphics
Ms Wang, architect
Mr Liu, intern
Ms Yu, intern
Ms Li, architect
Mr Zhao, architect
Ms Yan, architect
Mr Guo, architect
Ms Yao, architect
Ms Liu, assistent
Mr Li, HR
Ms Du, administration
Ms Du, PR
Mr Bai, planner
Mrs Liang, engineer
Ms Wang, marketing

Mr Yao, engineer
Mr Wang, 3-D graphics
Mr Gu, engineer
Mr Song, engineer
Mr Lu, architect
Mrs Guo, planner
Ms Yan, architect
Mr Zhen, engineer
Ms Tu, assistant
Ms Shi, marketing
Ms Zhang, PR
Mr Shi, model maker

March 2010

尔多斯东胜区20⁺10项目签字仪

JvdW

Mr Wang, client for government

November 2010

Mr Jiang, architect

Mr Huang, director

Fuzhou City Government

December 2010

JvdW

Mr Jiang, architect

June 2011

JvdW

Ms Zhao, interviewer for CCTV

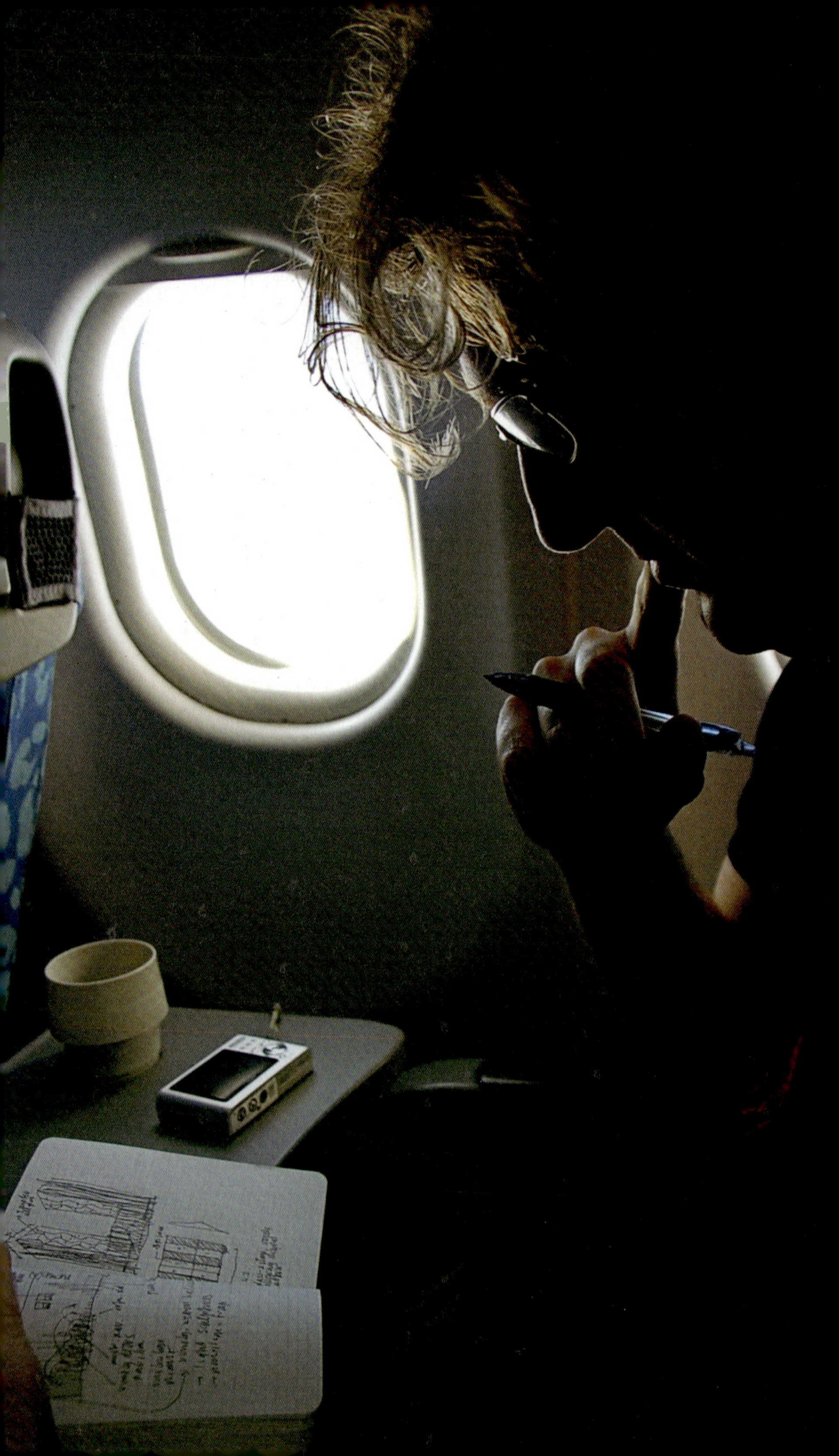

You Can't Change China, China Changes You

JOHN VAN DE WATER

010 Publishers, Rotterdam 2012

Preface *19*
1. Intuition *21*
2. Dialogue *67*
3. Freedom *141*
4. Synergy *165*
5. Vision *192*
6. Reflection *229*
   Epilogue *250*

Preface

'BUT ... WHERE DO YOU BEGIN?'
Rotterdam, Netherlands Architecture Institute, 2008

'What's the secret?' The Dutch architect looked at me impatiently. His second question followed in the same breath: 'How does NEXT manage to get so much built in China?!'
He had already approached me before the lecture 'about the possibilities in China'. And before posing these questions at the conclusion, he had already summarized my lecture by deliberating out loud: 'Architecture in China ... What risks. But what opportunities!'
I smiled and replied: 'There is no secret.' The second part of my answer visibly disappointed him: 'And there isn't a manual or anything like that.'
'But ... where do you begin? So where are you to begin as a Western architect?!'
I thought about it. My own search for an answer to this question flashed through my mind.
Then I concluded out loud: 'I found the beginning in myself.'

You Can't Change China, China Changes You is the story behind this conclusion. Far from seeking to be a manual, it describes a Westerner's quest in China for an architecture embedded in Chinese values and developed on the basis of contemporary Chinese conditions. It is a quest for an architecture made both for China and in China – a quest that would ultimately change me and my ideas on architecture for good.

1. Intuition

QINGDAO

October 2004, 7 o'clock in the morning. It was my first week in Beijing and the telephone went.

'Hi John, how are you? It's Huan. Are you busy?'

An hour later I was standing next to Huan in a small, dark cubicle in the basement of the Faculty of Architecture at one of the most renowned universities of technology in China. The cubicle measured about twelve square metres and was stacked with computers. People had unquestionably been working overtime there for days on end. The air was thick with the smell of sweat, and Chinese youngsters, stretched out in front of the computers, stared with sleepy eyes at the screens. Cigarette smoke rose from ashtrays filled to the brim. Food scraps and empty noodle packing lay everywhere.

A small Chinese man manoeuvred through the stack of computers in our direction. As he did so, he attempted impatiently to keep his eyes on the computer screens. He greeted us heartily in Chinese, turned around, said something to someone at one of the computers and turned back to us to apologize in Chinese. He looked at us with tired eyes.

Huan introduced me to Mr Xia, who with renewed energy cordially greeted me once again in Chinese. Mr Xia immediately put his hand in his jacket pocket, pulled out a small pile of business cards and gave one to me with two hands accompanied by a little bow. I sought in one of my pockets, discovered my business cards and repeated the gesture. While he studied my card, I studied his. From the combination of Chinese and English on his card I understood that he was a PhD student. Through Huan, who translated his Chinese into English, Mr Xia told me his story.

For three weeks, Mr Xia had been occupied full-time on a large project for the Olympic Games in Beijing. The project consisted of four stadiums, a conference centre and a residential district, about

1,200,000 square metres in all. The site was in Qingdao, a city with around seven million inhabitants on the Chinese coast, a little more than an hour's flight from Beijing. It was a project in the context of an international architectural competition. Initially, 'they' were to collaborate with a 'famous' Canadian architectural office, but, according to Mr Xia, the collaboration had 'unfortunately never really got going' and had proved 'difficult'. And now 'they' were desperately seeking a Canadian architect who could hold the presentation for them.

Inquisitive eyes looked at me: would I take on that role?

In the taxi to the university, Huan had partly informed me about what I could expect there. I knew that I would be asked if I would be prepared to present a project for 'a friend'? Rather naively I had asked him why I, as an outsider, was needed. He had smilingly limited his response to: 'Because the foreign moon is rounder than the Chinese moon.'

I was of two minds. To a Dutch architect like myself, his request was contrary to my idea of professional integrity. Without giving him a definite answer, I first asked if I could have any influence on the design. My question surprised him and he seemed to recognize more advantages than disadvantages in the idea. 'No problem!' he simply reacted. That, too, didn't wholly comply with my Dutch notion of integrity: how could he decide so easily here, without consulting the Chinese architect responsible?

What Huan hadn't told me in the taxi was that I was to represent a Canadian architectural office. And what I also didn't know was that it would involve four stadiums, a conference centre and a residential district totalling some 1,200,000 square metres. We had never worked on such large briefs in the Netherlands. And we had had no experience with that type of project. The idea of consenting was as tempting as it was unsettling, especially when the last piece of information emerged: the presentation was to be held the following day, in Qingdao.

Temptation won. In the whole surreal scenario I saw a huge opportunity to gain experience. I looked at Mr Xia and, without hesitation, I replied to Huan 'No problem!' Two enormous grins appeared spontaneously. Mr Xia combined his grin with an uncomfortable shaking of my hand and seemed to have decided never ever to let go.

'May I see the design?' I asked, grinning in turn.

We moved past the screens and I was told that the guys manning the computers were from a 'rendering company'. Renderings – presentation drawings generated on the computer – were important links in the negotiation process in Chinese building projects. Mr Xia asked the guys to display the renderings. I was surprised by the dramatic perspectives and astonishing sunsets. The stadiums looked like curious attention-grabbers. I had only been in Beijing for a week. A fresh and unadulterated Westerner, I asked for concepts, strategies, a position, that sort of thing. Large eyes stared at me and at first there was no response at all. Huan reacted uncomfortably with the translation of a remark by Mr Xia: 'Qingdao lies on the coast, that is why the stadiums resemble large fish.'

'How can I justify that during a presentation?' I thought immediately, and the face I pulled must have spoken volumes.

One rendering was ready, on one of the computers at the back of the cubicle. The render boy summoned Mr Xia, who was only too pleased to escape the uncomfortable situation. The three of us looked at the rendering and Mr Xia exclaimed 'Yesss!!!' He threw his arms in the air accompanied by a second 'Yesss!!!'. The render boy looked proud and happy at the same time.

We manoeuvred to another computer and Mr Xia showed me designs for completely different stadiums. Via Huan he said that this was the submission from the first round. To me, these designs appeared to bear no relationship whatsoever to the designs they were currently working on, and I wondered why they weren't elaborating the designs that had got them through the first round. So, via Huan, I asked about the relationship between the two plans. Without waiting for an answer I declared that, in the Netherlands, the second round involved a more concrete elaboration of the ideas displayed in the first. However, without translating the question for the benefit of Mr Xia, Huan stated with a smile: 'Chinese clients like to choose.' Huan continued by asking whether I had any suggestions for improving the new design.

I looked around the cubicle and saw the fatigued eyes of the boys from the rendering company. I compared the design from the first round with that from the second. The design had nothing in common with what our office, NEXT, stood for. But this was not a NEXT project and I would not be representing NEXT. I briefly considered a last-ditch attempt to try to make it a NEXT project. But the presentation was the following day; there was simply not enough time.

'No, don't change a thing', I replied. Mr Xia again began to shake my hand.

When Huan and I took our leave of him, he walked with us quite a distance through the long corridor towards the exit. When he turned back, I looked round to see him go. He didn't walk back to the cubicle, he ran.

The next morning I showed the taxi driver the handwritten note bearing the address where we were to meet. The driver nodded and drove off with an air of concentration. I lived near the West Third Ring Road, and the small red Xiali drove across Beijing's ring roads to the North Fourth Ring Road. The high-rise buildings flashed past us and I tried to recall what Beijing used to look like.

Years ago, as NEXT, we had visited Beijing for the first time. When we arrived in the evening and looked out of the plane window, the city was practically unlit. We visited Beijing as a part of a photographic study of the changing appearance of world metropolises; in the preceding weeks I had visited Moscow, Mumbai, New Delhi, Singapore, Kuala Lumpur, Hong Kong, the Pearl River Delta and Shanghai. It was an overwhelming experience. Chinese cities in particular had conjured up a feverish energy in me. There seemed to be so much going on in China, and even more at stake. But despite this positive idea, the first impression of Beijing, the unlit capital of the Middle Kingdom, promised very little.

When we visited the city after the first night in our courtyard hotel, Beijing in the winter turned out to be as cold as ice. Smog irritated my throat, and the pungent odour of the many coal-fired heaters hung heavily in the streets. The air was dry and there were no colours: Beijing was grey. Endless variations of grey in the streets, on the façades of the buildings, in the clothes – even the sky was mostly grey. This impression was strengthened by the absence of green: all the trees were leafless.

We visited many corners of the city, on hired bikes, walking, in taxis and by public transport. We got lost in the *hutongs*, the old structure of alleyways and courtyard houses, and visited with some disapproval the alternative, the white modern high-rise blocks in park-like compounds. We looked down on the city from the tallest tower and visited an 'underground city', built on the orders of Mao with an eye to a possible nuclear war with the West. We found the most recent building projects, all of which seemed to be the victim of a limited choice of materials: tiles. We stared for ages at the first high-rise projects that had been realized in Beijing: all the towers had been allocated a temple-like peak. They seemed to be the first results of a quest for a new, modern Chinese architecture, where the architect hadn't progressed beyond a radical combination of building typologies: a Western type of tower and a traditional Chinese temple type of roof.

From every point of view, Beijing seemed to have advanced less far or to have found less direction in terms of modernization than other cities had done, such as Guangzhou, Shenzhen or Shanghai, which we had visited in the previous weeks. An erstwhile correspondent of a Dutch newspaper put Beijing's development in perspective by informing us of its recent history. People in China worked six days a week; the idea of leisure didn't exist at that time. By no means every family in Beijing had a television, and people generally went to bed early so as to practise shadow boxing, *taijiquan*, early the next morning, especially on the free, seventh day. The *danwei* or work unit was the central focus of life. This was where the public showers, clinic, meeting place and dining hall were located, with a film show on Friday evenings. The *danwei* organized work, food, housing, recreation and education. The correspondent concluded: 'People were owned by the *danwei*, as it were, which had authority over marriage, the right to divorce and education.'

Five years after that visit, a new Beijing now whizzed past. Tiled buildings had made way for miscellaneous forms and new material use. LED façades shouted out their messages, every new building demanded attention, new abutted old, high embraced low.

    My thoughts were interrupted by the taxi driver stopping at a junction and making it clear to me, in a combination of Chinese and sign language, that we had reached our destination. The taxi disappeared into the traffic, whereupon I looked round the junction but couldn't see any of my travelling companions. I tried to suppress the notion that I had got out at the wrong place. Exactly at that moment, Huan came running up, and a car of a type I didn't know mounted the pavement. Mr Xia was at the wheel and an older woman was sitting in the back. Huan directed me to the front passenger seat and the woman was introduced to me as Professor Deng. Huan mentioned that she was Mr Xia's professor. I looked at her and greeted her again in a friendly way. She responded heartily in Chinese and the business-card custom took place in the car, albeit with some difficulty.

There was a silence, and I asked Huan what we were waiting for. He told me that the scale model, panels and project books still had to be delivered. Not long after that, several more cars mounted the pavement, our boot lid was opened and a box containing a scale model measuring 1.2 by 2 metres was thrust into the car. The box practically propelled Professor Deng onto the front seat and I insisted that I should take her place. However, everyone assured me that I was the guest and therefore I was obliged to remain in the front seat. After Huan's argument that foreigners have longer legs, I conceded, even if it was purely because of the fact that we were already under way.

The traffic was against us. We needed a little more than an hour to get from the North Fourth Ring Road to the airport, which was about thirty kilometres to the north-east. Mr Xia became increasingly agitated with the slow traffic. We drove in the emergency lane for the last kilometre. 'Will we make it?' I asked Huan. 'No problem,' he assured me, after which he stated with a smile: 'This is China!'

Parking at an angle, we unloaded everything at the airport. Hectic moments followed, during which looked for luggage trolleys and the check-in desk. Our scale model turned out to be too big and had to be checked in as excess baggage. Eventually we passed in chaotic fashion through the security controls and walked straight onto the plane.

It was a little more than an hour's flight to Qingdao and while Mr Xia and Professor Deng slept, I asked Huan how this project was organized. Huan told me that projects like this were typical of a university. In addition to giving regular education, professors also had their own architectural offices where students worked directly in everyday practice. 'Studying during the day, working at night', he joked. PhD students were responsible for the projects and thus earned 'a little extra'.

I tried to get a discussion going about the value of academic assignments in relation to real-life practice, but it failed to take off. I then asked him if I could see the presentation of 'our project' and he answered: 'Later, no problem!'

Having arrived in Qingdao we were picked up with great cordiality by Mr Jia, an old friend of Mr Xia. Grinning broadly, he shook my one outstretched hand with both of his. While the scale model was being loaded, Mr Jia said that the presentation had been moved back a day. Huan mentioned en passant that we would therefore be staying in Qingdao overnight. No one reacted much to this news, so I didn't either. Having checked into a hotel, we were invited to lunch by Mr Jia. Huan smiled, we would go to the 'most famous' fish restaurant in Qingdao. The mood at the table was elated, drink flowed abundantly and there were constant toasts and laughter. Professor Deng and Mr Xia caught up on some sleep during the rest of the afternoon while Huan and I went into the town.

Qingdao turned out to be a misty city, right on the coast and full of historical buildings dating from the time when Germans had settled there. This was also the first time that Huan had visited this city and we were both intrigued by the way in which the old German architecture had acquired new significance as a result of Chinese adaptations and additions. Despite all this, I couldn't really take in the city, being too preoccupied with the coming presentation. At one of the city vantage points I asked Huan if he knew when the presentation would take place. Huan said with a neutral expression that this wasn't known yet.

That evening we were invited over to Mr Jia's home. He lived in a winding street with houses on the edge of the sea. His house was large and was partly used as a studio. The interior was filled with art: paintings, figures and objects. In the studio I was introduced to Ms Yu, a slight girl who worked for Mr Jia. Not long after that I learned from Huan that Mr Jia was an artist, but one in the broadest sense of the word; Mr Jia also 'dealt' in buildings and 'bits of city'.

Mr Jia stood next to Huan, who translated, and Mr Jia grinned just as he had done during our first acquaintance. Via Huan, he went on to say that he was a good friend of one of the mayors of Qingdao. This had made it 'easier' for us to take part in the second round of this competition. He had also shown the jury 'our design' on 'several occasions' so as 'to be able to improve it'. His smile became even wider when he confirmed that the jury was very pleased with our design.

We sat in the double-height living room with a view out across the sea. As Mr Jia was pouring more red wine, the doorbell rang. He went to open the door and I asked Huan if he also had the idea that there was something wrong with the wine. Huan, who had studied in Paris for two years, told me that the Chinese *nouveau riche* enjoyed embracing new things from the West but often didn't know how to cope with these 'novelties'. He confirmed my suspicion: the bottle of wine had been opened quite some time ago.

Mr Jia came back excitedly with two A0 panels bearing two dramatic renderings of what most resembled a greatly magnified fish. Grinning, he told us that, just to be on the safe side, he had also produced a proposal for the main stadium. Mr Xia looked at the panels sceptically and remarked that the lake that had been planned in front of the stadium would never fit into the available space. Mr Jia smiled: 'It's only a concept.'

The karaoke machine was switched on and the rest of the evening was spent singing, dancing and drinking. After a duet by Mr Jia and Ms Yu, Professor Deng stood up abruptly and, with a few words, the evening was concluded. The presentation would take place at 11 o'clock the following morning.

I asked Huan again about the presentation, but his response was brief: 'Tomorrow morning.'

After a restless night I broached the subject of the presentation again. I asked Huan if I could see the presentation, what our strategy would be, what I could expect, where I should place the emphasis and which Canadian office I was actually representing. Huan translated my questions to Professor Deng and she said, through Huan, that she would be doing the presentation. I could add something at the end and could answer the questions.

Via Huan I told her that I had very little information to be able to add anything let alone answer any questions. Huan translated, but Professor Deng didn't answer. I repeated my questions, Huan was silent and Professor Deng repeated her smile. I smiled back in a friendly way. 'No problem', concluded Huan. Breakfast was finished and we agreed to meet in the lobby ten minutes later. We would then be able to visit the site before the presentation.

During the journey there, the image of the city changed from a mixture of old German and Chinese low-rise into typical Chinese high-rise, and then into a blend of poorly maintained low buildings with new high-rise, medium-rise and cleared areas. This last image lasted for about half an hour on our drive. When we reached our destination, I was astonished to see that there was already a stadium at this site. We drove around one time, and to my fellow travellers the most important outcome of this exercise seemed to be the site's orientation and an apparent axis that was to run through the area. To my further astonishment, the presentation was to be held in the stadium itself. We were cordially received at the entrance. The panels, model and project books were taken to a room where two scale models by other architectural offices were already laid out on a ping-pong table. Their panels were lined up along the wall. Three other offices turned out to be competing: two coalitions of Chinese and South Korean architectural offices and a coalition between a Chinese and a French office.

While Professor Deng made an in-depth study of another office's scale model, 'ours' was unpacked. For the first time I could get an overall picture of what the brief involved, of the scale of everything and of what 'we' had designed. The scale model was much more detailed than those of the other offices and Professor Deng complimented Mr Xia on the result. Mr Xia played down the compliment by stating that the scale-model production company had indeed produced very good work.

The scale models were compared more closely and then came a moment of astonishment. Our model had no highway exit, which was there in all the other models. Mr Xia was clearly mortified, Professor Deng looked stonily at the absent exit. I asked Huan whether or not this was a problem. 'Maybe this is a problem', he replied.

A second moment of astonishment followed: the scale of the model of the French office was not 1:1000 but 1:2000. I suggested to Huan that this could work in our favour. 'Perhaps they knew they had a better chance so they've invested less energy in their model', was his response. Mr Jia was the only one who remained calmly smiling, despite all the excitement.

One of the ladies who had met us at the entrance informed us that the jury was waiting for us. A light panic seized me – and my 'team-mates' as well, I noticed. We left the scale models and walked along a corridor some forty metres long, sharply lit by bright fluorescent lamps, towards a leather-padded door. In the dark space behind it there was an enormous table around which, I estimated, some twenty men were seated in huge easy chairs. I was escorted to an easy chair at the table's extremity and 'my team' followed. While Mr Xia connected a laptop to the beamer and Ms Yu placed the A0 panels with the renderings against the wall panelling, I let my eyes meander through the room, somewhat uneasily. It was thick with cigarette smoke and the wall panelling was only half visible. Three vast chandeliers hung from the ceiling. Some ten ladies with notepads sat along the walls. Two cameramen stared at me from a corner. An enormous camera was pointed straight at me.

A strange form of nervousness descended upon me.

I tried to move my much-too-heavy chair towards the table a little and looked at the people seated there. They were all dressed in dark suits with white shirts. Two of them were speaking softly to one another, others drank tea from lidded mugs filled with tea leaves. Yet others were playing with their mobile phones. None of them displayed any expression.

I had no idea who represented what here and in which function. I asked Huan, who looked at me in a way that I took to mean that he had no idea either. Spontaneously I decided to tell a story about a globalizing world in which local identity is increasingly coming under stress. None the less, Qingdao had a number of unique qualities in comparison to other Chinese cities: the splendid situation on the coast and the historical architecture. In stadium designs for a 'global event' such as the Olympic Games, the translation of just these local features could lead to a striking result. I realized that, in this way, the enlarged fish represented a certain logic, at least for myself.

My thoughts were interrupted by a balding man seated in the middle of the table, who told me something in Chinese. Silence fell, and I understood that we could begin our presentation. Intensely concentrated stares were directed at me. I looked questioningly at Professor Deng, she looked back and took the initiative. Huan whispered that he would try to translate everything as well as possible.

Professor Deng explained that the plan we would present was the result of intensive international collaboration between a renowned Canadian architectural office and their university. Because the time available for this presentation was 'limited', she continued, she would present the plan herself, so that no time would be lost with the translation. After Huan had translated this, I nodded in approval. After only a few sentences I was fascinated to observe that Professor Deng had suddenly adopted a very subservient attitude. She seemed to present the plan as a 'possibility', rather than as a precise response to the client's brief. This was fascinating, as the last-named attitude is far more common in the Netherlands.

The presentation consisted of three parts: first of all there was an analysis of the site that was limited to the entrances, the importance of an orientation to the south and an urban axis. In the Netherlands, this type of analysis would be done at a greater scale and from different angles of approach. So as I saw it, the historical context of the site was lacking, as well as the link-up with the infrastructure, functional and spatial analyses and the site's position in the perspective of a larger master plan.

The second part of the presentation consisted of a series of renderings of the stadiums and the conference centre. With each rendering, a precise description was given of where the entrances were situated, the size of every component and a suggestion for the materials to be used. In the Netherlands, we would have explained the brief much more from the inside, from the aspect of organization, and then have concluded with the images.

The third part of the presentation covered the residential area, where the renderings were again presented first. This area was a green oasis with a series of white high-rise blocks on the edges of the green space. After the renderings, we were shown dozens of floor plans for housing, all filled with small rooms. The explanation was full of catchwords such as 'luxury', 'comfort', and 'practical'.

The total presentation lasted about forty minutes and could roughly be divided into five minutes for part one, twenty minutes for part two and fifteen minutes for part three. Professor Deng thanked the jury and stated that she was willing to answer questions of any nature.

Mr Jia sat at the back of the room. In the silence that followed, he whispered something to the person sitting next to him. This person said something to the balding man in the middle of the table who in turn said loudly that another design would be presented. A different laptop was connected to the beamer and Ms Yu began playing nervously with her laser pen. The PowerPoint was started up and I saw the Sydney Opera House appear full-screen. Then followed the Eiffel Tower, Big Ben, the Empire State Building, the Pyramid of Cheops and many more icons. As last of all appeared the enlarged fish: the stadium of Qingdao as a logical conclusion to this series of world icons!

The balding man in the middle thanked us for the presentations. Then he announced that, because we had given not one but two presentations, there would be no more time for a round of questions. I looked at Huan in surprise and asked quickly whether or not I should add something. 'Maybe not necessary', he replied. A few minutes later we had left the room. I hadn't said a single word to the jury during the entire presentation.

We walked back through the corridor to the room with the scale models. Then I realized that the jury hadn't seen the model at all. I looked at my 'team mates'. Everyone was silent. A few minutes later, the silence was broken by someone entering the room. It was the person to whom Mr Jia had whispered something in the jury room. Mr Jia approached him heartily, greeted him and shook his hand intensely. This person vanished again after about ten minutes and Huan reported what had been said. The man turned out to be a Mr Ma and he had said that the jury was most satisfied with our design. Mr Jia had then invited Mr Ma for lunch, several times in fact, but Mr Ma was much too busy to accept.

So we went for lunch without Mr Ma. After driving around for a while, we entered a street that led us to the middle of a vacant patch of land. The road was a cul-de-sac and a two-storey building stood at the end. That turned out to be our destination. Far in front of the entrance, large trays of fish and shellfish stood ready for consumption. We were welcomed and accompanied to a 'VIP room', as Huan referred to it. The room was fabulous: thousands of shells had been inlaid in the floor, walls and ceiling. We had a view of the sea, which lay no further than twenty metres from the restaurant.

I was invited to sit next to Mr Jia and was given a glass of Chinese rice wine, probably most comparable with Dutch gin. Mr Jia directed his words to me through Huan. It turned out that he had designed the VIP room and knew the owner of the restaurant well. He asked me what I thought of the patch of land that we had just crossed.

What could I say? Beautiful? Bare? I smiled just as Professor Deng had done that day and waited until Mr Jia continued. He told me that the land measured three square kilometres and that he owned it. Then he asked if I would be interested in making a design for it. I was surprised and via Huan I replied that of course I would be interested!

Mr Jia grinned. I wanted to exchange ideas immediately about the commission but, again to my surprise, the subject was not raised again during the rest of the lunch.

Two hours later, Mr Jia asked for the bill. I wanted to pay it, but that wasn't allowed. I asked Huan what else was on our programme and he said that we would visit a tea plantation in the mountains. A good friend of Mr Jia had invited us there.

The surroundings were splendid, the atmosphere was unbelievably tranquil. Classical Chinese music was being played in the glasshouse in which we were sitting. Fascinated, I observed the tea ceremony. Shortly afterwards, I was introduced to the owner of the tea plantation. Huan told me that the owner would very much like to build a hotel next to the plantation, and perhaps I had some 'suggestions' about that? A feeling of euphoria began to wash over me: it was so difficult to acquire a commission for an actual building project in the Netherlands. Everything seemed to happen automatically here. Of course I was interested!

During the tea ceremony, Professor Deng began to discuss the presentation. According to Mr Jia, everything was cut and dried. But Mr Xia had his doubts concerning the fact that the jury had not asked any questions. Professor Deng turned to me and asked, via Huan, if I had an idea about how we could realize the main station in structural terms. I asked her to draw a cross-section, since I had not seen that in the presentation. Paper and pens were brought out and Professor Deng began to draw an enormous span as a roof. I said that my knowledge of Chinese building practice was limited but that I could think of two possibilities. I drew a static diagram and proposed, as the first option, that the roof should largely be prefabricated. The second option was to make everything on site, but this seemed rather unrealistic to me because everything would have to be supported by scaffolding. Professor Deng looked at the diagrams, nodded several times, and smiled in a friendly way.

The consultation stopped just as quickly as it had begun. Huan informed me that we would return to Mr Jia's house for some karaoke sessions. But once we arrived there, it was apparent that there would be no singing. In the studio, Ms Yu was busy with a number of colleagues at several computers. Rendering lines crept slowly downward on various screens.

Not long after, an entire urban area full of skyscrapers loomed into view. I saw dozens of towers and the proportions indicated that they must have been between 200 and 250 metres tall. An enormous axis ran from the city to the sea. With no more explanation than a couple of sentences in which words such as 'landmark' and 'modern' kept recurring, my suspicions were confirmed: this was the vacant patch of land we had crossed on our way to the restaurant that afternoon.

Mr Jia looked at me with eyes wide open and asked Huan: 'What does he think of it?'

'Of what?' I wondered. 'The image?' The entire plan layout was a complete mystery to me.

All eyes were on me. Professor Deng seemed especially interested in what I would say. I hesitated between 'Don't change a thing!' the as yet unspoken sentences about 'a globalizing world', and a more critical approach. This time I opted for the critical approach and I began, by way of Huan, on a sermon about totally planned cities, about diversity and changeability, and ended with the question as to whether Mr Jia had any ideas about organizing the necessary infrastructure of the area. Before responding, Mr Jia asked the opinion of Professor Deng. Out of the corner of my eye I had seen that she had been nodding during my whole speech. Via Huan I then heard a speech resembling my own, with similar arguments. Mr Jia responded that it was only a concept and that he would first have to convince the government because it had imposed a height restriction of 18 metres on the entire area.

The bottle of red wine, which still wasn't empty, came round again. This time I refused politely. Professor Deng said that it was late and that our flight would be leaving early the next morning. A moment of hearty farewells followed and Ms Yu gave me her business card. If I were interested in learning Chinese, or ever returned to Qingdao, I certainly had to call her. All exchanges occurred via Huan, because she spoke no English.

Via Huan I repeated to Mr Jia that the project greatly interested me and I emphasized that I would like to work on it. Mr Jia grinned, nodded and shook my hand.

That same evening, in my hotel room, I made the first sketches for Mr Jia's project and the hotel for the tea plantation.

Back in Beijing, I thanked Huan for the experience and asked him to maintain contact with Mr Jia and the owner of the tea plantation.

He promised to do so, thanked me, and suggested going out for dinner sometime in the near future.

Months later, having informed several times about the outcome of the Qingdao competition, the result was finally announced. The Chinese–French coalition had 'probably' won. Nevertheless, a positive feeling reigned: Mr Xia had 'probably' received the commission for the residential district.

The owner of the tea plantation? Never heard from him again.
And Mr Jia? Never heard from him again.

HOW DO YOU START A DESIGN?
Delft, Holland, twelve years before Qingdao

One of the more elementary questions students of architecture ought to ask themselves is: 'How do I start a design?' During my education at the Faculty of Architecture at Delft University of Technology, this issue was consistently approached in a semi-scientific manner. The education was based on modernist or, to be more accurate, functionalist principles. Beauty was no goal in itself: ideally, all exterior features of a building were a reflection of functional starting points. Thus, if there were mention of beauty in architecture, it lay embedded in the function. This concept was made clear to me during one of the first design studios I participated in. A fellow student presented his project and volunteered, as the reason why he had chosen a particular option, that he found the result attractive. The teacher sneered: 'That's only an opinion!' He continued, visibly emotional: '*Why* is something good, *why* does something work. *Why?*' And he repeated loudly: '*Why?*'

To find answers to the issues of *Why?* and *How do you start a design?*, my strategy was to develop a frame of reference that was as large as possible. In the search for references during my first year of study, I soon became acquainted with the future partners of NEXT architects: Bart Reuser, Marijn Schenk and Michel Schreinemachers. Together we organized workshops and exhibitions on the most diverse topics, as well as foreign excursions such as 'A hundred buildings in ten days'. With our 'self-initiated education', the Faculty gave us the leeway to set our own tasks and select our own teachers. Delft allowed us space and freedom, of which we made grateful and intensive use.

In my third year, I interrupted my studies for a year in order to represent, as board member of the Stylos Student Association, around 1500 students on a full-time basis. Reuser and Schenk had been board members the previous year and, within Stylos, Schreinemachers and I had produced the first Faculty yearbook. My task on the board was focused on organizing lectures and excursions. More than fifty lectures and ten excursions were the result, and if quality can be measured by attendance figures, the lecture given by Renzo Piano when he came to the Netherlands to accept the Erasmus Prize was the absolute highpoint.

After Stylos, I felt an urgent need for practical experience. I had a work placement for six months with Christian Rapp, who had just won the Rotterdam Maaskant Award for Young Architects. Rapp was the architect of the Piraeus Building in Amsterdam, in collaboration with Hans Kollhoff. I once dared to refer to this building as 'one of the better housing complexes in Europe'. However, there was no opportunity whatsoever to gain any practical experience there, work being limited to making studies and draft designs. The commissions portfolio of fledgling architectural offices in the Netherlands consisted mainly of studies, I was told. And it also became evident to me that the freedom we students claimed in projects was of a different order to the freedom an office could claim in real-life practice.

Back in Delft, Schenk, Reuser, Schreinemachers and I increasingly began to collaborate on projects. The four of us – the name NEXT would only come later – first moved into a former police station now allocated to anti-squat residents, and later into a classroom of a former school. We referred to the space as our 'studio' and worked both individually and jointly on our graduation projects. A graduation project was the summit of an educational programme and, ideally, all the knowledge and expertise gained should now converge in a clearly articulated design to which you gave your full backing. It was the last project in which you could enjoy total freedom and draw up your own brief, as one of the teachers warned us.

In my case, it concerned a design for a housing complex at Amsterdam Schiphol Airport. Due to the confrontation between the apparently opposing functions of dwelling and travelling, I hoped to visualize a quality that seemed to me to be under-appreciated at the time: the atypical urbanity of airports. Graduation became an architectural quest for the possible mutual added value of combining a housing complex with an airport.

The design process began with an analysis of the immediate context of Schiphol: the space, accessibility, organization, functioning, facilities, traffic flows, development and plans for future expansion. I extended this analysis to airports in a wider context on the basis of, among other things, texts by the French anthropologist Marc Augé on 'non-places'. These were characterized by their uniformity and lack of social coherence: 'non-places' looked the same the world over and you were there only temporarily. The increase in 'non-places', which was an inevitable result and characteristic of what Augé called 'supermodernity', had far-reaching consequences for our society, in his view. 'Non-places' made much human interaction redundant and could thus entail a new form of loneliness.

The second part of my analysis involved empirical research. For example, I found evidence that the noise pollution at the centre of Schiphol fell within the margins of the Dutch Housing Act and that the air quality at Schiphol was better than, say, in the centre of Amsterdam.

I began the translation of analysis and research into a design by projecting Le Corbusier's Unité d'Habitation on site. This 'machine for living in', this 'vertical village', was confronted by the 'machine for travelling' and the 'non-place' of Schiphol. This confrontation between the Unité and Schiphol led to a series of transformations. A three-dimensional square from which all functions could be accessed acted as a social 'intermediate level'. I sought a high degree of flexibility: three basic living-working types could be varied and combined as 68 distinct units. The central notion behind the design was that as long as loneliness was facilitated as a choice, this also represented a quality.

My graduation project gave me a provisional answer to the question 'How do you start a design?'. With this project, I sought to visualize qualities through confrontation. The route to the result had begun with analysis and research. I had translated their outcomes into an architectural design by means of a number of transformations. Lastly, the design was enriched by the flexibility in variations and combinations.

THE IMAGE OF METROPOLIS
Amsterdam, five years before Qingdao

Schenk, Reuser, Schreinemachers and I graduated virtually during the same period. During a lunch at our studio, we realized that the claustrophobic reality of real-life practice lay just around the corner. The freedom that we had assumed until then seemed to be shrinking fast and, in an ultimate attempt to enlarge our frame of reference to the maximum, we conceived the idea of taking a trip to all the great metropolises in the world. This was mid-1999 and almost every self-respecting discipline was engaged on the 'issue of globalism'. In our discipline, the scenario of Rem Koolhaas's generic city was exceptionally relevant. The world's urban population was on the verge of surpassing the rural population in number. What did this apparently unbridled urbanization mean? And to what extent were cities worldwide taking on identical features under the influence of globalization?

We embarked on a quest for 'The influence of globalization on the appearance of the world metropolis'. We analysed, in a project plan, the manifestation of a city in seventy themes, varying from 'suburbia' to 'international architecture' and from 'wedding' to 'McDonald's'. We would record each theme in each city along identical lines. Besides a photographic section, we wished to collect a series of media expressions and to do interviews. The ultimate aim was to generate a matrix which would enable a systematic comparison between the appearance of world metropolises. We called the project 'The Image of Metropolis'.

With this project we transcended our studio's autonomy and took the first steps towards becoming an office. We asked for a subsidy for the project and to our great delight it was granted.

With an open outlook we travelled the world in various combinations. Via e-mails and a website, we informed one another of our findings and discoveries. With Schreinemachers I visited Moscow while Schenk and Reuser were in Cairo. I met Reuser in Mumbai, and we encountered Schenk and Schreinemachers, who had just come from Johannesburg, in New Delhi. Together we travelled via Chandigarh to Bangkok. Schenk and I visited Singapore while Reuser and Schreinemachers were in Kuala Lumpur. We met one another again in Kuala Lumpur and together visited Hong Kong, Shenzhen, Guangzhou and Shanghai. Schenk flew to Tokyo and Osaka alone. Reuser, Schreinemachers and I visited Beijing at that time. We met one another again in Tokyo. Schenk and Schreinemachers went to Mexico City, Reuser and I to Los Angeles, from where we travelled on to San Francisco and Las Vegas. Reuser flew to Mexico City, going from there to Santiago de Chile and Buenos Aires with Schenk and Schreinemachers. I flew via Washington to New York and met the others in São Paulo. In Brazil we also visited Rio de Janeiro, Belo Horizonte and Brasilia.

At the beginning of January 2000 we landed at Schiphol. We had acquired an endless quantity of experiences and impressions, spoken to hundreds of people, made dozens of interviews, and collected masses of media expressions.

A few days after landing, we met in a grand café in Amsterdam to discuss how we could assemble all the information into an exhibition. In addition, we had obtained a commission during our trip: two studies for two urban expansion projects with two exhibitions on our work and thinking. This new commission was another step on our way towards attaining our own office. We soon had the office's name: NEXT *architects*, to promise ourselves and the world to continue to operate in the direction of the future.

The question we had posed ourselves with 'The Image of Metropolis' could be relatively easily answered: yes, the image of the world metropolis was largely being levelled out. The proof was undeniably given by the systematic image matrix we had made. But this was merely the outcome of a superficial inventory. The idea that the appearances of all world metropolises resembled one another conflicted greatly with our experiences, in which the same image in all those different cities could have infinitely many different meanings. Interpreting these different meanings became the basis for speculation in which we predicted and described a series of urban phenomena.

The task we had set ourselves, however, was so all-embracing and permeated so many disciplines that we could never succeed in describing the wealth we had uncovered. At the end of a collective lecture at the opening of the 'Image of Metropolis' exhibition in the Netherlands Architecture Institute in Rotterdam, Professor Carel Weeber reacted critically: 'You allow yourselves to be too surprised by what you have encountered.'

That remark remained in my head for years.

During an appearance on Dutch television I was asked the following question, as sharp as it was obvious: 'To what extent will this journey influence your work?' I avoided giving a direct answer by saying: 'Our designs will certainly not have Chinese temple roofs.'
In retrospect, exactly why I referred to China was quite unclear to me. It was probably due to the enormous contrast we had experienced between the Netherlands and China and, related to this, the realization that what we had seen in China couldn't possibly be introduced unadulterated into a Dutch context.
The real answer to the question concerning the extent to which the trip would influence our work could not yet be given. However, with our newly acquired worldwide frame of reference, we had found the broadest possible basis and new freedom for input for both our work and our thinking.

1%
Amsterdam, one year before Qingdao

With the success of 'The Image of Metropolis', the fact that Schenk and Reuser won *ex aequo* first prize for the best graduation project in the Netherlands – Archiprix – and a number of almost effortlessly obtained commissions, NEXT architects seemed to have become a reality. The office's merit was that it had never been planned but had simply arisen out of a shared interest. Almost immediately after NEXT was founded, a common friend drew our attention to the risks of 'four captains on one ship'. His remark was quickly qualified; all four of us were convinced of the added value of shared authorship. The notion that an architectural office can only operate successfully when 'every idea issues from the pen of a single architect' was, to us, an archaic idea. Moreover, there was a second basis for our collaboration: complementarity. Within NEXT, Schenk represented the 'train of ideas', Reuser 'the essentials' and Schreinemachers was the 'critical force in the background'. I was typified as someone who had 'little resistance to taking on challenges'.
Increasingly, we began working in a multidisciplinary capacity – for example with sociologists on the project entitled 'The Atlas of Cultural Ecology'. A large-scale multidisciplinary study on 'The Working Landscape of the Future' earned us second prize in an international

architectural competition, the OSCUR Award. We won several design competitions with, among other things, designs for two bridges, a watchtower and an enormous sloping circular path in a 'museum forest'. We were approached by Droog Design, and designed a range of doors and fences for the Milan Bienniale in which the chosen design brief was the boundary between individual and public space. We designed furniture and products such as a slow-lamp: a lamp filled with coagulated soy oil that only slowly began to emit light. We designed interactive software to confront users critically with their own tastes, and an architectural game with '1000 questions on modern architecture'. This is only a small selection from an exceptionally broad portfolio.

NEXT nurtured the shared conviction that our office would gain added value from the interaction between research and a building practice. It became increasingly clear to us that research made an essential contribution to practice and vice versa, that experience from real-life practice could function as a fundamental input for research. And with the ongoing enlargement of our frame of reference, we hoped to develop a 'mobile perspective' by means of which we could approach design briefs from various angles.

At that time, the crown on our work was its inclusion in the exhibition 'Tomorrow's Elite?', a selection of new architectural offices which the curators felt were on their way to a golden future. We deliberately presented our work there as part of an endless quest. The space allocated to us, one square metre, two metres high, was used for a stack of Styrofoam, a material often used to make draft scale models. The projects we had created until then were cut from the volume, the material that remained providing scope for further quests and findings.

However, after four years it became increasingly evident that our building practice was lagging behind our research practice. Although we did have commissions for small-scale building projects – mainly interior commissions – true architectural commissions remained beyond our reach. And it proved complicated to go looking for commissions with our broad portfolio, the exceptional architectural projects and our lack of building experience. We gave a high priority to seeking out concrete building projects and it brought Reuser and I to the DHV consultation and engineering office. DHV had also

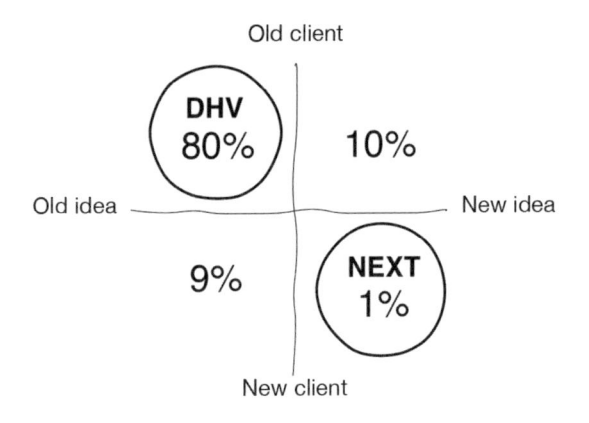

```
                    Old client
                       |
            ╱─────╲    |
           │ DHV  │    |
           │ 80%  │   10%
            ╲─────╱    |
Old idea ─────────────┼───────────── New idea
                       |   ╱─────╲
                  9%   │  │ NEXT │
                       │  │  1%  │
                       |   ╲─────╱
                       |
                    New client
```

Sword of Damocles

competed for the OSCUR Award and had ended fifth. DHV operated worldwide with more than 5000 employees in more than seventy offices. They had every conceivable kind of infrastructure at their disposal, and we were full of ideas. The idea of combining our qualities was brought up. A combination of DHV and NEXT appeared very enticing, at least to us.

We agreed to meet again at the DHV headquarters to get better acquainted. Full of conviction, we presented our work and notions and illustrated these on the basis of our portfolio. The manager of DHV listened attentively and occasionally jotted things down. After our introduction we waited tensely for her reaction.

She opened up a world that had been closed to us until then. She called it a 'well-intended little lesson in marketing'. On a piece of paper she drew a coordinate system and wrote at the end of the coordinates 'old client' – 'new client' and 'old idea' – 'new idea'. According to her, there was a demonstrable connection between these: there was an 80% chance that an 'old client' would accept an 'old idea' and a 10% chance that an 'old client' would accept a 'new idea'. The chance that a 'new client' would accept an 'old idea' was 9%. And the chance that a 'new client' would accept a 'new idea' was 1%.

She placed a circle in the 'old client, old idea' quadrant and said: 'This is DHV.'

She placed a circle in the 'new client, new idea' quadrant and said: 'This is NEXT.'

That was a wake-up call.

That one per cent hung like the Sword of Damocles above our heads. The added value of interaction between a research practice and a building practice was obvious to NEXT. But how could we connect the two, as we stood such a small chance of actually putting our ideas into practice? To me, it was clear which direction we had to take: we had to go for the building practice. But where could you start a building practice equipped only with ambition and without the relevant building experience and references?

CHINA, CHINA, CHINA
Amsterdam, six months before Qingdao

The subject of the e-mail was 'Are you interested in a project for the Beijing Olympics?' The name of the sender consisted entirely of strange computer characters. I couldn't resist the challenge and opened the e-mail in the expectation that it would be a new kind of spam for architectural offices. But I was wrong – it was a message from Zhou Huan, a Chinese architect with whom I hadn't spoken in an age.

I had become acquainted with Huan three years previously, during the 'Image of Metropolis' trip, at a dinner organized by the head of the Cultural Department of the Netherlands Embassy in Beijing. In addition to Huan, three other Chinese architects had been invited. A number of themes had been prepared as discussion points. The first theme was 'Andreu's Egg', the new national theatre that was to be realized right next door to Tiananmen Square. The issue was whether 'the Egg at this location would fit within Chinese culture and architecture'.

No one dared to open the discussion. So I began with the remark that such an exceptional location demanded an exceptional design, but that it was difficult for me to estimate what kind of significance this design would have. Huan replied that it was a most exceptional design but that there was resistance to it particularly from the academic world, primarily due to the costs: it was a lot of money for a developing country like China. He then remarked on the clash between the design and traditional Chinese patterns of thought. In order to make the curvature of the egg and to fit the auditoriums into the shell, the building would have to be 50 metres tall. However, it was not allowed to be taller than 47 metres, the height of the Chinese parliament building. For this reason, the Egg would have to be sunk into the ground. The entrance was now a stairway that descended in a glass tunnel that would run beneath an artificial lake to the Egg. However, descent is linked with death in Chinese thinking. The notion of the design as a tomb was further reinforced by the fact that the auditoriums would be installed as independent volumes in the space below the shell – exactly as Chinese emperors had been buried in bygone days. And, as a final point, Huan mentioned the artificial lake: Beijing suffered from a chronic shortage of water, so why was such an enormous lake necessary?

Huan intrigued me because he dared to adopt a stance. The other Chinese architects were reserved and silent. They had – or pretended to have – difficulty with English. Huan contradicted the cliché that Chinese never spoke out and always – at least in the eyes of Westerners – lived in 'a state of harmony'. It later turned out that Huan had studied in Paris and was currently working on his PhD. For the rest of the evening it was most interesting to hear his ideas about the differences between Asian and European cities, the opportunities and challenges for Beijing, and suchlike.

The contrasts between Europe and China appeared to be greater than those between Europe and any of the other countries I'd visited. To me, these contrasts, combined with the unprecedented modernization that left visible traces all over its cities, made China more than fascinating. The issue of the Egg also touched upon a theme that I found most intriguing: a 'developing country' with an extremely long history, faced with an unparalleled modernization process. What position could you, as a foreign architect, adopt in such a context?

I spoke to Huan again, a year after our first meeting. The 'Image of Metropolis' exhibition had its international première during the 'Urban Futures Conference' in Johannesburg, South Africa. Afterwards, it moved on to other cities: Delft, The Hague, Eindhoven and Kuala Lumpur. At the beginning of 2001, I was engaged in intensive talks with Huan to enable the exhibition to be shown in Beijing and Shanghai. In March 2001, I followed the exhibition to those two cities in order to present our journey and findings in lectures, just as I had done in Johannesburg. Huan was waiting for me at Beijing airport. Together we took an old city bus to the university and on our arrival there we immediately went to see the exhibition, which had been installed in the lobby of the Faculty. Huan told me proudly that the dean was most interested in the exhibition, and had given the order to photograph everything systematically. On the same day, a poster bearing my name hung everywhere around the campus: tomorrow someone from NEXT architects would come and give a lecture.

The next day, I saw that the auditorium was crammed full of students. The lecture was due to begin at 3 p.m. but ten minutes before the start we first went to a room adjoining the hall. An entire row of professors was standing there waiting for an audience. The head of the Cultural Department of the Netherlands Embassy was there too. One after another the professors gave me their business cards and I exchanged a few words with each of them. By now it was 3.30 p.m. and I didn't understand why we still weren't going into the lecture hall. I waited until I was whispered to in Dutch that it was time to begin. I didn't want to be the first to pass through the doorway but I was told, again in Dutch, that I should do it. It was the custom in China to allow the guest to enter and leave the room first.

The dean announced me in Chinese. There would be no translator there, I was to present everything in English. When I ended forty minutes later with the remark that I would answer any questions, hundreds of eyes stared at me in surprise.

The first question, in broken English, was: Had we visited all those cities by plane?

I was surprised by the question and replied: Yes, by plane.

After some hesitation came the second – and last – question: Where had we obtained all that information about those cities?

'From internet, books and interviews', I replied. I had made all the wrong assumptions about my audience and had had a glimpse into an utterly different world. Very little indeed of my story had been understood, I realized with conviction.

After the lecture I was invited to dine with some of the professors. At the end of the dinner, the idea of possible collaboration between NEXT and their companies was raised. I was surprised by the questions and had no idea of what this collaboration might entail. An editor of one of China's few architectural magazines of those days was also present at the dinner. He was very interested in publishing our story, but didn't have the funds to do so. The story was never published in China because it was only years later that I understood that his words meant that we should organize the funding ourselves.

The next day, I visited an architectural office with which Huan was on friendly terms, where I displayed our projects. I showed a sculptural apartment complex measuring 21 by 18 metres with a 12-metre columnless span, which could be implemented as a Vierendeel girder through the façade. One of the architects couldn't grasp that such a span was possible. Then it turned out that he had read the drawing as 1:1000 instead of as 1:100, so that he thought that the span was not 12 metres but 120 metres. I observed that people in China thought at a completely different scale. Despite our small projects, this office was also interested in collaborating: 'Together we can build many towers.'

After Beijing, Huan and I flew to Shanghai where the exhibition had been installed at Tongji University. I had now structured my story in a different way and I believe that this enabled it to come across much better. Here, too, we had a dinner with the professors after the lecture, where the topic of possible collaboration was again raised. And again the following day we visited architectural offices that also wanted to collaborate with us.

One of these offices was run by a PhD student. His office was brand new and only half fitted out. We drove there in his car, whose seats were still covered in plastic. 'New', he confirmed in English. He too was interested in collaborating but he only wished to use our 'name and business licence'. How much would that cost? The question alone was unthinkable in the Netherlands. Avoiding giving an answer, I asked about his portfolio. He started up his computer, opened a folder and then clicked on dozens of renderings. Every time an image appeared he gave a laconic chuckle, which I didn't understand: 'hospital, haha', 'office tower, haha', 'museum, haha', 'school, haha'.

The journey lasted ten days, and on my return to the Netherlands, when I recapitulated on the events, eleven offices had shown a willingness to enter into a collaborative relationship. I had attended eight karaoke evenings, had eaten in nine revolving restaurants on hotel towers and was laden with gifts. NEXT had only been operational for a year, we were working on our first projects and we lacked the relevant building experience. How could we possibly 'build many towers together'?

The sense of reality triumphed. We let our chances slip and, with this, our contact with China faded. Until I received that e-mail from Huan.

Full of enthusiasm, I informed the others. Were we interested in a project for the Olympic Games in Beijing? Sober reactions, combined with scepticism and a reserved interest: 'Tell us about it...' The project concerned a badminton stadium in a city outside Beijing. As a condition for taking part, the university had to form a team with an international architectural office. This was a major opportunity – of course we were interested and I asked Huan what he needed from us. He asked for an office portfolio. I then asked what was the important aspect of it we should emphasize. 'Koolhaas' was his answer: 'Koolhaas is very popular in China'. Without having a clear idea of what we could do with this information, we prepared our portfolio and mailed it to Beijing. After waiting a long time and making subsequent enquiries, it turned out that the selection committee had found us 'too light'. After even more enquiries, it turned out that celebrities such as Zaha Hadid would 'probably' take part in the competition.

Despite the disappointment, this was the moment that China again became a live issue for us. Six months after the '1% deception' at DHV, it was even topical enough for me to suggest to my colleagues that we should perhaps open an office in China. My NEXT partners looked surprised; we briefly discussed how that could possibly work but were soon faced with everyday reality. At that moment, China still seemed very far away.

A month later I was sitting with one of my NEXT colleagues in the auditorium of the Netherlands Architecture Institute in Rotterdam. It was full. China was the topic for that evening. The speakers were 'China experts', spatial planners and sociologists. The evening was filled with stories about Chinese projects and ambitions, both of which were megalomaniac and monolithic by Dutch standards. Then I knew for sure: 'We ought to be a part of that', I decided resolutely. The lure of China steadily became stronger and stronger.

Via Huan and various other contacts, I approached a number of Chinese architectural offices on an informal footing.

A few weeks later, I had had invitations from four Chinese offices. While on excursion with students in Berlin, I received a fifth. I phoned the office in Amsterdam and asked them to book flights from Amsterdam to Hong Kong and from Beijing to Amsterdam. Two days later I was back in Amsterdam and the following day I flew to Hong Kong, open-mindedly looking for collaborative ventures.

*Hong Kong, Shenzhen, Guangzhou, Shanghai and Beijing,
five months before Qingdao*

During the landing in Hong Kong, with a view across the skyscrapers of Hong Kong Island, Kowloon and the dynamic of the harbours, the faded but still familiar feelings about China resurfaced. Behind the customs gate, someone was waiting for me with a large board emblazoned with 'NEXT architects'. We drove to the hotel and during the journey I received a phone call from my first contact. Could I perhaps come to the office first? I changed clothes in the back of the moving car and forty-five minutes later we arrived at the office. The 'human resource manager', as the lady introduced herself, welcomed me cordially. At that moment the CEO wasn't at the office but one of the associate directors was, and he would like to meet me before leaving the next day on a business trip. The associate director, whose name was Jason, entered with a large stack of rolled-up A0 drawings.

'Human resource manager', 'CEO', 'associate director' and 'business trip': these were terms that were pretty remote from the world in which NEXT thought and operated. However, such corporate jargon proved to hold considerable significance for architectural offices in Hong Kong. We were introduced and there was an exchange of business cards, after which the package of drawings was spread out. Jason was engaged in a large housing project and had not yet designed a number of components. His request was whether or not I could help him with these. I had my doubts about taking part in this test, in view of the fact that I had not yet met the CEO and therefore could not estimate what kind of status had been attributed to my visit. I asked him if he knew why I had come to Hong Kong. Jason was somewhat startled by my directness. He said he knew why, and apologized if his request was inappropriate. I, in turn, was surprised by his reaction and immediately responded: 'No problem!' I continued by asking if he could explain his project to me.

Relieved, he began to tell me about the housing project that had been organized along an axis kilometres long, which, as I saw it, ran from nowhere to nowhere. The axis followed a platform that stood one and a half metres above ground level. Under the platform was a semi-sunken car park. What he had not yet designed was the boundary between the platform and the ground plane. Could I possibly make some proposals for that, tomorrow? I said that

I would and repeated 'No problem', a remark that seemed to please him.

After an extensive lunch, a guided tour, a dinner and a sleepless night, I began on the project the following day. I had three hours before the meeting with the CEO and, due to the time difference with Amsterdam, where it was night, I would have to organize a proposal for the boundary without the aid of my NEXT colleagues. I limited myself to two proposals: one with an enormous stairway that would sharpen the boundary, and one with a meandering garden with paths that would break it down. As I had some time left, I designed something of the layout of the axis itself. By projecting a diagonal axis with trees over the Chinese axis, I took the edge off the space's monumentality. And in shifting a number of residential buildings, I broke up the monotonous march of buildings and made room for a large public space in the middle of the plan.

I drew the ideas in 3-D on the computer, printed everything out and awaited developments.

The telephone on my desk rang and the human resource manager asked me to come to the CEO's office. I did so and, without saying a word, the CEO bent over his desk to offer me his business card. Across the desk, I gave him mine. He was in his late fifties, early sixties, I estimated, and had an air of boundless energy about him. Then the HR manager told me that the CEO had undergone a dental operation and was not allowed to speak for the rest of the day. While she said that, the CEO had written 'Design?' on a piece of paper and had pushed it towards me across his desk.

I picked up the prints, slid them to him and told him about the ideas behind them. On seeing the two proposals for the platform-ground plane boundary, he nodded and wrote on the same piece of paper 'Sketch?'. I asked him what he meant by that and he wrote 'Can you' in front of 'Sketch?' I confirmed that I could, but I didn't understand the relationship with my proposals. I then showed him my spontaneous idea for the axis. I told him about shifting the housing blocks and he wrote 'Not allowed'. At my proposal to weaken the monumentality of the axis, to create a central point and more variation, he wrote 'I don't like this'. Then he wrote 'Thank you' and the HR manager escorted me from his office.

What was I to make of that?

The next day I was treated to a helicopter flight over Hong Kong Island, guided tours, food and karaoke, all expenses paid by the office, until I was completely worn out. That evening I had an appointment with the CEO in a revolving restaurant above a hotel tower. To my relief he was allowed to speak by now, but this relief soon made way for something rather different.

The conversation was stiff and came generally from his side. I had the constant feeling that I was being tested by challenging questions. When I asked how he foresaw our collaboration and how we might be able to attune our aims substantively, he responded: 'Very, very difficult'. This was not a conversation about collaboration on an equal basis, I silently concluded. While I attempted to suppress this thought and looked for an opening to give relevance to our intentions, he apologized. He looked once more at his watch and said he had another appointment. After a cordial farewell I remained behind with a number of senior associates and the HR manager. No one was eager to stay much longer and the evening quickly came to a close. That night, the question continued to resound in my head: what could the agenda have been, and why were we invited to Hong Kong at all?

In the morning, the HR manager came straight out with a proposal: would I – I alone – be willing to work for them? The answer was 'Nee!', as Dutch as it was resolute. My negative response contained a measure of irritation, because in a sense I felt cheated. Or naïve. Or a combination of the two.

I took the experience as a wise lesson with me across the Chinese border and visited offices in Shenzhen, Guangzhou and Shanghai. Every visit was filled with similar meetings and customs, and with astonishingly similar portfolios and projects. A test had been prepared at every office. A good exemplary was the megalomanic brief in Guangzhou: make a design for 300,000 square metres of housing in one day. And, added en passant, an office building for the project's client. I turned first to the office building, as we could make more of it from a design standpoint, and mailed all the information and the first computer models through to Amsterdam. After some consultation by phone, I awoke the following morning with a whole range of office building designs in my mailbox. It is amazing how effectively you can make use of the time difference, especially if you've been working together for years. The Chinese office seemed impressed by the tower designs but they also asked casually about the proposal for the housing.

By the time I reached Shanghai, I had become so convinced of the fact that we ought to have an office in China that I e-mailed the Chinese School in Amsterdam, found via Google, asking if they gave intensive courses in Chinese. In the plane to Beijing, on my way to the last of the offices, I drew up a top three of possible partners among them.

In Beijing a driver was again waiting for me, with a large board with our name on it. Speaking no English, he guided me to his car and brought me to a hotel where I was received by someone from the Chinese architectural office. She was a friendly woman in her late thirties who introduced herself as Mrs Li. She apologized, she was not an architect. Immediately after I had checked in, we visited a number of projects that the office had realized. The first was a Richard Meier-like office building, the second consisted of young people's housing in enormously thick towers, and the third was a housing project that was a year old but already showed signs of wear and tear.

After lunch, we continued on our way. The car stopped at a small office building and I was accompanied to the fourth floor. The Chinese office, I was told, had its seat on the fourth, sixth, seventh and ninth floors. On the fourth floor I was guided past the 'Wall of Fame', which consisted exclusively of renderings. As had so often been the case in the days before then, I waited patiently in a presentation room for what was going to happen. In my thoughts, I counted the number of large tables at which I had been seated since my arrival in China.

Mrs Li entered, followed by six others.

I was introduced to Mrs Hu, a lady with an unrivalled charisma. She was the CEO of the company. Everyone sat down opposite me at the table and Mrs Hu asked me in English what I thought of their projects. 'Good', I said, more positively than my actual experience had been. My response seemed to surprise her. She browsed through our portfolio and asked me what I expected. I referred to the letter that was enclosed in it and asked whether she had had time to read it. She picked up the letter, ran silently through the points one by one, and said: 'No problem, good'. Now it was my turn to be a somewhat surprised.

'Is there anything else?' she asked. I answered that I would like to work with them for a day, the next day in fact, to test out our potential collaboration. She thought that that was a good idea and asked what kind of project I would like to work on. 'Public building', I said. 'Good', she responded.

The ease with which she said 'good' sounded promising and aroused in me a further yearning for building briefs. With difficulty, I tried to conceal the combination of excitement and adrenaline while I thought back to the Dutch Sword of Damocles, outlined to us by DHV. One of the six others at the table, Mr Chen, the 'vice general manager', invited me in English to take a guided tour. A few minutes later I followed him through the building, which had clearly been in use for quite some time and was choc-a-bloc with people. The departments seemed to have been randomly spliced together. In Mr Chen's extremely small office – two people could barely share the table, free movement was virtually impossible – I asked him for a portfolio. Just as curtly as in Shanghai, we rushed through a great number of renderings. After the final rendering I was invited for a dinner in yet another revolving restaurant at the top of a hotel tower. That night I slept like a log.

The following day, I was collected from the lobby of my hotel. At the office, a small room measuring around five square metres had been cleared out. In it, a table and three chairs stood next to a computer server. Two of the chairs were unusable because nobody could sit between the glass wall and the table. A sketch roll and dozens of felt-tip pens and pencils lay on the table. This was to be my work space for the day. Mr Chen entered, greeted me heartily, and said they had a very interesting brief for me: a hotel of around 50,000 square metres, in the mountains, adjacent to a lake! The project manager joined him and was introduced to me as Mr Jiang. The three of us leafed through the drawings, which I felt contained very little information. There were no photos of the location.

Because it was still night-time in the Netherlands, and I would discuss the plan that same afternoon internally, I would have to tackle this proposal without input from Amsterdam. And in this case there was even less information available than there had been in Hong Kong. I asked about the programme components, preconditions, site boundaries, the wishes of the client... but 'You can design freely' was the invariable answer. I repeated the question and told them that I needed some information about the brief in order to begin... Questioning eyes stared at me, and then came the answer: 'You can design freely'.

With an air of uneasy indifference, I began 'freely' on the design for the hotel.

I thought a thousand rooms would be sufficient, determined a size for one room, and organized them all along a single-sided corridor. I assumed that eight floors would be ideal, so that the hotel would not make too big an impact on the surroundings. On the basis of this assumption, the building would be 1500 metres long. As the third step, I halved this length by using both sides of the corridor. The building was now 750 metres long: still impractically long. As a fourth step, I created an inner courtyard by connecting the ends of the corridor. The building was now 180 by 60 metres, more practical and an acceptable scale for China, I thought. The next step consisted of 'cutting open' the block to enable relationships between the inner courtyard and the 'magnificent surroundings'. The last step was to include a self-conceived programme of conference halls, restaurants and offices, organized along a public street. This street began at the entrance, rose to the top floor and ended at the other side back at the entrance.

I modelled everything three-dimensionally, specified a number of camera views, and printed out some wireframe models, as I had done in Hong Kong. I cut through the three-dimensional model several times and worked up the cross-sections to clarify the different relationships between the context, the courtyard and the programme. I had now been working for three hours and, just as in Hong Kong, I waited to see what would happen next.

Shortly afterwards, Mr Chen came along to invite me to lunch. I needed some feedback and asked him to look at the plan first. He asked a number of senior architects to join him and we all went to sit at a large table, outside the glass room. I explained my design steps, showed them the wire models and waited tensely for their reaction. It was quite some time before the first response came, so long in fact that I began to wonder if what I had presented had any merit at all.

The reactions arrived very slowly: 'Very good!' said one of the architects, 'Very, very good', confirmed the others, one by one, after this first judgement. I found the compliments not particularly useful and I wanted to know what they thought was good about the design. But the desired discussion never really got going. According to the architects, the plan was 'enough' and, in their view, 'the design steps could also be presented to the client as various options'! I repeated this last remark in my head. The remark was as surprising as it was inconceivable in a Dutch setting. Why would you present design steps that lead to a single result as different options? That evening we again dined extensively and this time I became acquainted with the rest of Mr Chen's design department. The mood was high-spirited and there was plenty of laughter and conversation. I wondered why this office with more than a hundred employees had only a few architects, and for the rest only engineers and draughtsmen. But I didn't articulate my surprise. I thanked Mr Chen heartily that evening and concluded that this was the office I preferred. NEXT had the most conceptual freedom here, and the Chinese back office was large. Although critical discussions seemed to be difficult, my intuition told me that we would have the most opportunities here.

The office was called Huanyang, and Huanyang was going to be NEXT's new partner. The following day, after a short discussion with Mrs Hu, I thanked her cordially and told her I was eagerly looking forward to our collaboration. It was mutual, she said. We agreed that I would return to Beijing as soon as possible.

Amsterdam, four months before Qingdao

Back in Amsterdam, my partners in NEXT were equally enthusiastic about developments. We were about to take part, from the inside, in what had been so intensely highlighted from the outside: the unprecedented modernization of China. Practical matters were arranged, I followed an intensive course in Chinese and I became increasingly convinced of the value of the steps that had been taken.

One evening, on the balcony of Schenk's apartment, we philosophized further about how this should all work in the future. The idea arose of each of us alternately doing a six-month shift in Beijing, but at the same time we saw the weakness of this idea. Having to build up knowledge and experience every time would not be productive. We concluded that the centre of gravity in NEXT should remain in Amsterdam. I would send commissions to the Netherlands and with the feedback from Beijing this should make specific NEXT projects possible in China.

In China I had imagined an ideal working model between NEXT Amsterdam and NEXT China on the basis of a schedule in which the working hours in Amsterdam and Beijing could be added together. By making positive use of the time difference – six or seven hours, depending on summer time – this enabled effective working days of at least 21 hours. Mrs Hu had smiled amiably when she had seen the schedule: 'Do architects really work such long hours in Amsterdam?'

I had also presented our ideal model for collaboration to the Chinese offices. This ideal was illustrated by a combined Chinese-Dutch flag. It represented a division into four building stages – 'concept design', 'design development', 'construction drawings' and 'execution supervision' – based on a proportional division of time. This division had been prompted by the way Chinese building processes are organized. Although Huan had told me that in the typical Chinese building process 'execution supervision' was not a part of the architect's brief, I had nevertheless added this part in the conviction that an architect ought to be involved in a project right up to the last moment.

The flag was divided on the basis of the degree of responsibility that NEXT and its Chinese partner ought to have, respectively, in each stage of the process. NEXT would concentrate on the concept development and, as implementation approached, the Chinese partner would assume more responsibility. Both parties should be involved in the project from beginning to end. Input from the Chinese party in the concept stage was essential, as was the presence of NEXT during the implementation.

To us, this was the ideal model for collaboration, and we attempted to emphasize that by making an analogy with yin and yang: complementary opposites in a larger whole.

Mrs Hu had again smiled amicably on seeing this diagram.

A NEW HOUSE
Beijing, a week prior to Qingdao

Having arrived at Beijing airport, I passed through the glass sliding doors towards a wall of waiting Chinese. There were dozens of signs with names in English, Russian, Chinese, Japanese, Korean and other languages. I sought my name, but couldn't find it immediately. Then a small girl came up to me and greeted me heartily in English: 'Hi John, welcome in Beijing!' She introduced herself with her English name, Amy, and brought me to the car park where a driver was waiting for us. He took my backpack and laptop and placed them in the back of the car. On the way to the city, the adrenaline surged through my body; this was the beginning, the beginning of the adventure called 'China'. We would give it a try for four months, after which we would evaluate whether or not this step held any kind of future for us.

During the drive, Amy asked if Dutch people liked to cycle. I didn't understand the question, but replied positively: yes, certainly, especially because it was not practical to have a car in many of the older Dutch cities. Then I remembered that I had borrowed a bike the last time I was in Beijing, in order to explore the vicinity of the office. Amy interrupted my thoughts by cheerfully recounting that Huanyang had bought a bicycle for me and that I could now cycle from home to the office every day. At the moment she said that, we drove past a typical Chinese carrier tricycle, which was used to transport almost anything one could imagine. As a joke, I asked if it was a cycle like that one. It was a joke she clearly didn't understand because she then asked me what I wanted to transport.

We were on our way to my new apartment. Three weeks previously, when I was in Latvia, I had received an e-mail from Beijing showing four photos of an apartment they had found for me. 'Renjishanzhuang is a very famous project in Beijing', I was told. 'The prospect is a beautiful view over the park and lake.' There were photos of the view, the kitchen, the bathroom and the living room. From Latvia, I wrote back that it seemed to be a perfect apartment, although I couldn't find Renjishanzhuang when I googled it and I had no idea where the apartment was situated.

'There is your apartment!' said Amy pointing it out from the car. I looked at the two salmon-coloured towers with an enormous gateway in front flanked by two huge stone lions. My new home was on the 17th floor.

The living room was directly behind a large wooden door. To the left of the door was the bathroom. A small kitchen was reached off a small corridor and the bedroom was at the end of that corridor. The bedroom had a loggia where the photo of the view had been taken. The apartment was about twenty metres deep, and the living room had only one small window in one of the enormous recesses in the tower. Everything was new, parquet covered the floor, photos of New York at the turn of the century hung on the walls. 'Beautiful', I said to Amy, while recalling my Amsterdam apartment in a building dating from the beginning of the 20th century.

We went to the underground bicycle parking facility to admire my new bike. The guards were astonished to see a foreigner ride a couple of rounds in front of the entrance. Amy smiled and explained their surprise: 'You are the only foreigner here.' I had no idea how I should react, so I simply smiled back.

After saying goodbye, I went upstairs to unpack my things. Half an hour later I rode on my new bike through my new city. Beijing was of a totally different order to Amsterdam. Fifteen million inhabitants compared to 700,000; six ring roads instead of one. The list of statistics became longer and longer in my head. The scale of the roads and the buildings, the number of people, the colours and odours – they were so different.

There was so much to discover here.

A BIG ONE

On my first working day, again everything proved to be excellently arranged. A kind of bamboo plant, a 'lucky bamboo', stood in my small room and I was told that the faster this grew, the faster I would become rich. At that moment I couldn't think of a plant in the Netherlands with a similar significance.

I sat in my new office chair and only then did it become evident that my office was right at the end of the corridor. Everyone who entered the premises, just as almost everyone at every workstation in the office, could see me behind the glass wall. I made a remark to Mr Chen about how prominent my desk was and he said: 'Yes, everyone can see the panda!'

Just as Amy hadn't understood my joke in the car about the bicycle, I couldn't quite grasp this one.

Mr Chen was called away and disappeared from my doorway. From my chair, I looked around me. Pens, sketch rolls and an enormous calculator lay ready for use on my desk. When I took my laptop out of my bag, Mr Chen came back to accompany me to the 'large' meeting room.

Two somewhat older Chinese men were waiting there. I was invited to take a seat and Mrs Hu entered shortly afterwards. She welcomed me heartily. Mr Chen spoke, and told me that the two gentlemen were also 'vice general managers'. He asked me to introduce myself, and NEXT, to them. I nodded to the older gentlemen and told them quickly about NEXT and about the ideas behind our projects.

The introduction lasted less than ten minutes, I looked at two men and waiting for their response, or possible questions. Silence fell and then Mr Chen told me that they didn't speak any English. By agreeing to his request too soon and by talking much too quickly I had robbed Mr Chen of every opportunity to translate what I was saying.

Fortunately, this uncomfortable moment was neutralized by the proposal to give me a more thorough tour of the office. I agreed and we visited the various departments, while I was informed about the responsibilities of each one. When we went past Amy's department, Marketing, and Mr Chen had a brief conversation with someone else, Amy told me that she was going to leave Huanyang because she didn't feel completely at home in the 'architecture market'. I had no time to respond: Amy saw Mr Chen coming and hastily retreated to her desk. It was one of my first encounters with Chinese office hierarchy.

Mr Chen continued his guided tour and we stopped at a massive scale model that stood uneasily on a number of half-size archive cabinets. The scale model had just been delivered to the office and was still half wrapped in plastic. Together, we removed the rest of the plastic. A huge project of five towers on a podium loomed into view.

'This is a Big One', grinned Mr Chen. I asked him what a 'Big One' was. 'This is a Big One', he repeated, grinning, and he continued with gleaming eyes: 'More than 200,000 square metres.'

Back at my desk I installed the webcam that would make it possible to contact Amsterdam. During this operation I thought about the 'Big One'. Why had he placed so much emphasis on this project? It seemed to me to be of little interest to an architect. Where was the architectural challenge in a massive commercial project such has this? Then I remembered an office visit to OMA Hong Kong during 'The Image of Metropolis'. A project leader displayed the design for a high-rise project for Hong Kong Island. 'This architecture is 30 centimetres deep', she said. Everything behind the elevation was pure economics, she added. 'How do you make 30-centimetre-deep architecture interesting?' she then asked herself out loud.

From behind my desk I looked through the glass wall at the other workstations. While it buzzed with activity, Mr Chen had described the working ambience as 'relaxed'. The following week would be a Chinese 'Golden Week', and the whole of China would have a week's holiday.

At around six o'clock I cycled homeward, slowly, absorbing my new surroundings as much as possible. In the streets I saw almost none of the Chinese characters that I had learned in Amsterdam. Later that evening I tried a dumpling restaurant not far from my house. I couldn't read anything on the menu and I tried in my best Chinese to order something from the waitress. She didn't understand me and continued to repeat her questions, which I, in turn, didn't understand either. After a number of attempts, she stamped off. Ten minutes later I was served with one and a half kilos of dumplings.

CONSTRUCTION BEGINS IN FOUR MONTHS!
One week after Qingdao. E-mail to NEXT Amsterdam

'Men, time for champagne!'
Today I received the official announcement: The first pile of NEXT's first China project will probably be driven into the ground in four month's time! And the great thing about it is that the project still has to be designed!

Incoming project: Liuming, meaning something like 'good reputation', is a sales centre, a kind of information pavilion, 2300 square metres in size, maximum of twelve metres and three storeys tall.

It is typical here, before projects are completed, to build a sales centre where potential buyers can be enticed by what is going to be on sale there. Much money is invested in such centres, in view of the fact that customers seem to believe that the quality of the sales centre is representative of the quality of the project itself. Exceptional concepts and materials are possible for these centres. It is a matter of commercial glorification: everything is geared to selling the product. Enormous scale models will be exhibited and even 1:1 mock-up spaces of apartments, for example.

Liuming is due to become a housing district near the West Fifth Ring Road. It is a singular district, planned to look like a villa neighbourhood but with a higher density. They call them 'townhouses' here. The location seems to have much in the way of quality: there are many old trees and a view of the mountains. An old tree in China represents history and mountains have much mystical significance, I have been told.

We have two weeks' time to come up with a concept design, then we have the first presentation for the client. After this, we may have

the opportunity 'to adjust the design once', and a month later the final design must be ready.
Make it a good one! J

re: Construction begins in four months!

Today we had an internal presentation. Mrs Hu, Mr Chen, Mr Jiang and Mr Zhen, senior architects, were all present. I had told them about the idea of retaining as many trees as possible and of adding the building to the site as a kind of arboreal ceiling. In this way, old routes are maintained and interesting new relationships arise because some trees now come to be situated in patios and half-open courtyards.
'Very interesting!' was the reaction!
Carry on, in other words. Tomorrow I will receive a CAD file indicating the position of the trees, so that we can determine the precise outline of the building. I'll begin on the façade studies today – could you initiate an elevation point study? How to connect the ground floor with the first floor (in China they're called the first and second floors) in an interesting way?! [...]

re: re: Construction begins in four months!

I have just come from the presentation for the client. He is called Mr Ma and had brought about six assistants with him. It is difficult to estimate how they regarded our 'Silver Forest Building'. He seemed particularly confused by the diagrams of the building's organization and seemed to wonder what, if anything, he could do with them. The only real question was: 'Is this modern Dutch architecture?'. The only real doubt was expressed by one of his assistants: 'Will this building also look good in the winter when there are no leaves on the trees?' Mr Ma said that he could not take a decision, he would report everything to his superior and would then give me feedback.
Once back in my office, Mr Chen told me that we should continue quickly. Mrs Hu came in and asked me to show her the design proposal. Then she asked Mr Chen something in Chinese, probably about how the presentation had gone. I didn't understand the dialogue between them, but during the conversation I typed 'green light' on my translation computer and had it translated into Chinese. Mrs Hu and Mr Chen smiled!

So, keep going! I'll draw up a to-do list and see you all on the webcam! [...]

re: re: re: Construction begins in four months!

I have now done three presentations for Mr Ma and the 'Silver Forest Building' has been officially rejected.

A moment ago, Mr Chen came into my office and told me that they couldn't approve it 'after all'. Too many square metres on the upper storeys and 'few' at ground floor level. The abstract leafy façade would cause 'problems'. And, building next to the existing trees was 'difficult'. Actually, these remarks have undermined everything the project stood for.

Unbelievable that that has only now come to the surface.

I asked Mr Chen if that meant that we had to come up with a new proposal, and he answered: 'Well, maybe.'

Mr Ma will come to the office tomorrow to look at a new design. Huanyang is now also making a proposal. While I'm typing this, I'm looking at the screen of Mr Guo, a senior architect who is copying an American golf club with a book on his lap.

If you are awake, can we make a quick call to sort things out? [...]

re: re: re: re: Construction begins in four months!

'You worked the whole night through?!' asked Mr Chen surprised. We were on our way to the meeting room where Mr Ma and all his assistants were waiting. Mr Guo was there, his laptop at the ready. When Mr Chen and I sat down, Mr Guo began his presentation. He explained the ground plan from bottom left to top right, without any logic that I could see. Then the CAD elevations were shown. And then dozens of reference images. In an ingenious way, he had managed to sample all the references into his design.

Then it was my turn. I explained the new idea in three steps. First of all: a projection of the functions on site — exhibition space, offices and services. Subsequently, the exploitation of local qualities by positioning the exhibition part on the office volume, while the service volume was 'thrust' into the ground. And as the third step: the introduction of a public route across the roof to a vantage point, and an internal, ascending route along the scale models. The ascending route referred to the nearness of the mountains, and the new housing estate could be viewed from the vantage point.

Mr Ma looked distrustfully at our section. He said to Mr Chen that they would like to use the sales centre as a coffee bar later and that our design seemed difficult to modify for that purpose. I argued that the route was so relaxed that a table with chairs would easily fit onto every tread. He said that an electricity pylon near the site was probably visible from the vantage point. That was a disadvantage for sales, added Mr Chen. I argued that people would be able to see the mountains from the vantage point.

Mr Ma concluded that he couldn't make a decision, he would report everything to his superior and would return with feedback. It is painfully unproductive when clients are so non-committal in the dialogues.

Summing up, I can only remember one moment when I could read a judgement on Mr Ma's face. That was when I repeated a standpoint for the third time.

To my great surprise, a fence was to be installed around the entire area. An enormous fence as well, one that would even have to be designed by an architect. The idea of closing off the entire neighbourhood from the city and vice versa was completely contrary to my architect's belief in public and urban life. I spoke from experience: I myself now lived in the unreal world of a gated community. But despite this conviction, I initially kept my opinions to myself: I was in China and perhaps enclosure was a kind of quality I had not yet discovered.

However, I was unable to withhold my opinion on the main entrance to the compound. A number of facilities – a supermarket, restaurants and suchlike – were to be placed behind a large gateway. But by having them behind the gateway, they would be accessible to the residents only and would contribute nothing to the surroundings. Wasn't it better to move the entrance gate and to make them publicly accessible, with all the potential advantages that would bring?

My remark was made in the context of the general question: 'Do you have any suggestions for Mr Ma?' When I had explained my position, there was no response. I raised this view again on my own initiative at the next meeting. The reaction then was, as translated by Mr Chen: 'They will consider it.'

On the third occasion, I again advanced the suggestion at my own initiative, and this was my last attempt. I tried to convince Mr Ma with both old and new arguments. His face spoke volumes and this was my first experience with Chinese annoyance. Irritated looks flashed across the room but consistently avoided eye contact. There was a slightly raised voice speaking a language I didn't understand but from which I could deduce, purely from what I normally heard, that there was some agitation. Altogether, it was a most distinctive play of expressions that lasted perhaps ten seconds and ended in an irritated look from Mr Ma to Mr Chen, who in turn threw an irritated look at me.

My relationship with Mr Ma seems to be everything but productive, and as a consequence, my relationship with Mr Chen seems also to be coming under increasing pressure.

But there is no shine without friction, and it is the perfect way to discover limits. [...]

re: re: re: re: re: Construction begins in four months!

'Liuming' is no-go.

'Too strange', according to Mr Chen. He referred to an old Chinese saying when he told me that many Chinese clients 'liked dragons until they saw one'. And when they saw one, they became afraid.

'Are our ideas dragons?' I asked edgily, wondering what I should make of his remark.

He avoided my look and continued with an extremely subtle but practical observation: 'Perhaps your renderings are not suitable for the Chinese market.'

After some questioning, a piece of advice emerged: 'Chinese clients like to see many details, much reality in the renderings, with light, flags, colour and suchlike. They don't like renderings to be too simple!' More clarifying words of advice followed, and this time about project books, 'Thicker is better', and scale models, 'Bigger is better'.

Not too simple? Thicker is better? Bigger is better?

I kept my opinions to myself – this advice was well-meant. How could I summarize them in my own language? 'What a Chinese client gets is what he sees, no more and no less'? [...]

THE SKY IS NOT THE LIMIT

At first, the lack of design feedback from our new Chinese colleagues seemed to allow total design freedom. But after three months and three projects, this freedom proved to be our greatest restriction.

In the Netherlands, I was used to being critical, seeking discussion and designing in dialogue. NEXT had been founded on that principle: designs were drawn up in team settings and the result was always greater than the sum of the parts. In addition, it ensured that the results were ego-less. But ego seemed to mean a lot in China and this, combined with the fact that 'the foreign moon was rounder than the Chinese moon', appeared to imply that only I 'was allowed' to take decisions. And those decisions were not openly questioned. However, without discussion, it was impossible for me to design and develop and to chart the boundaries of what was possible. I sought dialogue with my Chinese colleagues where I could, but when it came to designs, the feedback was no more critical than 'Very, very good'. After some time I mentioned the pointlessness of this to Mr Chen and, as a consequence, he had introduced 'a new system of feedback': projects were now (1) 'good', (2) 'very good' or (3) 'very, very good'.

The absence of feedback carried the risk that all sense of reality would be lacking. Add to that the cliché, now discredited, that everything was possible in China. 'China is a playground for architects', a Chinese architect once said to me in Shanghai. My experiential world was different, and I now wondered whether he had only said what I wanted to hear. Or had I perhaps simply heard what I myself wanted to hear?

I was of the firm opinion that many of the ideas I tried to convey simply didn't get across, due to the translations but also due to the fact that our ideas didn't seem to refer to anything in China. Recently, in a presentation, my explanation of a concept, formulated in about ten sentences in English, was translated as: 'This is the entrance.' With her laser pen, the translator randomly indicated the projected diagrams.

'This is the entrance.' At least I knew that much Chinese by now.

I was constantly seeking the right way to present a project or an idea. The value of a 'concept', or 'gainian' in Chinese, seemed without parallel. Everyone seemed to be looking for 'new concepts'. But what people in China understood under the term 'concept' was different to what we understood. Whereas in our terminology concepts were primarily related to conditions, in China they were much more concerned with image and form. Often, a 'concept' in China was a completely materialized and detailed – in short, fully rendered – building.

There was another existential uncertainty that had increasingly begun to concern me. What was the overlap in the architectural ambitions of NEXT and Huanyang? Now that I had gained more insight into Huanyang's portfolio, their ambitions seemed to lie primarily with 'Big Ones'. I had my doubts about such projects, because there was so disappointingly little satisfaction to be gained by an architect whose design ambitions extended further than the elevations.

As yet there were no answers, only uncertainties, of which the greatest was whether or not I would ever penetrate the Chinese surface.

During a dinner, a German working for BMW told me that they had wished to introduce a new model onto the Chinese market. For the introduction they 'tested' the commercial on dozens of potential buyers. The film showed eight pilots. Eight is a lucky number in China, he explained. The pilots arrive in futuristic planes and subsequently perform impossible stunts. They land, step into eight BMWs, and race away in different directions. When the makers asked the potential buyers what kind of associations this commercial evoked, the collective Chinese reaction was: 'This is a car for pilots.'

There were six Westerners present at the dinner, of whom I was the only architect. But our surprise was unanimous: our association was not just a little different, but *utterly* different. Wasn't it obvious that there was a direct relationship between the experience of flying and the experience of driving a new BMW?

On a previous occasion, I had dined with a group of foreign architects who had been working in China for varying periods. There were several French, two Germans, a Swiss and an Italian. It turned out a most enjoyable evening, especially as more and more experiences with language problems, powerlessness, uncertainty and other cultural misunderstandings were exchanged.

The Italian architect left us at one at night because he had an appointment with a rendering company. It was a promising project, he said, a villa quarter near a small river in a city a few hours from Beijing. Architecture in China was hard work, he continued, because 'Chinese clients *can smell* whether or not much energy has been invested in a project.'

At the office of one of the Germans they had produced an alternative Chinese–German dictionary. The idea came from an American

company where, due to frustration with the continuous miscommunication, they had made a 'cultural dictionary':
  'ming bai' means 'there is understanding about what has been said'
  'ke yi' means 'it is possible'
  'tong yi' means 'agreed'
  'dui' means 'correct', 'good' and 'I see'
  But all of these can be translated as 'yes'
  'ye xu' means 'maybe'
  'ke neng' means a little more 'maybe'
  'maybe' can be understood as 'yes', 'no' or 'maybe'
  And 'maybe difficult' means 'no-go', but I already knew that from my own experience.

One of the French architects had cultivated an exceptionally ironic attitude. He had been working two years longer in China than we had, and had 'found a method' to cope with his 'powerlessness'. In a project in Hangzhou, a city with a population of millions to the south-west of Shanghai, he worked on a project for a central square for a new urban expansion. After a comprehensive analysis of the significance of squares in China, he developed a proposal for a red square with an abstract pattern of stars, which referred to the Chinese flag.

The client was enthusiastic, but after the presentation he was informed that 'maybe' the red square was too loaded politically. After all, this was also a square for commerce.

After a new attempt to convince the client, the idea of a red square proved untenable. The client did appreciate the star pattern and regarded it as very 'glamorous'. It reminded him of the Walk of Fame in Los Angeles.

Disappointed, the French architect designed a star pattern for the square on the basis of the Braille text 'I want to be red!'. Without telling the client, he presented the new pattern. The client liked it and the square is currently under construction.

I had listened in fascination to the story. But, with that story came the realization that such an attitude represented a position in the architectural spectrum that was diametrically opposed to the one I hoped to occupy.

2. Dialogue

MAINSTAYS

Courtesy, hospitality and friendliness are the mainstays of personal relationships in China. A fourth, no less important foundation is modesty. These are established tips on Chinese etiquette that are communicated to every foreigner and are widely mentioned in Western media, often accompanied by anecdotes about business conflicts that are the result of ignoring this etiquette.

On my birthday, Huanyang had reserved an enormous table in a Western restaurant. We sat there, almost thirty of us, and shared the same food, in much the same way as a family in China shares its food. Everyone held a short, flattering speech in English and ended with the wish that they hoped to learn a lot from me in the future. After every speech I thanked the speaker amicably and put the flattering words in perspective by expressing the wish that we could actually learn a lot from each another.

I had brought along several bottles of champagne and we jointly raised our glasses to a long and happy life. 'Happy every day!' someone said. After the meal, we went to the karaoke bar where we sang together until daylight. 'Life should always be like this', said someone else.

A few weeks later, on behalf of NEXT, I gifted a self-designed ceiling element to Mrs Hu as a sign of 'friendship and mutual understanding'. It was a large, abstract road map, measuring five by five metres, of the typical concentric urban structure of Beijing. The map had light sources at sites where Huanyang had worked on a project. And much space had been left open on the map so that a light source could be added for every future joint project.

Mrs Hu seemed surprised by the gesture.

I attempted to take advantage of the moment by deliberating out loud on the projects that future lights could possibly represent, and I asked Mrs Hu about what ideas she had about the future lights.

She gave me a friendly smile and responded: 'I hope in the future there will be many!'

NEW COLLEAGUES

MRS HU was the proprietor and founder of Huanyang. She was about forty years old and had studied some kind of architecture management programme, as I understood it. Some ten years before my arrival, she had founded Huanyang and now employed more than a hundred people.

Mrs Hu was the personification of Chinese charisma. She was gentle on the outside and as hard as nails on the inside, a side of her you only saw at the negotiating table. She was exceptionally self-disciplined and radiated an authority that required little verbal communication: one look from her was enough to get the assistants running.

She seemed to be desperately searching for a philosophy for her office, but I had trouble fathoming the parameters that she was applying. Thus, for example, her office philosophy was exceedingly flexible, even adaptable to the possible wishes of different clients. The central idea was to provide 'service'. And the emphasis invariably lay on the mastery of an 'efficient working method'.

Huanyang was run according to the 'American model', so I was told: everyone worked in accordance with fixed protocols and responsibilities. Efficiency was generated by the repetition of fixed duties. What exactly was typically American about this remained a mystery to me. Nor did I understand what advantages this model might bring to an architectural office.

MR CHEN was the vice general manager and architect, and arrived at Huanyang soon after its foundation. I estimated him to be in his late thirties. Within Huanyang, he was responsible for the 'scheme department', which comprised several architects and an auxiliary staff of dozens of employees. Mr Chen was the person with whom I was most involved. He briefed me and was the contact person with clients for our projects. He became one of my few sources of feedback.

Mr Chen was a fox with his heart in the right place. He and I were inextricably linked. To him, I was both an opportunity and a threat. I was an opportunity in the sense that his department could work more efficiently, because he was obliged 'to learn from my working methods'. On the other hand, I was a threat because I represented change. Change in China is synonymous with problems, and people preferred to avoid problems. The opportunity-threat factor that I embodied was never directly articulated by Mr Chen: he was cordial, explained things to me calmly, but never gave an outspoken opinion on precarious issues.

Mr Chen was exemplary of the flexibility of a Chinese manager: with the change of course and reorganization in the office around the time of my arrival, he also changed from an employee in traditional dress, via an everyday conservative suit, to a most fashionably dressed manager, sporting a new 'fashion haircut', all within a period of three months.

He was very kind to me and I began to build up a strong bond with him.

MR GUO was born in a small village somewhere in the west of China and first saw a real live foreigner when he was nineteen. As a senior architect, he was responsible for Huanyang's more ambitious projects and was the back-up for our joint projects. When we came up with a proposal, he made alternatives to increase the chance of obtaining or keeping the brief.

Mr Guo was simultaneously indolent and hyperactive. Ninety per cent of the time he sat slumped at his desk and watched DVDs on his computer. Before watching the DVDs, he would play a kind of Chinese 'battleships', but that probably cost too much energy. I could follow these developments in detail, due to the fact that I had a full view of his screen from behind my desk.

In his mid-thirties, he represented China's new middle class: he had a fast car, was constantly busy with mobile phones, had let out his second apartment to an American ex-pat, was married, had a son, and, I suspected, was having an affair at the office.

He could be quick, terrifyingly quick. He was 'rolled out' if a project had to be finished by tomorrow: he could stamp square metres into a master plan, build volumes and sample elevations. He had studied urban planning, but now did everything: interior, architecture, urban planning, master-planning and landscape design. He had lots of architectural and structural knowledge and was ruthless in copying because he maintained that, with 5000 years of culture, the origins of all ideas by definition lay in China.

I developed an ambivalent relationship with Mr Guo; I admired his efficiency but failed to understand his nonchalance towards our discipline.

MR JIANG was a senior architect, also in his mid-thirties, and had grown up in a remote village in the Province of Henan. Of the estimated 100 million inhabitants of Henan, only eighty were admitted to Tsinghua University every year. Mr Jiang was one of these eighty. And, as such, he represented to me the idea that, regardless of how small the opportunity in China appeared to be, that opportunity had to be seized.

Mr Jiang was responsible for the lion's share of the housing stock that Huanyang added to Beijing every year. The year prior to my arrival, this had been around one and a half million square metres. It was heavy work, because the unpredictability of the market was inherent in the unpredictability of the clients, while to me there seemed to be little architectural freedom in housing. When I voiced this suspicion, Mr Jiang reacted with the greatest conviction. Since graduating he had realized almost three million square metres of housing. More than 30,000 families lived in those houses. It was for those people that he made architecture, not for his 'own artistic ambitions', as he called it.

His position was difficult to contradict without lapsing into the argument that architecture should at least serve more than one goal.

On the basis of this healthy variance, I began to build up a strong bond with Mr Jiang.

QUESTIONNAIRE

To get to know my colleagues better and to synchronize references, I organized a small questionnaire in the office. I experienced the short office lectures that were given now and again as being too much one-way traffic, because individual opinions were seldom given in company. This seemed to issue from the theme of hierarchy and hierarchical thinking, an uneasy area for Dutch people. The idea for the questionnaire grew out of that experience: by enabling people to respond individually to straightforward questions there would be leeway beyond the claustrophobia of hierarchy.

Via Ms Jia, I distributed a questionnaire to about thirty colleagues. The results were as follows:

01 TOP FIVE CHINESE ARCHITECTS?
    1 I.M. Pei
    no other names

02 TOP FIVE INTERNATIONAL ARCHITECTS?
    1 Jacques Herzog
    2 Rem Koolhaas
    no other names

03 TOP THREE DECEASED ARCHITECTS?
    1 Frank Lloyd Wright
    2 Le Corbusier
    3 Alvar Aalto

04 BEST ARCHITECTURE CRITIC?
    no responses

05 BEST MODERN BUILDING IN BEIJING?
    1 Bird's Nest (main stadium for Olympic Games)
    2 CCTV (head office of Chinese state television)
    3 Water Cube (swimming stadium for Olympics)

06 BEST MODERN BUILDING IN THE WORLD?
    1 Bird's Nest
    2 CCTV
    3 Water Cube

07 BEST HISTORICAL BUILDING IN BEIJING?
    1 Forbidden City
    2 Summer Palace (Yiheyuan)
    3 Temple of Heaven

08 BEST HISTORICAL BUILDING IN THE WORLD?
    1 Forbidden City
    2 Summer Palace
    3 Temple of Heaven

09 WORST BUILDING IN BEIJING?
    no responses

10 WORST BUILDING IN THE WORLD?
    no responses

11 MOST BEAUTIFUL MATERIAL?
    1 glass
    2 steel
    3 wood

12 VILLA, TOWN HOUSE OR APARTMENT?
    1 apartment
    2 town house
    3 villa

13 CAR, TRAIN, METRO, BICYCLE OR PEDESTRIAN?
    1 car
    2 bicycle
    3 pedestrian

14 THE CHINESE DREAM IN ONE WORD?
    1 happy
    2 colourful
    no other responses

15 THE FUTURE OF BEIJING IN ONE WORD?
    1 happy
    2 colourful
    no other responses

If this result can be taken as representative, we could draw at least two conclusions. First of all, that the architectural references scarcely extended beyond the boundaries of China, and further, that architecture criticism in China appeared to be poorly developed.

The first outcome completely contradicted what I had imagined to be the case. The bookshelves here were filled with books on architecture. Book salespeople came to the office several times a week with trolleys laden with stacks of books. These were books that were probably not even available in Amsterdam.

Architecture books in China contain very little text but lots of images. And, without exception, the quality and price made one suspect that there was an enormous infrastructure in selectively copied architecture books. I once saw Mr Guo in complete ecstasy: it was now possible to buy DVDs containing scans from books. And these were substantially cheaper than the books themselves: 'Paper is more expensive than a DVD!' And because everything was on DVD, the pages themselves no longer needed to be scanned! In this development, he recognized the opportunity to reinforce his status: he proudly administered the largest image library in the office. And the library was not only in his computer; mentally he also had an almost encyclopaedic overview of modern architecture worldwide.

If the body of references was really much larger than the outcome of the questionnaire indicated, how reliable was my second conclusion?

Older colleagues were often extremely reserved and, as a consequence of their frequently more poorly developed verbal knowledge of English, only limited dialogue was possible. 'Good or not good?' was often my typically simplified question. 'Good' or 'not good' would then be their answer, which was invariably qualified by the addition of the word 'maybe'.

'Maybe' was a short English word that every Chinese person seemed to know and invariably used. As a result, the life of a foreigner in China was shrouded in uncertainty.

The language skills of young colleagues were much better. Nevertheless, I wittingly and unwittingly simplified my English in their presence too. By avoiding an intellectual smokescreen of expressions such as 'hypothetical truth', 'iconic noise', 'symbolic realm' and 'post-modern traditionalism', brief but penetrating dialogues became possible. Particularly in face-to-face discussions, a number of younger colleagues with whom I built up contact were so outspoken that they could almost be characterized as thinkers in black-and-white by Dutch standards. Judgements about the most diverse situations were often formulated in fractions of a second and often displayed little qualification.

Why didn't this show up in the results of the questionnaire? This was filled in exclusively with answers where 'the head did not rise above the grass'. Was that because 'he who stands outside the group is first attacked', as a Chinese saying goes?

Something suddenly occurred to me. When I had requested Ms Jia to translate the questionnaire and to distribute it to my colleagues, she asked 'Do you want people to write their names on them?'. Good idea, I thought. By linking the answers to a particular person I would have a point of address for later discussion.

'And is there a prize we can win?' she then asked with a smile.

I assumed she was being funny and I answered jokingly: 'Maybe!' But could it be that my colleagues really thought that this was a prize competition? In that case, within Chinese trains of thought, as I had increasingly come to see, a personal opinion would by definition be less suited than a strategic estimate of what the jury would like to hear. And in this 'competition prize', I was the jury. My suspicions materialized: a few days later, Ms Jia subtly enquired whether or not a winner had emerged.

With my questionnaire I had gained more insight not into the personal ideas of my Chinese colleagues but rather into the collective picture they had of me. And that picture of me was probably just as limited as my picture of them.

MASLOW
Conversation with Mr Chen during lunch

J: Have you ever heard of 'Maslow's hierarchy of needs'?
C *(thinking)*: Maslow? I have!
J *(drawing the diagram)*: I believe it's quite an interesting diagram, let's think, how did it work again ...
C: Right, five parts, how's the top called again?
J *(checking Google on his phone)*: It goes from physiological Basic Needs like health and food at the wide bottom to Safety, Belonging and Esteem. Self-actualization is on the narrow top. Where would you put yourself as an architect, now, in contemporary China?
C: Here, between Belonging and Safety. You?
J: Wow, I don't want to be arrogant, but I hope to be here, in the top, self-actualization.
C *(surprised)*: Are all architects in Holland in this position?
J *(thinking)*: I don't think so, but probably most. What about Chinese architects, are they all in your position?
C *(still smiling)*: You have to understand, John, China is a developing country.
J *(also smiling)*: I know.
C: But do you really know the meaning?

J: Please tell me.
C: You know, China has a large population. And there is very little security. If you get sick and need to go to a hospital, the personal costs are severe. If you lose your job, there is no more money for you. Young people bear a large responsibility towards their parents, to take care of them when they grow old. And most of us are only allowed to have one child, so this child grows up under tremendous pressure to extend the family bloodline and prosperity. The Chinese path in life is full of worries and uncertainties and we cannot rely on the government for paying for the three mountains: education, medical care and housing.
J: My background is so much more privileged, the Dutch government supports all 'three mountains'. And for me, there was an abundance of choices, where to study, to travel, to discover... to live and think freely.
C: You know, I built my first building when I was a student?
J *(surprised)*: What kind of building?
C *(smiling)*: A hotel. My professor got the project but he was too busy. So he asked me to design it.
J: Was it built?
C *(sketching)*: It's built, it's not too bad.
J: Do you have any pictures of it?
C: I think so, I will try to find them.
J: You know, when I finished my study, I had no idea of how to make a building. The most important thing I learned, I think, was analytical and conceptual thinking.
C: You're free, that's why you are in the top of the Pyramid! *(worrying:)* I hope my son later can be there too!
J *(smiling)*: Me too, me too.
C *(silently thinking)*
J: You know, Mr Zhen told me last week that my life in China was pretty good. I asked him why, and he told me that I only had to worry about architecture. And in his opinion there was 'nothing to worry about architecture'. Do you have any idea what he tried to say with this?
C: Chinese society, John. We live in a society where: 'A dog needs a rabbit and a donkey needs a mill.'
J: I don't see your meaning.
C: You are interested in architecture, that's very good, but other people have more basic worries. They have to make sure they are

needed, how do you call this, indispensable? Just like the 'dog needs the rabbit', no rabbit, no need for the dog. If the dog kills the rabbit, no need for the dog.
J: You're saying that some people are pretending they are working?
C *(smiling)*: I'm saying Chinese people are very smart and architecture is not the most important thing in life for some people.
J: NEXT is so different. In Amsterdam we are friends with a common objective: architecture.
C: Sounds like a very good life! Have you ever heard of the Chinese word 'guanxi'?
J: Personal relationship and mutual benefit: it's more important to know 'who' than to know 'what'.
C: That's it. It's the most important aspect of Chinese society, only through 'guanxi' things can be done smoothly. And 'guanxi' is the secret of Huanyang. Mrs Hu's relationships are very good so her service for clients is very good. That's why clients find her.
J: You're telling me that the asset of such a large company lies in the hands of a single person and this 'service' also has little to do with architecture itself?
C *(smiling)*: I'm saying architecture is not the most important in life for some people.
J: Are you also saying that architecture isn't on the top of Huanyang's list of objectives?
C: For some people architecture is not goal but means.
J *(thinking for a long time)*: Is there anything that you can recommend me?
C *(thinking)*: Beijing is not China and the office is not Beijing.

VICTORIA

'Hi John, I'm Victoria, if you have any questions, you can ask me!'

Victoria's English was exceptionally good. She stood uneasily in the doorway and apparently had moved heaven and earth to come and tell me this.

'My Chinese name is Yuan, but Victoria is more easy for you to remember', she continued.

Victoria had studied architecture in Shenzhen and in all matters concerning architecture she appeared to understand immediately what I meant. Even better, she learned so rapidly that when we were leaning over drawings or staring at computer screens she sometimes anticipated my questions before I asked them.

As a result of her good English and her acute architect's mind, she became my most important direct access to more insight in China, besides Mr Chen. She did not translate information literally, but explained how this information could be interpreted in various ways. When we had time she taught me Chinese because, in her opinion, it was only by learning Chinese that I would be more capable of understanding China.

She was particularly keen on translating presentations and, in the run-up to these, she posed a seemingly endless stream of questions to get to the underlying ideas.

Her questions provided answers to the questions I had not yet discovered or articulated.

Unfortunately, the inevitable moment arrived much too soon. She told me that for 'her career as an architect' she would like to study abroad. 'Where do you want to study then?' I asked, interested. 'Delft', was the resolute answer. 'I recommend Delft to her, and her to Delft', I wrote in my letter of recommendation.

Before moving to the Netherlands, she married her boyfriend, adhering to the serious advice of her family. She asked me to hold a speech during her marriage. 'I hope that the Netherlands will be a genuine enrichment for her, and vice versa,' I said, meaning every word.

'Thank you John,' she said at the conclusion. 'Thank you, thank you!' said her parents, who were standing next to her, in Chinese. I said 'Not at all!' in English, but what I really wanted to say was 'Come back soon!' in Chinese.

FACE!

After 'Liuming', our first, not particularly successful project, Huanyang allowed us time to 'digest' the process and the results. I guessed that this was a strategic move to defuse any possible mutual friction at the root. A part of this strategy was that the project was swathed in silence. Huanyang didn't express the slightest suggestion of performing any kind of evaluation. But this silence led nowhere and for that reason I repeatedly sought answers, especially from Mr Chen, in order to learn more about why some things work in China and some things don't.

I sought responses at a deeper level than his well-intended advice on form, deeper than his suggestions about adapting renderings to a certain taste or about building larger scale models so that the designs would make more of an impact. However, my questions were too complex to be answered simply. In fact, they seemed to be increasingly unwelcome, going by Mr Chen's reaction. Nonetheless, undesirable or not, not only I but also my colleagues in Amsterdam were looking for substantive arguments.

The dialogue between Huanyang and NEXT, between China and the Netherlands, in which I functioned as the pivot, was critically tested whenever we took part in architectural design competitions. All the basic information for a project came via Huanyang. I filtered and assessed the information and passed it on to Amsterdam, along with the first diagrams. Amsterdam took stock of the information, consulted me, developed one or more concepts and sent them back to Beijing. I presented them to Huanyang for feedback, developed the ideas further and sent everything back to Amsterdam again. This process was repeated until the absolute deadline for production had been reached. From that moment onward, Amsterdam and I directed our efforts towards preserving the conceptual points of departure as much as possible.

That was the theory.

But real-life practice was more erratic, as transpired in a design competition for a head office for the Chinese IT company Watchdata.

Watchdata was an 'instant' company. Ten years ago it didn't exist and within two years it was to occupy a new head office of 55,000 square metres. I had visited the client's present office, an anonymous building, and there I had received a briefing in the form of one A4 page with the most general list of programme components. And I had visited the site, a razed expanse of land where an 'Electric City' was to rise. Unfortunately, there was as yet no design for this 'Electric City'. Nothing about the visit to the office, the briefing, or the visit to the site provided any kind of foothold for a design or for the start of a design process.

Mr Chen had mentioned en passant that our chances were slender, in view of the fact that we didn't know the client well and that therefore we could expect few 'interim suggestions' from his side. The remark called to mind Mr Jia, who had shown the design to the jury several times before the presentation in Qingdao. This type of 'advance knowledge' was at odds with the Dutch moral framework of our profession. However, Mr Chen had no moral worries at all. For him, the 'disadvantage' of the lack of 'interim suggestions' primarily caused him to wonder how we could manage to make a 'good' design. In his view, Huanyang was ideally an intermediary between the client and NEXT, his 'suggestions' were the client's 'suggestions' and this position released him from any form of responsibility.

But without 'suggestions' from the client, Huanyang itself was our only source of starting points for the design and, moreover, the only sparring partner on whom we could test our ideas. Mr Chen's dilemma was that he had to furnish us with input without being held to account later if his input turned out not to be in line with the wishes of the client. And my onerous task was the unproductive quest for useful input for Amsterdam, where the project was to be developed.

Huanyang's 'suggestions' were often not relevant enough for us. In most cases we were shown a reference project that bore no relationship at all, in my view, to the design we were working on. 'Suggestions' about design proposals were not particularly constructive. Ideas were subtly but resolutely dismissed in an instant with the argument: 'Maybe difficult in China'.

With some of the 'suggestions' I only saw the hidden negative connotation much too late, such as the remark that a proposal for a façade referred to Japanese windows. The value of this remark was graphically explained by Mr Guo, who told me about a washing powder advert on Chinese television. A white sheet with a large red spot is put into the washing machine and taken out again after a short wash. The red spot had disappeared. 'Did you get it?' asked Mr Guo smiling: 'We washed the Japanese flag!'

In short, all 'suggestions' were sublime examples of Chinese rhetorical gymnastics in which direct statements are avoided. For me, they nurtured the urgent necessity to discover verbal and non-verbal substitutes for evaluations.

The friction became tangible: Amsterdam was becoming increasingly critical because the consistency of the design process was constantly being undone. And my questing attitude was increasingly unsettling Huanyang, as they expected NEXT to assume a more leading role.

Then Huanyang responded subtly to a draft model by mentioning the theme of 'face'. Sensitive to all forms of information, I asked about the relationship to our project, as this wasn't clear to me.

To me, 'face' referred to the cultural concept of 'mianzi': the rigid system of values behind the social interaction of taking on a face, giving face, and the far-reaching implications of causing someone to lose face. Wasn't the essence of this inter-personal: always acting in all aspects in agreement with a position in a hierarchy?

My Chinese colleagues smiled in a friendly way and told me that 'mianzi' was not only something human, but that companies and, as a consequence, buildings too had a relationship with 'face'. The explanation went further and was more specific: in Beijing, the south façade, following the principles of feng shui, was the most important façade of a building. A north façade could be treated 'more economically'.

This was again information that was difficult to fit into an Amsterdam mindset. Feng shui was of little importance to us, and concentrating only on a façade was contrary to the integral mode of designing that we represented. But a point of no return had now been reached, the deadline was rapidly approaching and, with little other practical information, we had to choose the direction in which we wished to take the project.

We were in China, this design was for a Chinese client, for a Chinese organization, and we had information from our Chinese partner that was controversial but useful in some measure. The logical choice was to lean towards the 'suggestions' advanced by Huanyang. Feedback from Chinese colleagues had never been so clear: the 'face of Watchdata' was taken as the starting point.

The programme comprised offices, 'research and development labs', production facilities and ancillary services such as conference and sports amenities. The idea of 'face' was translated into the zoning of functions according to their degree of representation: from the south – first the offices, then R&D and then the production at the farthest part of the site. In this way, four gardens in which two pavilions could be built, one for sport and one for conferences, were inserted in the space between R&D and production. The office volume was moulded to include terraces and to guarantee daylight in the R&D volume. The logo of the company was worked into the construction and the façade.

On the basis of two different impulses, the design process moved into the fast lane. Amsterdam worked on the idea of connecting the zoned functions on the first floor (in China the second floor) by means of a central square with overhead bridges. A visitor route would begin and end as a roundabout on this square and lead past the gardens with the conference and sports pavilions. To Huanyang it seemed as if the priority lay much more with the exterior, and approval of the direction in which they appeared to see the project going was echoed in the suggestions: 'Good, but make the south even bigger!' and: 'Shape the south even more!'

In the meantime, the south elevation had grown to become a 'face' more than 180 metres long and 40 metres tall.

The project had to be presented to the client at 7 p.m. on Sunday evening. In the car to the client's office, I ran through the presentation with Mr Chen. He suggested spending less time on explaining the organizational diagrams of the building: 'It's better to explain the building with the renderings' was his advice. 'How can I explain a building with a rendering?' I asked him concernedly.

It was the second time I had run through the presentation with him. On the basis of the previous discussion and his suggestions, I had altered the structure of the story. Instead of starting with the conditions for bringing added value to the way Watchdata was organized, the agenda of the presentation had been changed to 'Eight steps towards an international landmark'. This aim had irritated me, because it was about the image rather than about conditions. 'International landmark' – it was a term that meant nothing to me. But I surrendered, not least because Mr Chen emphasized several times that an 'international landmark' was precisely what all Chinese clients wished to have.

We were close to the client's office. Mr Chen smiled, but his eyes betrayed annoyance about the smouldering discussion. 'No problem', I said to him. 'There will be more time for the renderings.'

We waited with three other architectural offices in a small room for our opportunity to enter the meeting room. Outside the room stood the scale models of all the participating offices. Mr Chen and I examined them all attentively and he concluded with a smile: 'Maybe we have a good chance.'

The presentation room was full of people who were introduced to me as 'specialists'. The presentation lasted half an hour and the renderings were the main component of my line of argument. Excitedly, I waited for the first reactions from the client. They came in the form of a question: 'Why did you make such a big building?'

I didn't understand the question – wasn't this to be the head office? Surely it deserved the 'face' of an 'international landmark'?

A short discussion in Chinese followed. The presentation was quickly rounded off and, when we were back in the car, I was told that something had probably gone wrong in the communication. We had missed the 'interim information'. The client 'probably' now wanted several buildings. The space that his company didn't need right now would be independently rented out to other companies. 'Maybe that is difficult in a big building.'

We were awarded second prize. 'We lost!' was Mr Chen's reaction, while he avoided the questioning look in my eyes.

Not only the project but an entire team of colleagues had lost face. The chaotic three weeks in which the project had been developed flashed through my mind. I had largely set aside our own integrity and consistency and allowed unsuccessful priorities outside our own frame of reference to prevail. If the concept of *mianzi* were to have any significance to us Westerners, I would also have lost much face in Amsterdam.

ADAPTING

After Watchdata, Huanyang followed a strategy similar to the one followed after Liuming. There was enough time to digest the results but no room for evaluation. Instead of seeking dialogue, I made use of the space on offer to reflect, during a short stay in New Zealand, upon our China experiences until then.

I sought frantically for a fitting relation between Dutch and Chinese values and for an appropriate ratio between the input from Amsterdam and Huanyang. But if I looked critically at the projects up to that time, they seemed increasingly dominated by a spontaneous assemblage of different ideas and interests. It did lead to designs but, as had been the case with Watchdata, the Chinese values of *feng shui* and 'face' had little in common with the Dutch pursuit of 'added value for the organization'.

That assemblage of divergent ideas and interests was the direct result of my questioning attitude, which probably could be characterized as typically Dutch. But it was also the result of the relatively free access we gave to Chinese values in our designs. However, it was precisely this probing attitude that met with increasing resistance from our Chinese colleagues. In their view, they were not the ones who ought to provide the answers – that was our role. And the inclusion of misconstrued Chinese values met with increasing resistance in Amsterdam, where the added value of these ideas could not be easily estimated.

The provisional conclusion, therefore, was that for Huanyang I should communicate our ideas more resolutely and for NEXT I should be more uncompromising in my support of those ideas.

I landed in Beijing early in the morning and was at the office a few hours later. I first distributed the sweets I had brought from New Zealand for my colleagues. It was a custom I had observed among Chinese colleagues who returned from a journey. The unknown tastes were eagerly tried, followed by verdicts ranging from 'delicious' to 'not good, it tastes like traditional Chinese medicine'.

This coincided with an announcement about a new project. Huanyang was involved in designing a large-scale housing project in the north of Beijing. While they concentrated on the tower blocks, we were asked to design the accompanying children's day care centre.

I could scarcely conceal my excitement: a new project, of a type that we had never even been close to getting in the Netherlands. There was a short briefing outlining the planning preconditions. I was given a copy of an illustration of a typical Chinese childcare centre from a kind of Chinese Neufert, an encyclopaedic volume giving a typological overview of Chinese buildings. Brief discussions with colleagues enabled me to construct a more accurate picture of the brief. In China, childcare centres are crucial places in the raising and training of children, perhaps to a greater extent than in the Netherlands. 'Day care centre' was actually an erroneous description because children stayed overnight there. In the most extreme cases, the parents brought their children here on Monday morning and only picked them up again on Friday evening.

I heard various stories. Due to China's one-child policy, many Chinese children grew up as an only child. The lack of interaction with brothers and sisters could be 'compensated' in this type of care centre. Another Chinese colleague described it as a necessity because parents in China were 'too busy' with their work. And yet another colleague could only conclude that such child care centres were 'incredibly expensive'.

All the information I gathered was sent to Amsterdam as an e-mail and a fax. The fax showed a sketch of a typical childcare centre, facing south and consisting of one volume of facilities and one of classrooms. The only exceptional space that could provide an impulse to develop this diagram further was the desired communal area serving the centre as a whole. This is where the children were to eat together and sing together, among other activities.

Ultimately, the jet lag took its toll and I left for home feeling exhausted.

The next morning, a fax was waiting for me on my desk. I looked at it and a strange feeling came over me. After six years' intensive work as NEXT architects, fourteen years since we had become acquainted and had collaborated increasingly on a range of projects in and out of our educational programme, almost six months since I had moved from Amsterdam and had tried to put down roots in Beijing, one day after I had sent the fax to Amsterdam with a typical diagram for a children's day care centre, there was this extraordinary moment.

The sketch was brilliant.

The collective area had been 'thrust' through the volume of facilities, creating an amphitheatre-like inner space. This space contrasted with the formal spaces of the volume and could become the place where children could informally learn, play and discover things.

Adrenaline. I hadn't been at the brainstorming session in Amsterdam, but nevertheless I was now looking at a proposal that dovetailed exactly with my idea of a good building. In fact it was the purest example of how we had envisaged our work in China: I would give the initial impulse from China and Amsterdam would translate it into an architectural proposal.

Mr Chen entered my work office and reacted coolly to the sketch.

Ignoring this omen, I resolutely worked it up in Beijing. Slowly but surely Mr Chen began to thaw and the feedback became more concrete. Increasingly, Huanyang seemed to see more risks than opportunities in the design. There was relatively little money for childcare centres because the developer had to finance the building and not the government. It was difficult to achieve fluid forms in China, and the spans and the glass roof were very expensive, I was told in no uncertain terms.

My arguments were quite clear: more economical alternatives were of little relevance at this stage of the project. We had not even received a building budget, so how could we opt for a more economical solution? At this stage, economics were less important than architectural quality and the possible intrinsic added value for the childcare centre, I maintained.

I used the same arguments in a casual discussion with Mrs Hu about the project. She told me that the architect's task was to save money for the client. I argued that the architect's task was to enable quality for both the client and the users. The impasse was complete when I said that not every quality could be expressed in money.

Probably as a consequence of this impasse, Huanyang openly began to develop an alternative proposal for the project. I was sceptical about this move, but acquiesced to Mr Chen's statement that Huanyang would undoubtedly give preference to our design at the presentation. He even defused the situation brilliantly by saying that the purpose of their design was only 'to show the client more options'. It called to mind Huan's remark that 'Chinese clients like to choose'.

The presentation was a week later.

I introduced our design with a series of analyses of different schools, both Dutch and international. The translation of the analysis into the design, and the design itself, seemed to meet with approval. Discussion at the end of the presentation seemed limited to our proposal, which I thought was a good sign. Mr Chen confirmed what I had suspected when he whispered: 'They think your design is very good.'

I again experienced a rush of adrenaline when the announcement came that our design had been chosen.

The euphoria dissipated immediately when it was also announced that it was not yet possible to make a final decision. This could only be made further up in the hierarchy. An extensive discussion had preceded this conclusion, with the two top managers debating the issue of which proposal was cheaper. Our glass roof was expensive, but Huanyang's proposal, with an enormous free-floating steel roof of steel spanning the school, was 'very expensive'.

I concluded from this that our design had been given the benefit of the doubt. There were alternatives to our glass roof, but if the steel 'canopy' were to be omitted, nothing would remain of Huanyang's design. We were given a number of 'suggestions' for improvement, which concentrated on looking for ways 'to optimize the design'. Huanyang was requested to design two new alternatives so as to 'give the leaders more choice'. My previous 'benefit of the doubt' now made way to incomprehension about this commission for Huanyang.

Back at my desk I sent an e-mail to Amsterdam with a detailed report of the presentation and the remarkable hierarchical struggle between the two most important managers. 'Hold on to this project!' was the response.

At the following presentation, a few days later, two new 'specialists' were present. Besides the managers and assistants who had attended the previous session, there was now a lady who knew 'all about childcare centres' and a man who knew 'all about finance'. The lady appreciated our design: the fluid forms and the atrium were expensive but could provide a very positive environment for children. The man was particularly critical and seriously questioned the financial feasibility of our project: the costs were substantial, much higher than those for 'normal childcare centres'.

Again no final decision was possible. This time, all the proposals that had been advanced until then would be presented to the local government. The client would 'probably suggest' our proposal, but if the local government had other ideas then 'these would have to be respected'. While waiting for the definitive decision, we were all requested to look for 'more economical solutions' to achieve 'the same effect', because money was 'limited'.

'Can we meet the local government to present the design?' I asked Mr Chen excitedly. He responded with a smile and said: 'For now, finding ways of saving money for the client is more important.' With this, he almost literally quoted, consciously or unconsciously, the words of Mrs Hu, while repeating the wishes of the client.

Again a detailed description of the presentation was sent to Amsterdam. And there, just as had happened to me in Beijing, the feeling arose that we had taken a step towards realizing an extraordinary design.

But then it became very quiet on the part of the client.

After some time, it became clear what was going on. The entire project of which the childcare centre was part, had been sold to another developer, one we didn't know and with whom we had no connections.

There were three ways for a developer to make money, stated Mr Chen. The first and most lucrative way was to sell a paper project with all the right permits to another developer, as had just happened to us. The second was to sell a complete, built project to another developer. The third and least lucrative option was to sell all the units to individual buyers.

Was the reason for the failure of this project an economic one? In retrospect, almost all the parties had taken economics as the dominant point of departure. I had been the exception and had even regarded the economics as being of 'little relevance'. Or was the reason for failure the fact that we had no relationship with the new client? In that case, he could at least discuss the design and any other wishes or requirements with us?

Not only the entire process, but also the priorities in this project were so different from our work and thinking in the Netherlands that once again a number of renderings and newly gained insights were the only results of our efforts. Building in China demanded more than a purely architectural agenda. Whatever the situation, building in China was always part of an economic agenda.

Convinced as I was of the quality of the design, and in view of the experience I had gained with Watchdata, this time I had excluded the influence of Huanyang and even of the client as much as possible. This was going to be a genuine NEXT project, one we could have realized in the Netherlands. But this strategy was extremely unproductive. We were not in the Netherlands, we were in a totally different context where different values and significances applied. We were in China for the purpose of building and, in order to realize this, it was necessary to adapt our thoughts and actions. And to make adaptation possible, it was not only useful to have more insight into China, it was absolutely essential.

THE ESSENCE OF CHINA
Conversation with an unknown man, when I was moving house

?: Hello, are you going to live here?
J: Yes, I am.
?: Welcome, I'm your new neighbour, you can call me Qing.

J: Hello Mr Qing, I'm John.
Q: Hello Mr John, where are you from?
J: Holland.
Q: Ah, Holland, a rich country, Philips, Shell!
J *(smiling)*: Holland is a small country.
Q: What's your business, Mr John?
J: Architecture, I'm an architect.
Q: Ah, architecture, very good, we need many new buildings in China! *(thinking:)* Many foreign friends have problems with their visa in China, what about you?
J: No problems, my visa is valid for four years, then I can renew.
Q: Four years? So long? You must be an architecture specialist, the Chinese government must want to have your knowledge!

A few weeks later. A conversation with Mr Qing, who was almost sixty and by now a familiar acquaintance. Mr Qing, or Lao Qing as I now called him on the basis of respect and friendship, turned out to have completed three university studies: English, International Commerce and Hotel Management.
J: Please explain me China better, Lao Qing.
LQ: Why John, you've been living in China for a long time, you must be an expert now.
J *(smiling)*: I'm not an expert, Lao Qing. My visa says 'Alien Residence Permit' and after many months I still feel alien.
LQ: What would you like to talk about?
J: Many things, for instance, is there something like an essence of Chinese culture?
LQ: You have big questions for a young man, John. *(thinking:)* What would you think the answer is?
J: I think your answer will be 'harmony'.
LQ: Correct, the essence of Chinese culture is Harmony.
J: What's the meaning of Harmony then?
LQ: Everything should be in balance: people, nature, the universe.
J: Do you think China is in balance, Lao Qing?
LQ *(surprised)*: Why do you ask me that, John?
J: Because I tend to see not one China but many Chinas. And most of the Chinas I see, seem to be more unbalanced than balanced.
LQ: Which different Chinas do you see, John?
J: Different Chinas between North and South, East and West,

between politics and people, between city and countryside, between rich and poor, between younger and older generations, between old and new values, between ... many ...

LQ: I agree, John. China is facing many challenges now, but our ultimate objective is Harmony. You know, some things can't be solved easily.

J: That's a political answer, Lao Qing.

LQ: You have big opinions for a young man, John.

J *(smiles)*

LQ: Many countries around the world, many people around the world, criticize China for our political and economic system. But look at the United States, for instance, people have to work until they are 65, both men and women! In China, my wife got her pension at 55, and I will get it when I'm 60. We're happy people, John, we have no terrorism, it's safe, and everything is relatively cheap. In China, we call this 'shenghuo shunli', a smooth life. It's what Chinese people wish each other: a smooth life! And the Chinese government makes sure China is safe and prospers because of our strong economic development.

J: But isn't that something like: 'food prevails over moral principles'?

LQ *(irritated)*: Moral principles? You think there's a problem with our moral principles? Didn't some years before in Europe hundreds of old people die because of summer heat? Isn't there any air conditioning for old people in Europe? Where are the moral principles in that?

J *(surprised)*: That summer was exceptionally hot, Lao Qing, typically, not all homes in Europe have a need for air conditioning.

LQ: Please explain me your meaning then.

J: I believe in the Chinese concept of Harmony, in a sense it's a beautifully idealistic and indisputable objective. But I think there a discrepancy between the idea that not all can be solved in a short period and therefore people have no other choice than to accept the situation they are in now. In other words, Harmony as an objective harbours a promise, which at the same time, could be used as a kind of excuse to make reality more acceptable.

LQ: Where are you going with this conversation, John?

J: Let's say, the objective of China is Harmony. Harmony can only be achieved by consensus, right?

LQ: Right.
J: Consensus leaves little room for different ideas and opinions. To achieve consensus, any 'noise' needs to be patronized. If patronized, the ideal of consensus is restored. If 'noise' can't be patronized, it needs to be excluded, fear of exclusion is often enough to restore consensus.
LQ: You're using big words, John.
J: I'm just trying to understand things better, Lao Qing.
LQ: Doesn't your country believe in Harmony?
J: Sure, but I think we prefer to call it 'compromise'. If you would ask me personally, I believe more in 'diversity' than in 'harmony'.
LQ: Diversity? Where's the advantage in that? How many countries are there now in Europe? Twenty-seven?
J: Europe faces many challenges too, both internally and externally.
LQ: Geographical division weakens, John. China had been divided for centuries. Now, being united, it makes us politically and economically strong. Many people reach higher living standards because China is united now.
J: Politically and economically strong, for sure. Higher living standards, definitely. But what about socially and culturally, Lao Qing? Can't you see the richness of diversity: different viewpoints, different ideas, different beliefs?
LQ: Your opinion expresses our cultural differences very well, John. Western people believe everything is about the individual, in China we believe everything is about the collective. I recommend you to read more Confucius, John.
J: There's no judgement in my viewpoint, Lao Qing.
LQ: You see ghosts where there are no ghosts, John.
J: I'm just trying to understand China better, Lao Qing.
LQ *(smiling)*: Thank you for your conversation, John, I learned a lot from you today.
J: I learned a lot from you too, Lao Qing.
LQ *(eyes distended)*: Sorry, I need to go now, I asked my wife to prepare me a turtle for lunch. Do you know why I like to eat turtles, John?
J: Eating turtles guarantees a long life, Lao Qing?!
LQ *(smiling)*: You're right, John!

'Qi is a fundamental concept within traditional Chinese culture. Qi is a component of everything that exists, as a kind of spiritual energy. Qi can be roughly translated as Energy Flow or, more literally, as 'air' or 'breath'. Qi has always been an essential part of Chinese philosophy, although the meaning has been subject to change in the course of time. Qi and Li, pattern, repetition, form, order, are fundamental categories, just like energy has been to the West.'

'The traditional Chinese art of designing and organizing space, feng shui, is based on the Qi flows, interaction between the five elements, Yin Yang and other factors.'

'The retention or dissipation of Qi influences health, wealth, energy, happiness and many more aspects of the user of space. The colour, form and position of each object in space influence the flow of Qi by slowing it down, distorting it, or accelerating it. Influencing Qi directly influences the energy level of the users.'

The necessity to acquire more insight brought me into spiritual worlds unknown to me. There were many impulses in this direction, such as the remark in the Watchdata project about the relationship between feng shui and the south façade of a building. And such as an interior project in which we suggested a combination of slanting lines. At first the client seemed genuinely to appreciate the design, but a few days later came the message that diagonal lines were not 'lucky'. 'Slanting' – 'xie' in Chinese – was pronounced in almost the same way as the Chinese word for 'accident'. The conclusion was that this design had 'bad feng shui', and therefore the design was unacceptable.

To me, as a sober Dutch architect, this kind of argument was difficult to assess. In my opinion, feng shui embraced 'reasonable argumentation', as Mr Chen referred to it, such as the orientation of buildings to the south to optimize the incidence of sun and daylight. But to make a direct connection between the pronunciation of a word and a design was rather subjective. And there was little leeway for subjective argumentation in architectural discourse in the Netherlands.

Within NEXT, too, subjectivity had been excluded as much as possible. Projects were developed as objectively as possible, and we wished to develop projects in China with this same attitude. But how relevant was rational argumentation like this when it was judged and valued irrationally?

An ideal opportunity presented itself. A client wished to visit a site with a 'feng shui expert' and had also invited me to accompany them. The published texts on what to me was a pretty impenetrable world were too abstract to be of any use. But now there was the opportunity to get some immediate answers and discover what was 'lucky', what was not, and why not.

For almost an hour, the client, my colleague Ms Qin and I followed the feng shui expert around. With the aid of a feng shui compass, the expert had given advice on the most diverse matters, such as the layout of the rooms, the organization of the departments, the necessity of having traditional elements in the interior, and the design of the landscape around the building. The client had asked a question now and again and respectfully accepted the recommendations. An assistant had jotted down the smallest details of the advice. All that time I had waited deferentially, but now my moment had arrived.

I showed the feng shui expert our design for the building and Ms Qin translated the ideas. I awaited his response with some trepidation. His first advice was to add traditional elements such as red lanterns to the design. 'Why?' I wanted to know. Ms Qin reacted uneasily, but translated the question that seemed so obvious to me.

The feng shui expert responded via Ms Qin in a friendly way: 'Feng shui is a very delicate art, it is the art of combining the heart and a centuries-old science.' He examined the design again and then suggested placing a wall in the interior, otherwise Qi would escape.

'Please explain Qi to me, and how it escapes', I asked via the increasingly uncomfortable-looking Ms Qin.

'Feng shui is a very delicate *Chinese* art!' was the response.

Open questions were proving to have little effect, so I tried questions that could provide more concrete answers. 'Which colours would you recommend?' Ms Qin translated the question, the feng shui expert thought about it for a moment and replied via Ms Qin: 'Purple'.

'Why?' I ventured, while looking first at Ms Qin and then at the feng shui expert.

There was no chance of any further 'dialogue' because the client subtly but clearly indicated that it was time to go. The feng shui expert was given a 'hongbao', a red envelope filled with money, for his services, and we said our farewells. Ms Qin and I had no transport, so the feng shui expert offered to drop us off at the subway station. We were pleased to accept his invitation.

The feng shui expert sat next to his driver, and Ms Qin and I sat in the back.

Q TO J: I would like to ask the feng shui expert some questions.
J TO Q: Then do it.
Q TO J: I'm not sure if it is appropriate.
J TO Q: Sure, no problem.
Q TO FSE: Excuse me Sir, can I ask you a question?
FSE *(turns his head towards the back seats)*: Of course.
Q: When do you think I should marry?
FSE *(thinking)*: When were you born?
Q: 1983, March 12.
FSE *(thinking)*: I think it's best if you marry in 2009.
Q: Thank you, I still have some time!
Q TO J: I still have time. I'll need to tell my parents!
J TO Q: Could you ask him if he has any advice for me?
Q TO FSE: John would like to know if you have any advice for him.
FSE TO Q *(looking at John, thinking)*: His heart is good, but in his mind are too many worries.
J TO Q *(after the translation, smiling)*: Why would I have too many worries?
FSE TO Q: He has so many questions. His head is not big enough for all his questions. He feels too much responsibility, I wish him for the future more 'gongzuo pingan' (relaxed work).

After the feng shui expert had dropped us off at the subway.
Q *(looking concerned)*: His advice is quite right, you're too busy with your work.
J *(smiling)*: Depends on what you think is important.
Q: Do you really think work is important?
J: Do you really think I moved 10,000 kilometres just to have more 'gongzuo pingan'?
Q: Then why did you do it?

J: To discover new things, new ideas, to broaden my perspective.
Q: You're just a, what is it called, a workaholic. And I'm not the only one in the office who thinks so.
J: Is a workaholic in China a person who loves his profession?
Q: A workaholic in China is somebody that never stops asking questions about his work.
J: OK, then you're right, I'm a workaholic!
Q: You see, the feng shui expert is right!

Smiling, Ms Qin and I took our leave of one another. When I got into the train I wondered about the extent to which subjectivity could be objectively understood. 'Maybe difficult', I concluded.

CONSCIENCE

'Beijing is not China and the office is not Beijing', Mr Chen had said to me. So whenever possible I seized every opportunity outside work to discover Beijing and to visit other cities at the weekends. And again wherever possible I sought a link with our professional field of action outside the immediate building practice, something we would have considered self-evident in Amsterdam.

As a result, I once found myself sitting in a communal student room on the campus of Tsinghua University. I was there for a lecture and, afterwards, I wanted to see the studios and the projects. When I was later presented with the choice between a lunch in a restaurant with several of the teachers or in the canteen with some of the students, the choice was quickly made: in the canteen with the students. After lunch, I had more or less invited myself into their living environment.

I sat on the lower half of a bunk bed, and looked around the room, about 12 square metres in size. Three bunk beds and six computers on desks made it almost impossible to move in the room. Students sat left, right and facing me, and were staring at me. So was a teacher who was there. The girls who had lunched with us had were not there. They were not allowed into the male living quarters, I was told.

I asked the teacher if it would be a good idea to start a small discussion. He quickly agreed, and asked me to suggest a theme. 'The future of the city', I said, without thinking about it for too long.

'In the future, everyone will be wearing a data suit!' said a boy to my right.

'Don't begin again about those data suits', sighed another boy.

'But just imagine', the first boy replied, 'all information is immediately available, everywhere!'

I latched on by asking what that might mean for the city: what influence would it have on living, working and recreation?

'No more city!' said the boy, 'everyone would live in a villa!'

After philosophizing about data suits for a time, I asked what would happen to the city if everyone lived in a villa. How would older generations, who lived in close communities, experience such developments? Could villas be a possible future answer to the old urban structure of alleyways – 'hutongs' – and courtyard houses – 'siheyuans'. And what would happen to the flats and high-rise blocks, commonly used building types that were now appearing everywhere?

It had gone quiet and the teacher gave me a penetrating look.

'I grew up in a hutong and in a siheyuan, and that was terrible! We had no running water, no bathroom, no washing facilities and no kitchen. In the winter the cold made it almost unbearable. Hutongs are fossils, they no longer meet the criteria of our times and they'll have to go!'

Surprised by this reaction, I tried to make the discussion more abstract by asking if it was possible to imagine a *modern version* that would express the social qualities of the hutongs in a modern way.

All the students were silent.

The teacher looked at me and repeated: 'Hutongs and siheyuans are fossils. Old Beijing is nostalgia for old people and foreign tourists.'

A few weeks previously, with Huan, I had wandered around the hutongs near Houhai, the lake to the north of the Forbidden City. Huan was doing research at Tsinghua University on the expropriation of siheyuan residents and on new models of hutong communities. He himself was sceptical about the possibilities, taking into account the fact that there were major obstacles. The density of this type of housing was much too low in relation to the ground price, and the alleys were too narrow for cars, often even too restricted to install drains.

We entered several siheyuans cautiously. We did so because I had the feeling that we were disturbing the privacy of the people there.

The living environment lacked the basic facilities. To our surprise we were invited into one of the siheyuans to drink some tea.

Through Huan, the story of the family unfolded.

The family had lived in the courtyard house for generations. To their horror, one day they saw the 'chai' character chalked on their wall. Huan explained: 'chai' is the Chinese character for 'demolition'. The family received an official letter stating that they had to move house. Financial compensation was offered and they could select a house from two different new projects outside town. The advantages were emphasized: the new house would have facilities that their current house did not have.

However, three things played a role for the family. First of all, the financial compensation would not be sufficient. Second, there was an unfair division: families that enjoyed good relations with the local authorities received considerably better financial compensation than those without such good relations. But their biggest fear was that they would be completely alienated in their new living environment. They were ground-oriented now, but 'there' they would be living in a tower. Here, their living environment was characterized by public life at street level, all the neighbours were acquaintances and their work was just around the corner. It was hard to imagine how all this would function 'there'.

The theme was not new to me, but I had never been confronted with it so personally, so directly. When we emerged from the siheyuan, I wondered about the extent to which we, through our presence in China, were accessories to such practices.

I confided my doubts to Huan. In my preamble I plied him with information well known in the West. Wasn't it the case that around 40 million people had lost their land to urbanization since the 1990s? And wasn't *how* this was happening the real problem? The local authorities expropriated land and leased it to the property developers. It was a win-win situation for civil servants and property developers but not for the house owners, who were bought off with meagre compensation and could offer no resistance because they didn't own the ground.

Huan listened patiently and when I had finished, he nodded without saying anything. He took me with him and, not far from the siheyuan, showed me a project in which the developer, government and architect were attempting to realize a 'modern version' of typical hutong life. It looked interesting to me but according to Huan it wasn't a success as it was 'economically impossible'.

We walked through the new living environment. Unlike the traditional siheyuans, the houses here were stacked. The apartments on the upper storeys were directly accessed from stairs leading up from a larger communal courtyard. I noticed that it seemed as if only foreigners lived there. Huan confirmed this – almost all of the houses had been rented out by the original residents.

So, was modern 'hutong living' a form of foreign nostalgia after all?

Not long after, another light was cast on the dilemma of China's inevitable modernization. A taxi driver told Huan that his former house had had to make way for 'modern Beijing'. But he said that when 'chai' was chalked on a house wall it was a 'golden day' for some families. In Beijing there were good opportunities to negotiate and it was a chance to improve life considerably at a stroke. Personally, he was extremely contented with the financial compensation and with his new home. He listed the advantages, but interrupted himself. Smiling, he said he would tell me a secret. Compensation was handed out to the family concerned. As soon as it had become clear that they were to be moved out, it was advantageous that the children should marry as soon as possible; in such cases, the 'compensation was doubled'. He mentioned proudly that he now owned three apartments, at different locations in Beijing. Huan translated the story with a neutral expression: the driver kept his eyes open for new opportunities to make a good deal in the real estate market.

Quite aside from the issue of how such a development model could be economically tenable, I was more interested in another question being posed in the Western media. Was it really a voluntary choice to move house? And was financial compensation sufficient justification for doing so?

In China they were called 'nail houses' – the houses of people ('nail families') who refused to leave, according to Huan. 'In China, the minority obeys the majority', he offered as an explanation. 'But they have the right to negotiate', he added in an attempt to defend what he knew was fairly indefensible.

'People don't know their rights, so how can they defend them?' I asked.

'It's a different viewpoint', he replied: 'Like the new dam in Chongqing. There, one million people will have to move in order to enable a water supply for 30 million. In China, the minority obeys the majority', he repeated. 'No person is more important than China'.

I doubted my own vehemence. Huan was not the right person to put critical questions to, in view of the fact that he was deliberately looking for alternatives in his research. The teacher was probably more suitable for that purpose because of his own experience and radical opinions. But again I had my doubts. Perhaps I simply understood far too little about China to assail the people here with critical, typically Western questions of conscience.

THE OLDEST CIVILIZATION IN THE WORLD

Why does modernization in China almost always imply a radical intervention which, in the view of a Western architect such as myself, seeks so little connection with the past?

'China is the oldest civilization in the world.'

The remark was intended for my ears and it was a favourite topic of my colleagues at lunchtime. With respect and interest, I listened to heroic tales about a seafarer who apparently discovered America hundreds of years before Columbus did, with a fleet that was 'tens of times larger and more advanced' than that of Columbus. And about how paper, printing, gunpowder and the compass had all been invented in China.

Often I just listened, occasionally I asked questions about the present-day significance of such a lengthy history and, more specifically, the cultural heritage. In the current building frenzy, all history seemed to be subordinate to the all-consuming modernization of China.

My questions invariably went unanswered, but now there was an opportunity to broaden my understanding in the shape of a new project. It was vast by Dutch standards, involving over 400,000 square metres of park, housing, working areas and commerce. It had been prompted by a new motorway that was to connect two ring roads; the site lay right up against the approach and exit roads to and from the new motorway.

To my astonishment I heard during the briefing that the site was still inhabited; it was occupied by a 'village within the city'. I asked what would happen to the inhabitants. They would be relocated to new apartment blocks two kilometres away, I was told. Mr Guo sighed resignedly when we heard this announcement and said that it could be years before construction could begin. 'Negotiations can take a long time', he added by way of explanation.

When several colleagues and I visited the site, we encountered a typically Chinese village. Small, single-storey wooden houses stood along unhardened streets. In the streets people were cooking, selling vegetables and doing their washing. Children were playing in front of a small run-down temple and animals roamed freely. I had an ambivalent feeling about it all: families lived here yet the houses were in an appalling state. Far too many people seemed to be living in far too small spaces. Rubbish littered the streets. The smell from the communal toilets was unbearable.

My Chinese colleagues looked at everything with repulsion. Everything seemed old and dirty to them. This was old China and it had to make way, in no uncertain terms, for new China. Once back at the office, they followed the well-known Chinese 'tabula rasa' approach and began with a proposal in which all existing buildings at the site would be swept away.

In all our projects before then we had been confronted with sites that had been emptied of everything. Now we had the opportunity for a restructuring task: our first chance not to disrupt the continuity of the place and the city, but to seek connections with what was there on site.

NEXT developed a strategy in which we dissected the site into various layers. Entrances to the site, streets and alleyways would be retained. The old houses would make way for landscape compartments that could be 'programmed' in different ways. Existing trees and the old temple would be assimilated into patios in these green 'rooms'. The required programme was proposed for the site's periphery, where it would link up with a major traffic axis and public transport.

During the presentation, I told a story about the cultural significance of history in European urban expansions. I showed examples of urban transformations in which old structures and new expansions were integrated seamlessly. I showed docklands that had been transformed into residential areas but had retained their former ambience. I presented old industrial areas that had been transformed into business estates with loft offices. I exhibited pictures of factories that had become cultural incubators, of old trees that had been integrated into the new architecture.

But the story made little impression: the client was not convinced of the value of history for the site. During lunch, my colleagues outlined this for me: 'The present is only a small moment in the sea of eternity that characterizes Chinese culture. Elements such as streets, alleys, trees and even the temple are negligible.'

But if so many 'elements' were negligible, where could you find the link-up with Chinese culture? How far back in history did you have to go to find an 'element of value'?

The question surprised my colleagues. An attempt was made to end the smouldering discussion in a single sentence. Mr Jiang responded: 'Value lies in the future.'

'But what is that value?' I ventured.

'Money and a better life for all!' he replied.

'And what about the history of that place, the memories, the continuity with the past?' I ventured again.

'A new beginning is better than bad memories!' he concluded.

It was a dead-end street, I thought, while another colleague changed the subject by making a remark about the taste of the food. We were sitting in a restaurant in Beijing where I regularly heard stories about the 'oldest civilization in the world'. He thought the food was marvellous and reinforced his opinion: 'The food in this restaurant has been prepared in the same way for centuries!'

Prepared in the same way for centuries, I repeated to myself as I picked up my chopsticks.

Other colleagues confirmed this: 'The taste of the food here is very good!'

I latched on, smiling: 'The taste of age-old Beijing is also very good!'

There was a wave of smiles and everyone ate on in silence.

CONFUCIUS

LQ: Are you reading Confucius, John?
J: I'm trying.
LQ: And what do you think?
J: There's a lot I don't understand.

LQ: Like what?
J: Besides the concept of Harmony, what's still present of Confucianism in contemporary China?
LQ: I'm sure it's a lot, it has similar meaning to religion in Europe.
J: To religion in Europe?
LQ: But we believe in 'li': proper behaviour and obligations to society.
J: The concept of 'li': the appropriate action for the appropriate situation?
LQ *(smiling)*: Correct.
J: I can see the concept of 'li', and even how it explains why, to a certain degree, Chinese people are instinctively unwilling to confront authority and question hierarchy.
LQ: So what's unclear then?
J: According to Confucius, are people essentially different?
LQ: Yes, there is a clear respect in hierarchy: a father is superior to a son, an emperor to his subordinates.
J: There's also a strict hierarchy in social status, right?
LQ: There is. The highest class are the Mandarins, the highly-educated bureaucrats of the country. Then, in hierarchical order of respect, come farmers, workers, soldiers and, at the bottom, business people. But very importantly: people could enter higher classes.
J: So, then I have two questions: how does a hierarchic Confucian society that aims for harmony fit in with a Marxist Communist society that aims for struggle? And secondly, as business people are the lowest in social respect, why does everybody in China nowadays want to become a businessman?
LQ *(surprised)*: Everyone wants to become a businessman?
J *(smiling)*: Actually, I'm quoting Chinese colleagues.
LQ: I think Confucianism is becoming more important again in China. You know, my generation studied revolutionary Marxist theories, very useful then, but not so much useful now. How would you call that again, dogma?
J *(smiling)*: You're not answering my questions.
LQ *(smiling)*: Sometimes silence is an answer.
J: …
LQ: You should understand that the advantages of Confucianism – emotional control and respect – are the most important things young children can be taught.

J: I'm not sure if these are most important in Holland.
LQ: Please explain.
J: I'm not sure about the education of children, but I can compare Confucian-influenced education with my own background more easily, I think.
LQ: Please do.
J: I have a brilliant colleague, her name is Ms Jia. Before she joined our company she studied industrial design in Holland. Like me, she studied a 'creative' subject and told me that 'creative education' in China and Holland are 'difficult to compare.'
LQ: Why?
J: First she mentioned the different attitudes in students. In China, students do exactly what a professor asks them to do. In Holland, students learn to formulate their own questions and answers, and therefore, they always do more than the professor asks them to.
LQ: And second?
J: More generally, that Dutch people are less flexible than Chinese people. She explained this by her discovery that everybody in Holland was walking around with schedules and organizers. She had to make appointments, sometimes a week before she could actually discuss things. In China you just knock on the door and discuss things, especially when things are small and take no longer than a few sentences.
LQ *(smiling)*: Chinese people are very smart people.
J: She was also critical about China.
LQ: Why?
J: In essence, 'creative education' in Holland is much more about what you do with information, and not so much about developing the capacity to reproduce information. She considered switching to this different system was very difficult, because all she'd ever learned at school was 'learning by reproducing', as she called it herself.
LQ: You're touching on a very delicate issue that the Chinese government is very aware of. How to modernize our educational system whilst keeping our core values?
J: The Chinese wife of a Dutch friend of mine formulated it less delicately: 'The Chinese government doesn't want people to become too smart.'

LQ: Putting down chopsticks after eating meat, then starting to complain.
J: I'm not sure if I'm getting you.
LQ: She must be from a younger generation than me, right? My generation ate rice and didn't complain.
J *(smiling)*: She's from a younger generation.
LQ *(nodding)*
J: But isn't this 'modernization issue' much older? Doesn't this question go back centuries?
LQ: Why do you think so?
J: A Chinese colleague explained to me that in the late Ming Dynasty China consequently chose for isolation, and as such, missed opportunities for development.
LQ: I don't like to admit it, but I think maybe your colleague is right and that maybe you are right too. During that period, during the late Ming Dynasty, society became strictly Confucian. Education was based on learning enormous amounts of information by heart. Skills were judged on the ability to repeat.
J: Could it be that the essence of such a system is conservative, based on looking backward, in contrast to a more progressive system that aims at looking forward?
LQ: I'm not sure if I see your meaning.
J: In other words and for example, could this be a reason why China never experienced an industrial revolution like Europe did?
LQ *(annoyed)*: You know, John, China is a great civilization.
J *(worried)*: I know, Lao Qing, the achievements are unprecedented and speak for themselves.
LQ *(annoyed)*: Did you know that your china, what's it called, Delft Blue, was copied from Ming Dynasty china? That's exactly the period you are talking about.
J *(worried)*: I know, people told me several times. I also know that my questions are probably very rude as I completely disobey Confucian hierarchy. And I'm also sure there are disadvantages in our educational system as well.
LQ *(smiling)*: You're a Western friend and you're not rude, you're just eager.
J *(smiling)*: I just want to understand China better, Lao Qing.
LQ: Let me think about your questions, John.
J: I'll think about yours, Lao Qing.

'Japan is twenty years more advanced in its development than China. South Korea is ten years further, and North Korea is the China of thirty years ago.' My Chinese colleague said it with conviction. It was a remark that put China's development in a broader context and in a different perspective. Prior to my arrival in China, I had visited various cities in Japan and South Korea and therefore I had been able to experience a fragment of China's possible future, inasmuch as you could formulate it this way. From the moment that colleague made this remark, I was most eager to experience China's past. I had carried the idea around with me for several months and now the chance had come.

Koryo Air departed with around thirty passengers from Beijing to Pyongyang. All the foreigners sat at the front; at the back there was a delegation of North Koreans, all of whom were recognizable by their pin with a picture of the Great Leader, or the Beloved Leader. The plane was full of reading material about 'foreign misunderstandings' concerning North Korea, the Korean War and an outline of the ideology of the Juche Idea.

'Juche' was the North Korean version of Marxism-Leninism and the brainchild of the everlasting North Korean leader Kim Il Sung. 'The Great Leader is a father figure to the people and leads the people. [...] The proletarian revolution is for the people and the masses must be led by the Great Leader. [...] The people, the proletariat, the farmers and the intellectuals are the centre of society. [...] Self-sufficiency and the economic independence of the people are fundamental.'

The people and the masses, I thought. I saw in my mind's eye Lao Qing's expressive face. With great regularity he would parry my questions and statements by declaring: 'You can't compare the individualism of Western I-thinking with Chinese we-thinking.'

In my thoughts, Lao Qing made way for an article in which the Juche Idea was placed above all other communist movements. The article didn't provide concrete arguments, so I attempted to make my own comparison with the Chinese variant of Marxism-Leninism, the Maoism of Mao Zedong. However, the similarity – the outspoken xenophobia towards the West – seemed to me to be greater than the difference. Mao's 'Better red than expert' was the complete opposite of the Juche Idea in which intellectuals were a fully-fledged part of the socialist revolution.

I thought about Lao Qing once more. He often regarded the 'ideological' thinking and acting of Westerners as being diametrically opposed to his own. So my trip to North Korea had a second agenda: to find answers to the question of the possible role and position of a Westerner in a completely different ideology.

The Tupolev landed at Pyongyang airport and stopped right in front of the terminal. The airport was empty. At customs, all mobile phones had to be handed over; we would get them back when we left North Korea. This was the beginning of an experience that would last ten stage-scripted days, organized right down to the finest detail. We were received by two guides and a driver, who would escort us during the entire trip. The bus left for the city and the collective tension of all the foreigners was tangible.

Pyongyang was spaciously laid out and the massive roads were empty. Inhabitants crossed the void on foot or by bicycle. Showy buildings radiated political power and their only objective seemed to be to make every individual feel exceptionally small. There was no advertising, the only pictures along the roadsides being those on propaganda posters. On the most exemplary poster, a gigantic blood-red North Korean fist smashed into some American soldiers.

In the next few days we were driven from one monument to another; we were not allowed to leave the group, just as we were not allowed to leave the hotels in the evening. At every attempt to do so, we were literally whistled down by 'policemen' in civvies, who kept a constant eye on us.

Every day we ate excessively. At every mouthful I remembered that probably only a few kilometres from us there was scarcely any food at all.

We visited the Arirang 'mass games' where, with synchronized precision, tens of thousands of dancers embodied the ideology that individuals ought to blend into the collective will of the nation.

We visited the Palace of the Children, where 'model children' played revolutionary songs for us on musical instruments. I tried to gain eye contact with a girl in the first row. In vain; she looked right through me, expressionless; she seemed switched off.

Under the Palace, in the bookshop, I found among the revolutionary literature a mathematics schoolbook that had been translated into English. One calculation was roughly as follows: The Revolutionary Army of our Beloved Leader Kim Jong Il travels with a speed of 30 km an hour towards the army of the American Imperialist Bastards. The army of the Imperialists is travelling at 12 km an hour. They are 200 km from one another. How long will it be before our Revolutionary Army defeats the Americans?

Back in Beijing I spoke to Mr Yang, the husband of Mrs Hu, about this visit. He concurred with what I had told him: 'That was China thirty years ago. And Pyongyang was the Beijing of thirty years ago.'

Since he had been raised with this type of indoctrination, as our clients had also been, how could they now fully embrace Western ideas? Or was a full embrace a fabricated illusion?

In my office I looked at my Chinese residence permit and read aloud the English words, printed in gold letters: 'Alien Residence Permit'. 'Alien' was the official description of a foreigner in the People's Republic of China. The more common term was 'laowai', which was the informal variation of 'waiguoren', which could be translated as 'foreign person'. In essence, 'laowai' was not a positive, not even a neutral term, a Chinese person once told me. The term was open to many interpretations and could be used to make jokes about someone's 'amateurism'. But 'laowai' was certainly better than 'yangguizi', or 'foreign devil', which was the term for foreigners prior to the opening of China in 1978. And, to me, 'laowai' was also better than the more affected 'waiguo pengyou', or 'foreign friend', used since 1978.

During the age of Maoism, the Chinese world picture had been 'coloured red' by propaganda. The Chinese were the happiest people on earth, as a consequence of class struggles and socialism. By comparison, the West was poor under the yoke of capitalism. But the threat was more real than the ideological distinction. A genuine danger lurked in the influence from the West; it was aimed at undermining the socialist system. Lao Qing regularly told me how 'educational' films, with grainy images of poverty and protests in American cities, underscored the truth of the socialist dream.

For foreigners in China freedom of movement was limited, even after Mao's death. Outside Beijing there were signs with warnings in Chinese, Russian and English stating that the area was 'Forbidden to Foreigners'. Foreigners could only live in certain allocated compounds and couldn't pay for things with normal Chinese money.

Interaction between the local population and foreigners was avoided as much as possible: even the very idea of it inescapably led to a person being treated as suspect.

Decades later, little of this attitude is noticeable, at least on the surface. The surprising and almost mystifying aspect of China has been its successful adjustment to the rest of the world. Surprising, because a city such as Beijing thirty years ago was just as empty as Pyongyang is now, and currently, due to reform and the 'opening of the doors', only sporadically evokes memories of those times, at least at first sight. Almost mystifying, because the country was totally closed between 1949 and 1978 and subjected to the same xenophobia as that which now characterizes North Korea.

I tried to imagine Beijing being empty, with cycling or even walking as the ultimate means of getting about, with roads constructed for military parades, and with architecture aimed at expressing political power. Present-day Beijing is anything but empty. Military parades have made way for endless tailbacks of new cars on the six new ring roads. And architecture now expresses a different form of power, namely, economic power.

Two aspects clearly topped the list of status symbols of modern-day prosperity: a car of your own and an apartment of your own. With the words 'Why do you travel in the subway every day, it's so busy', Mr Yang once encouraged me to buy a car. When I avoided the suggestion by explaining that in the metro I could get to know the potential users of our projects better, he looked at me inquiringly. I attempted to reinforce my explanation: 'If I can't understand them, I can't make a good design.' The inquiring look seemed to increase. I tried a different approach: 'I prefer to experience things, not to own things.' The inquiring look had now become as large as life.

The conversation died away, and I thought that enjoying a material life in combination with 'min yi shi wei tian' – food is the people's heaven – characterized the China of the 20th century. But I had taken Mr Yang's suggestion the wrong way. A colleague later explained that in China there was a connection between the brand and type of car of an entrepreneur and his or her degree of success in business. Cars imported from abroad in particular were a sign of status. Not only buildings but also cars gave 'face', I realized.

In North Korea it seemed impossible to enjoy a material life. Even art, literature and music were entirely in the service of socialism.

Individual expression seemed to be excluded as much as possible. As a way of testing the significance of the change in China, I once said provocatively to a Chinese colleague that life in North Korea appeared to be bare and impoverished. Without referring to North Korea, the response was that present-day life in Beijing was 'more colourful' due to 'China being more open'.

I wondered whether the words 'more open' could be replaced by 'subject to greater influence from outside'.

With regard to architecture, my colleagues often also stated that Beijing had become 'more colourful' due to 'China being more open'. Could this too be replaced perhaps by 'subject to greater influence from outside'?

This 'being more open' had led to China's intriguing adaptation to the rest of the world. But how did this embrace of Western ideas relate to Chinese culture and history?

With this new question, I was voluntarily opting for a stretch on the intellectual rack.

I sat at my desk and looked at our department through the glass partitions. It was relatively quiet. Many male colleagues were busy with MSN and its Chinese variant QQ, while my female colleagues were on Taobao, a kind of Chinese e-Bay, searching for clothes and make-up. Some were working with AutoCAD, others were adjusting renderings in Photoshop. There was a discussion going on between a number of engineers, a project manager and some project assistants. To the rear, several people were working on a preliminary scale model. I grinned when I saw Mr Guo: he was leaning back in his office chair, watching a Will Smith film.

I took a gulp of tea and tried to run through 5000 years of Chinese history in leaps and bounds. Right then I could only think of two stages of adaptation, or reformation, when China had no choice but to open up to Western influence. The first stage was imposed from outside and occurred in the late Qing Dynasty, in the 19th and early 20th centuries. The second had taken place voluntarily and had been initiated from the inside by Deng Xiaoping, at the end of the 1970s.

The Qing Dynasty was China's last imperial dynasty. But the reign of the 18th-century Qing Emperor Qian Long was also one of China's most glorious periods. According to Mr Guo, Qian Long was one of China's most successful emperors. His reign, lasting decades, was marked by economic prosperity, as well as almost doubling the country's population and expanding its territory to the largest China has ever been. 'No other country in the world could match the economic and cultural power of China', Mr Guo stated with pride. He was surprised when I asked him where this firm conviction came from. Surely that was obvious, if you compared the history of China with that of the rest of the world? China had been economically and culturally superior for centuries before then. He was referring to the emperors of the Han and Tang Dynasties, eight centuries apart. They were extremely conscious of their superiority and confidently opened the gates for commercial exchange with other countries. China flourished, but there was no question of cultural influence from outside; everything that entered China was automatically 'Sinicized'. 'The power of the Chinese civilization was too strong to be influenced.'

Mr Guo made a leap through time to illustrate this viewpoint with a story about the renowned Chinese seafarer Zheng He. The story was one of his pet subjects, but this time he told it in more detail.

'Over 600 years ago, Zheng He led a number of great expeditions, the furthest of which took him to America. The fleet consisted of hundreds of ships, the largest of which was more a hundred metres long. Columbus only discovered America a century later with a fleet of a few ships, the largest of which was only a few dozen metres long.' But despite their superior power, Mr Guo stressed, China essentially has always been a peaceful society. 'Zheng He was the leader of the largest fleet the world had ever seen, but he conquered not one square centimetre of foreign land. He brought other countries tea, silk and technology. He brought them harmony, peace and civilization.'

With Zheng He, Mr Guo was referring to the early Ming Dynasty and thus to another 'golden period'. I asked him about the late Ming Dynasty, about the strict Confucian period which I had previously discussed with Lao Qing. What was the reason for the demise of the Ming Dynasty? Mr Guo looked uncomfortable: 'Chinese people were only interested in cultural life, nobody was interested anymore in technology and science. What was left of Zheng He's fleet was destroyed.' I had once read that the cause had to be sought in external circumstances. After the Mongolian occupation during the Yuan Dynasty, China had developed into an introverted country. There was little leeway for innovation, stagnation was symbolized by an emperor who was so fat that 'he couldn't stand on his own two feet'.

Mr Guo again made a rapid jump in time and stated that China had known another 'golden period' in around 1800, when it had the largest population, the largest territory and the largest economy in the world. He was now talking about the early Qing Dynasty, which followed the Ming Dynasty and was established after the conquest of Peking by the Manchus. After the two consecutive reigns of the great emperors Kang Xi and Qian Long, China again managed to develop to glorious proportions within 120 years. Trade with foreign countries increased. Then Mr Guo spontaneously explained: it was at that very peak that a new and serious threat emerged. In an extreme attempt to save the Middle Kingdom from disaster, reformers compelled the Chinese to study the West and imitate everything that could be useful. 'But the threat was too great.' I guessed the threat that Mr Guo was referring to was Western imperialism.

Europe's arrears on the economic and technological fronts in relation to China had quickly narrowed during the late Qing Dynasty, under the influence of the Industrial Revolution. Increasingly, Europe imposed its desire for trade upon China, and China, to the West's irritation, attempted to regulate its foreign trade by allowing only one port to trade with the West: Canton.

The reason to breach this restriction was found in Beijing's attempts to limit the import of opium. Two Opium Wars followed and parts of China had to be surrendered 'in compensation and for eternity'. In addition, Western states were assigned harbours and privileges in various cities that put foreigners in China above the law. Lao Qing described it as 'a bitter moment in China's history'. 'The first presence of foreigners in China was based on an unequal treaty, forced upon China by aggression', he stated gravely. And it even looked as though he still held me personally responsible after all that time.

This latent sense of injustice that foreign powers had imposed upon China still seemed deeply rooted in present-day Chinese consciousness. There were other moments when I was made aware of it. For example, one time I took a taxi in Xiamen, a metropolis in the south-east of China. The first thing the taxi driver asked me was where I came from. 'Holland', I replied without much thought. 'You once occupied Taiwan', was his immediate, indignant response.

The unequal treaty gave rise to a dilemma. In traditional Chinese thinking the emperor had been appointed by Heaven itself, so that his jurisdiction could not be shared with other rulers. The enforced diplomatic representations, and the growing presence of Western powers, led in the early 20th century to the Boxer Rising, a Chinese-nationalist movement directed against the influence of Western imperialist powers. The Boxers believed that Taoist rituals would make them immune to foreign bullets, but their rebellion was savagely put down by a foreign coalition.

At the end of the 19th century China had already lost parts of its empire and some of its face to Japan and, at the beginning of the 20th, after the Boxer Rising, an international occupation force dominated Beijing. According to Mr Guo, this period of foreign occupation was 'the clearest example of China's humiliation by Western powers'. He looked at me seriously when articulating these words. He seemed to hold me personally responsible for this as well.

By the early decades of the 20th century, the decline of the Qing Dynasty was complete and Sun Yatsen, the leader of the Kuomintang and 'father of the nation', became the first president of the Republic of China. When I visited Sun Yatsen's memorial in Nanjing, the presence of thousands of Chinese people was confirmation that the social change that he led was still held in great esteem.

In my thoughts I imagined Lao Qing before me, with his scepticism about this period. 'The new age had only a short life, the democratic experiment failed and, after a coup, China disintegrated into a collection of regions ruled by warlords.' To this day he has never explained exactly why the 'experiment' failed; it is an issue to which there is probably no straightforward answer.

The disintegration of China continued when Japan occupied the Province of Shandong during the First World War. But the start of a new era came when Mao Zedong and others founded the Communist Party in Shanghai in 1921. Conflict with the Kuomintang of Sun Yatsen, who had by now died, was inevitable.

The Kuomintang, now under the leadership of Chiang Kai-shek, was on the side of the industrialists and the better-off, whereas Mao's party believed in the class struggle and held the opinion that the revolution could only succeed with the help of the rural population. The clash between the parties culminated in the famous Long March, in which the Communists covered 10,000 kilometres on foot in a year's time. Lao Qing: 'The survivors were later declared to be Communists of the purest kind.'

The history is well known: after an opportunistic 'united front' which only existed due to the presence of a greater enemy, Japan, the conflict focused on the struggle between Mao and Chiang after Japan capitulated. Mao had won the hearts and minds of the peasants with promises of increased prosperity, while Chiang's supporters were the urban population, hard hit by inflation. After a bitter civil war, which was supported militarily and financially by the Soviet Union and the United States who according to Mr Guo 'fought out a struggle on China's back', Chiang fled to Taiwan. On 1 October 1949, in the Square of Heavenly Peace, Mao declared the founding of the Republic of China.

Mr Guo: 'Chairman Mao had reunited China, and China was again liberated from all foreign influence after a period of a hundred years.' Mr Guo placed the emphasis on the words *liberated from all foreign influence*.

After this liberation, China evolved into an almost completely isolated empire. During this development Mao sought to engineer society by instigating a series of large-scale reform campaigns and announcing the end of private ownership. Lao Qing: 'Mao was a great man, but when his power began to fade, he initiated the Cultural Revolution. His "destroy the old, create the new" policy cost around 30 million lives. China was on the edge of the abyss.'

Lao Qing always reacted reservedly to my attempts to find out more about this period. He himself was separated from his wife, and had to move to the inlands of Mongolia to learn about farming life in an isolated village, he told me. He didn't want to say more about his personal experiences, but he would say something about China's experience as a whole. He still became emotional when describing what had happened decades previously. 'Poverty and hunger, a thoroughly disrupted society, complete social mistrust, the almost total loss of everything of cultural value, and a lost generation as the result of all the schools being closed.' 'China was a cultural desert', he summarized: 'In the whole of China, the only performances were a few variations on the Beijing Opera, all dishing up the same revolutionary message.'

When Deng Xiaoping 'opened the doors of China to the world' after Mao's death at the end of the 1970s, China had just been through a period of almost thirty years of complete isolation. Deng countered Mao's 'Better red than expert' with 'It doesn't matter if the cat is black or white, as long as it catches mice it is a good cat.' This celebrated quote was one of the first pieces of wisdom that Mr Chen communicated to me in China. Until that moment, I had always thought that Deng was referring to the political dilemma with which China was faced: to hold on to strict communist values or to allow in a capitalist market. But Mr Chen made it clear to me, smiling as he did, that this mantra could be applied to every situation in present-day China.

Deng was a 'weida' or great person, as my Chinese teacher described him. At the end of the 1970s he liberalized not only the economy but also the mind. His vision of life was purely materialistic: 'Getting rich is glorious!' This mantra, too, was smilingly quoted by various colleagues on various occasions during my first month in China.

During a dinner with NEXT Amsterdam in Beijing, Mrs Hu explained the unparalleled energy behind the development of modern China by means of another quote by Deng: 'Some people may become rich first.'

With the opening of China's 'doors to the world', Deng hoped to modernize poverty-stricken China. But the necessary integration in the world economy also brought disadvantages. By opening the doors, Deng was confronted by the same dilemma as the reformers from the late Qing Dynasty: how to profit from the Western influence *and* regulate the risk of Western influence on the foundations of the state?

The superior qualities of the Han and Tang dynasties, which ensured that everything that entered China was automatically 'Sinicized', had lost their vigour. China's development was dependent on abroad more than ever before. Deng was keenly aware of the risk this entailed: Western technology and capital were welcome, Western culture and lifestyle were not.

By coincidence, Mr Guo entered my office just at that moment and I made use of the opportunity to ask him how that quote by Deng Xiaoping, the one less well-known abroad, went exactly. He smiled and knew immediately what I was referring to. 'If you open the window for fresh air, you have to expect some dust and mosquitoes.'

The comparison of our Western ideas with dragons now had a new metaphorical corollary, that of fresh air, dust and mosquitoes. But which part of these ideas was fresh air and which part dust and mosquitoes? Mr Guo interrupted this thought by unrolling a drawing on my desk and saying: 'Maybe we have difficulty.' I leaned over the drawing and light-heartedly imagined that he had encountered some dust and mosquitoes. Then I realized that Deng's quote was a political standpoint, referring to the possible risks of 'dust and mosquitoes' to the Communist Party.

I looked at the drawing.

Who decided in present-day China what was fresh air and what was dust and mosquitoes in architecture?

WHAT DOES THE CLIENT WANT?!

Mr Yang's voice resounded through the meeting room. 'The only question an architect should ask is: what does the client want?!'

For months I had been impressed by the fact that my Chinese colleagues could switch in an instant from, say, a project in 'classic style' to a project in 'modern style'. It was an ability that I, as a Dutch architect, had never learned or perhaps had never been willing to learn. However, although I was impressed, I was not entirely in agreement with Mr Yang's standpoint. Although architecture was a servant discipline, an architect also had a certain professional obligation to seek leeway for innovation. Innovation could bring added value not only to the discipline but also to the client and the users. Literally translating what the client wanted was simply doing what had already been decided and didn't require an architect. Architecture was also about finding unknown possibilities that the client had not yet considered. So 'What does the *architect* want?' was an equally fundamental issue.

The meeting was a part of the briefing on a new project. I stared at the brief – 'Splendid, grand, like a building owned by a rich tobacco company' – and wondered what this meant.

The client had provided two suggestions for the 'style' of the building. The first was 'modern European' and the second 'pure modern'. It was decided to divide these two 'styles' as design briefs 'to increase our chances'. The 'broad commitment' strategy had become our norm so as to offer an alternative to clients who 'liked dragons but still flinched when they saw one'. The 'modern European' proposal would be produced by Huanyang and the 'pure modern' one by NEXT.

Armed with this cryptic brief, sketches flew back and forth between Amsterdam and Beijing. Our design began by orienting as much of the programme as possible to the south. This gave us a volume measuring 50 × 50 × 24 metres. After that, a number of adaptations were made to optimize daylight incidence, emphasize the entrance and introduce roof gardens on the upper storeys. Different elevational treatments were used to emphasize different directions.

During the design process, Huanyang must have received new information because, to my surprise, they turned out to have adjusted their 'style' from 'modern European' to 'classic European'.

Before the presentation was to take place, we were requested to send the designs to the client via e-mail. I protested, as this was an exceptionally narrow form of interaction with a client. But I was told that the e-mail was only 'to keep the client up to date with the direction in which the project was developing'. The e-mail was sent and a verbal presentation proved no longer necessary: in the vicinity of Tongzhou, some time in 2010, a 'splendid landmark' would be realized to Huanyang's classic European design.

The fascinating aspect here was that Chinese architects had designed a classic European building in an extremely short time in the same office space in which I, a Western architect, had worked on a 'modern building' for China, in conjunction with my colleagues in Amsterdam. This surreal idea was so intriguing to me that I regularly dropped in on Mr Zhen, the Chinese project architect, during the design process.

When I asked Mr Zhen if it was easy to generate a design in 'this style', he answered resolutely: 'Easy'. He then nonchalantly continued by telling me that he had learned to design in many different styles during his education. He talked about his training as an architect. 'We learned how to make exact copies of classic European architecture, like the Pantheon, from memory. I still can draw everything: plans, elevations and sections in great detail.'

'I couldn't do that!' I responded, genuinely impressed, although I did wonder what such a study method could have added to my own curriculum. In my education, I had got no closer to classic Roman architecture than an assignment issued by Professor Hertzberger for an architectural addition to St Peter's Square in Rome. The difference was evident: the Chinese assignment consisted of learning to make a perfect reproduction, the Western assignment concerned the architectural dilemma of placing something new in relation to something old.

I asked Mr Zhen if he liked the 'classic European style'. He had obviously never entertained the question. He answered simply: 'Chinese clients like this style.'

Mr Jiang, sharp as he was, once stated that it seemed to him that Western architects 'could think less freely than Chinese architects'. He explained: 'Western architects always want to influence things. That's the limitation in their thinking. In my thinking, architecture has a social duty.'

'What's that duty?' I enquired.

'To make people's lives better', was his response: 'Architects should work for the people, not for their own thinking.'

'What's the best criterion for making better?'

'The market', he said to my surprise.

'Aren't you mixing up *social* and *commercial*?'

'Why?' he countered. 'Hasn't the market the best ability to judge what is or isn't great architecture?'

'Shouldn't we architects try to look beyond the transience of the market?' I tried.

'What makes you think we can do that?' he asked, surprised.

Back at my desk, I remembered that NEXT had once proclaimed that it wished to approach briefs free of dogma. It then struck me that Chinese architects were the ones who were genuinely free of any form of dogma. I had begun to jot down my experiences in China, and by now my notes and comments in notebooks and on sketch rolls, restaurant napkins and even on air sickness bags weighed more than two kilos. Browsing through the first notebook I saw on one of the first pages, as the theme for a meeting with Huanyang, that NEXT was not inclined to design 'classic architecture'.

Our standpoint was that contemporary architecture could no longer be categorized in styles. At most, classic elements such as rhythm could be applied as a tool in a design. The list of arguments filled an entire page. But the theme had never arisen. In retrospect,

I think I had already developed an instinct for avoiding restrictions and preconditions wherever possible. 'In China, problems can only be solved when they arise', I saw in another notebook.

I reread our viewpoint on classic architecture, smiled and looked from my workstation at Mr Zhen, who was proudly communicating something to his colleagues. He was elated, and the reason why was quite clear: the client had chosen his proposal on the strength of a design he had dashed off and sent by e-mail!

I began to nurture an outspoken admiration for the 'flexible Chinese design spirit'.

Looking back on our summary of reasons not to design classic architecture, I wondered if resistance to dogmas perhaps wasn't a dogma in itself.

Another dogma immediately reared its head: that of creativity and originality.

To the Western architect, originality was the highest ideal. In China, at least for the time being, the ability to reproduce what had already achieved a perfect form in the past seemed no less of an ideal. Mr Guo in particular was ruthless in his copying of reference projects, but this didn't appear to bother anyone. More to the point, his designs were successful and he was known internally as a 'smart guy'. He allowed himself total design freedom, averse to any moral convention whatsoever.

But where did the assumption of freedom violate the boundary of intellectual property? How could a country develop sustainably when everything was copied on a large scale? And not only in architecture; as Mr Chen put it: 'In China you can find anything copied that you can find elsewhere in the world original.' He continued: 'Chinese people copy everything, and if it isn't copied, then we have tried to copy it!' During this remark, Mr Guo stood next to Mr Chen, grinning broadly and nodding in confirmation. They even seemed to see only advantages in this practice instead of risks. 'Japan also copied everything after the Second World War, and look how developed they are now!' I was regularly reminded.

The next day, Mr Li, one of Huanyang's drivers, proudly showed me his new Nokia telephone.

'Original or imitation?' I asked him in Chinese, with a smile.

'Imitation', he replied, laughing.

'Why?' I asked him rhetorically. 'Because it's much cheaper?'

'Not only cheaper', he said while pulling out an antenna that was perfectly integrated in the phone. He turned to Ms Jia who translated for me: 'This has more memory and he can also watch television for free on it!'

A new stage has been reached: no more literal copies but imitations with systematic improvements that anticipated the requirements and desires of Chinese consumers.

'Chinese people are very diligent', said Mr Li in Chinese, smiling at me, meaning the producers of the 'Sinicized Nokia'. It was a remark I'd heard before. I smiled and nodded. Thinking of the Sinicized Nokia and Huanyang's classic European palace, it was, from a Chinese perspective, an irrefutable truth.

And the reason for this success became increasingly clear to me: these products gave an exact answer to the question: 'What does the client want?'

CLIENT OR USER

In China the client decides everything. An architect is accountable to the client, much more than to the users or even to the profession. The term 'user' was practically absent from Huanyang's vocabulary. That fascinated me because, in Amsterdam, the user was at least as important in the development of a project as the client. Proceeding from this belief, we increasingly involved future users in the design process of our Amsterdam projects, whether architecture or, say, urban restructuring. Participation was an ideal method to involve users in that process and to test, in a workshop setting, where priorities lay.

I sought an opportunity to integrate user ideas in our China projects, and that opportunity arose with a design competition organized by a university.

We passed a barrier and drove on into the campus. The urge to visit the location was surprisingly large, especially among my male colleagues. They grinned: the university was well-known for the many 'beautiful girls' who studied there.

Our brief was to design a student housing complex of 36,000 square metres. Four students would share a room of fifteen square metres and were entitled to a loggia as external space. My Chinese colleagues sighed; the facilities hadn't been anywhere near this good in their day. Then, everything was 'simpler'.

Another condition was the strict separation of boys and girls. I remembered the discussion with the students at Tsinghua about the future of the city. There, too, the girls were not allowed to enter the boys' building. Somewhat provocatively, I pretended to be surprised by this requirement. I asked no-one in particular how and where the boys and girls would 'meet' one another. Instead of answers, I received broad, almost shy, smiles. I couldn't resist the temptation and told them about my student days in Delft where, in a student accommodation, the boys and girls showered together every morning. There was general hilarity in the bus combined with utter disbelief.

We parked the vehicle and stepped out. I looked at the translated brief and read the third condition, the explicit requirement to have 'uniformity' on the campus. I looked around and could only conclude that the campus was full of massive buildings with enormous entrances and staircases.

I was extremely eager about this brief, in the light of the fact that in implementing it, we could perhaps connect to the way in which we developed projects in Amsterdam. Until that moment I had been unable to have any direct dialogue with the client, and not even an indirect dialogue with the users. And here was a golden opportunity, not only for input, but also to test our ideas on the future users. Indeed, not only were the users of this project known to us but I could communicate with them directly due to the fact that they all spoke English.

We visited the site, made a round of the campus, and returned to the office. The next day, I returned to the campus alone. With a number of questions and initial ideas it proved relatively easy to establish contact with the students. However, it was much more difficult to tempt them to articulate applicable demands and desires. My questions consistently evoked suspicion and the answers were restricted to 'I don't know'. After several fruitless attempts I got into a conversation with a young man who did seem to have outspoken ideas. Via detours such as football, cars etc., I told him about my wish to learn more about the students. This Mr Liang then phoned some friends and after an hour I went back to the office with a wealth of insight. Two days later, we had another meeting and the group had now grown to almost ten students, boys and girls. I showed them my first sketches and they reacted to them spontaneously.

Many of their wishes were beyond the architect's domain; they were centred on making more facilities available and on relaxing the rules. On the basis of still more discussions, it became increasingly clear that the outspoken requirement of uniformity specified by the university governors did not harmonize with the ideas of the students. The students found the buildings 'impersonal'. They sometimes felt 'lost', as one girl expressed the common feeling.

Sketches flew back and forth between Beijing and Amsterdam. We decided to allow the wishes of the users to prevail over those of the client, and to place individuality above uniformity. And we could not resist the temptation to take the possible tension between male and female students as our starting point. That tension was sought in creating a maximum distance and minimum connection between two point-symmetric L-shaped buildings. The two enfolded a pair of half-open courtyards, one for the boys and one for the girls. The courtyards were linked under a bridge connection with shared facilities.

The L-shaped buildings were oriented in such a way as to protect the courtyards against the harsh winter wind from the north-west, while offering sufficient shade from the bright summer sun. With the courtyards, we hoped to create a place for the students to linger and meet. To realize enough 'critical mass' for individuals and pairs to dissolve into voluntary anonymity, all the entrances were situated on these courtyards. In the buildings themselves, individuality prevailed above uniformity with every loggia shifted half a module. It was now possible, in a complex for 8000 students, to recognize your own space, your own place.

At the conclusion of the presentation, the jury stated that our design was exceptionally creative. The chairman concluded: 'It seems as if ivy is growing round the building.' Mr Chen judged the remark to be a very great compliment. No further content-related questions were posed and the result would be announced in a week's time because the board of governors of the university had to do the judging. In that period I received a text message from Mr Liang that said that they had seen the designs. The last sentence was: 'Your design is the best one!' This simple sentence touched an elementary feeling in me as an architect: the spontaneous appreciation of a user.

The final results were not long in coming. The board of governors concluded that the design didn't fit harmoniously into the campus. So we had to make do with second prize.
In China the client decides everything.

MEETING IMPORTANT PEOPLE

Some months later, Mr Chen mentioned that in retrospect the student accommodation project had been very poorly underpinned. I knew the reason before he uttered it: we had not had any 'interim contact' with the client. Aware of the change in my own value judgement, I smiled and nodded while looking at him.

'A conversation face to face with a client is ten times better than a telephone conversation. A presentation is a hundred times better than a face to face discussion. A dinner is a thousand times better than a face to face discussion. And a joint visit to a spa is 10,000 times better than a telephone conversation.'

Such Chinese comments were almost never throwaways. Mr Chen increasingly communicated scraps of Chinese wisdom in his own outspoken way. It was always done casually, but there was invariably essential information hidden in his remarks.

Presentations for, and discussions with, clients were critical moments in China. In fact, everything in a project hinged on such moments and these were the crucial points around which projects were organized, much more than in the Netherlands. They were moments when the capacity and expertise of the parties were tested. The client's feeling of contentment with a certain development or situation could be interpreted from the often non-verbal communication. And in discussions, a balance had to be found or confirmed between the different interests of the different parties.

Presentations invariably took place in 'meeting rooms'. The style of a meeting room said a great deal about the type of client. Very often they were dark and heavy-panelled spaces with pompous furniture. And often they were brightly lit 'modern style' meeting rooms typified by imitation Eames chairs. I regular entered temporary meeting rooms where a plant had been placed here and there and a Chinese painting hung on the wall. A number of clients had arranged their meeting rooms in classic Chinese style. I occasionally visited a baroque 'classic style' meeting room in which imitation Roman statues lined the walls. Or again I might be in a room laid out futuristically, illuminated by fluorescent light; almost the décor for a science fiction film. At such times, the laser pen used to point out features of the presentation took on a Darth Vader-like charge.

Discussions often took place in the office of the client himself. Other discussions occurred in private areas of restaurants. The cliché was true: dining and doing business were inextricably linked. Sometimes the more formal discussions were held in reception rooms of hotels. But there were others in teahouses, bars, clubs, during foot massages or karaoke, in a spa, in shopping malls, in cars. Occasionally, due to pressure of time, they happened on the way to the airport, along the motorway, in a parking lot or in a lift. And I regularly heard Chinese colleagues who answered their mobile phones on the toilet to speak to a client.

One day I had a discussion in a hospital. The client lay with a drip, sleeping, when we entered the room. With difficulty, her project manager helped her sit up. A small smile graced her lips when she saw me. She asked me about developments and continued with: 'Time is limited'.

Time was limited? In which sense – for the project, for her perhaps?

Due to the lack of space, she invited me to sit next to her on the bed. When I opened the computer, I wondered about how big the chance was that the laptop might disrupt the hospital equipment. 'Architect kills hospitalized client with keynote presentation'. Probably China was one of the few countries in the world where a newspaper heading like this would not cause much of a stir, at least not in the Chinese architectural and real estate world.

After half an hour we left the hospital while the project manager helped a contented-looking client back into bed and a hospital nurse checked the infusion.

We went to an office meeting. In Amsterdam we had weekly meetings, always on a Monday morning. Sometimes the discussions were short due to deadlines, but they were always at a fixed time. In China, they were often spontaneous and irregular. The gradually increasing number of meetings and the need to display productivity there differed markedly from the Netherlands. Mr Chen vividly described this culture as: 'Chinese people love the "meeting sea" and "paper mountain".'

During this office meeting, there was a new girl at the table.

When I saw her, I noticed that I had begun to develop a kind of nonchalance, a nonchalance that irritated me. Nine out of ten times there were new faces around the table at these meetings. And, in view of the large group of people who always participated in the consultations, I had become increasingly laconic about introducing myself. By no means all of the participants offered input, many were silently present and jotted down notes. Because it was simply not possible to maintain an overview, I increasingly followed Mr Chen's advice: 'Just focus on the important people.'

But my idea of 'important people' was not necessarily the same as his.

I was asked to give my opinion, and the new girl was told to translate for me. Her English surprised me. This was new to me, because I had become accustomed to 'Chinglish' and translations in which only the 'meaning' of a conversation was communicated. I had adjusted my English to a certain extent – something that I myself only became aware of when new foreign colleagues were not understood by Chinese colleagues and I reformulated their sentences in Chinglish. My own adjustment again became evident when I heard the new girl's perfectly formulated English sentences.

Her name was Ms Wang and at the end of the meeting I asked her if she had time to go with me to a briefing with a new client. We had been invited to participate in a limited entry competition for a research centre with a surface area of 55,000 square metres. During the drive to the client, which took about 45 minutes, I asked her where she had learned to speak such good English. She said that she had studied 'international business' in Canada for a number of years. I asked her what kind of architectural background she had. 'None', was her reply.

Nevertheless, Ms Wang provided a wonderful opportunity to establish real contact with a client. I informed her quickly about this project and the questions I wanted to put to the client. I told her that it was essential for me to receive specific answers, in view of the fact that these were the preconditions for starting the design. The better the preconditions were defined, the better the design would be.

I emphasized that it was essential to continue the questions until we knew enough about the brief. She nodded in understanding, thanked me for the compliment about her English, and we reviewed the questions.

We stopped in front of the client's office and looked at the dilapidated building. I began to wonder what kind of project this could be. When we entered through the run-down lobby, I asked if she had understood all the questions. Avoiding a loose tile in the floor, she said: 'Ask only questions that can be answered positively.' While we climbed the six storeys to the client, because there was no lift, I wondered what she could have meant by this remark.

Having waited in the meeting room for fifteen minutes, the vice general manager came in. It was a standard scene: a typical Chinese developer in a tieless suit with a potbelly and a hasty look, in a typical Chinese meeting room with a large brown table and heavy pompous chairs. He explained the preconditions in a few sentences: the function, the site, the necessary surface area, the maximum building height and the floor area ratio. All this took a maximum of three minutes, then he looked at me and asked if I had any questions.

I directed my words to him via Ms Wang and asked for confirmation that specific demands were still unknown at this stage. He confirmed this.

After a brief calculation that the ground plans would cover about 200 metres by 100, under the given conditions, I suggested that it would be important to guarantee daylight everywhere on all of the floors, probably in the form of courts or patios.

'Of course!' he responded.

Further, flexibility, both of the floor plans and the façade, should be a very important component of the plan, because the ratio between the research and office areas was still unknown.

'Certainly!'

The energy-saving aspect would have to be taken into account?

'Very good!' was the reply.

I thanked the client for the briefing. We took leave cordially and when we passed through the lobby on our way out, Ms Wang said: 'You saved his face.' The possible value of that was not apparent to me at that moment.

Two weeks later I presented the proposal. This time, too, I avoided critical dialogue and explained the proposal in an open and non-obligatory manner. In my mind I saw Professor Deng, who had presented the design in Qingdao as a possibility rather than as a precise response to the brief.

An hour after the presentation, the telephone rang. We had won the competition and construction would begin four months later.

I was overwhelmed by a mixture of feelings, but there was no hint of euphoria. In fact, there was no reason for that, for the project had been developed on the basis of a non-dialogue with the client and presented as a possibility, rather than as an answer. I phoned Ms Wang to tell her about the result. I thanked her by saying: 'A correct briefing by the client is important but the correct assessment by a colleague is crucial.' She came along to my workstation and we again congratulated one another. She made use of the moment to say that she would be moving to Dubai shortly, to work for a Chinese producer of glass façades.

To my mixture of emotions I could add the disappointment of losing another valuable colleague.

VISION

'The beginning of 1990 was the best period for architects in China.' Mr Jiang was referring to 'doing business', and explained: at that time, clients waited feverishly for their plans. Many clients even stood at the architects' desks to pressurize them into getting the plans done sooner. And when the plans were handed over, the architect was given a bag full of cash in exchange. Mr Jiang laughed: 'The clients then ran out of the office.'

Fifteen years later, reality was different, but the pressure was no less great. Mr Jiang talked about the rivalry between project developers to gain the rights to land. For instance, after a preliminary selection, fifteen developers competed for a project in Beijing, each of whom submitted ten proposals by different architects. Thus, the local authorities had 150 plans from which they could choose, in addition to the 'culture of relationships' that had characterized China for centuries. And after acquiring rights to the land, the fortunate developer was given twenty days by the local authorities to start construction.

In China, architecture seemed to be much more of a vehicle for development, and therefore have a different value, than in the Netherlands.

'We're a developing country, food and shelter first, all other things later', the director of a Chinese landscape architecture office with whom I was on friendly terms once said to me. He was responding to my remark that it was unavoidably complicated to realize high-quality architecture in China. When I asked him, with a smile, if that was the philosophy of his office, all he could do was smile back at me.

In the Netherlands, architecture offices crow about their 'vision', their philosophy. An architect works on the basis of a certain perspective on the discipline and sometimes even of society, a perspective that ideally is formulated as acutely and explicitly as possible. The vision was a professional oath, in a certain sense, to the profession and to clients. Critics of architecture tested the consistency between the vision and the realized work. But developers also had 'visions' and attached significance not only to what an architect stood for, but also to the extent to which an architect's vision fitted into their own.

Like so many architectural offices, NEXT was continually searching for the appropriate way to describe its motives. We consistently attempted to summarize the themes that were important in our work as compact 'mission statements'. The themes were often abstract and went further than architecture, but were without fail underpinned by architectural research.

For example, the relationship between mobility and urban development was an important theme in the first few years of the office. In later years, themes such as context and participation became more dominant. Such themes and developments were the mainstays of our office and provided the points of departure for architectural innovation. But they had also taken us around the world during the 'Image of Metropolis' project, and had subsequently helped nurture the ambition to set up an office in China.

In the run-up to projects or discussions I often asked about the portfolio of clients, about their realized work and about their 'vision'. Mostly the answers were limited to a series of photos of buildings, from which it was an almost impossible task for me to discover any architectural connection between them. This request therefore offered hardly any points of address for our designs. We had been in

China for almost a year and I had provisionally accepted this situation. The quest to learn how to build in China was directly related to the clients who had to make the projects happen. Accordingly, the quest to discover the motivation and goals of these clients was at least as important.

One day we were on our way to Liangxiang, a city two hours' drive to the south-west of Beijing. We had planned a presentation for a new client. It was a client whom I didn't know yet, although we had already produced a design proposal for him. In the run-up to the design, very little lucid information had been given in response to my request for a portfolio and a vision. As a result, the design had been created purely on the basis of our own ideas. For NEXT, I regarded it as a limitation that we couldn't develop a design from various angles of approach as we were used to doing in the Netherlands. My thoughts were interrupted by the excited remark of a Chinese colleague who sat in the front of the car: 'The client of this project was in my schoolbooks!'

We were on our way to 'the leader of an enormous construction company'. After 'China's doors had opened to the outside world', he had become a millionaire in a very short time by developing real estate. This information was known to me. But what I didn't know was that the client was renowned as a present-day version of a 'model socialist' rather than for his acquired capital. In his village of birth he had given every family a villa as a gift.

'He's a very famous Communist Party Member,' said the colleague.

I was very curious about this person and his philosophy.

I had had several discussions with Lao Qing about communism. He knew exactly how to reproduce the mission statement of the Party. 'The Communist Party works for the interest of the Chinese people, the Party doesn't have its own interest. It pursues the interest of all the people in China. The Party's ultimate objective is to achieve Communism. The Party tells us it's a long process, that it has to be divided into stages. We are now in the early stage of socialism. Our current aim is to become a prosperous xiaokang society.' The 'xiaokang society' was a society in which everyone enjoyed a relatively good standard of life in material terms.

If our client was a 'very famous Party Member', he would surely have outspoken ideas on how architecture, designed by Western architects, would harmonize with this kind of society. However, his reactions to the design were restricted to 'haoyong' and 'haomai': 'pragmatic' and 'readily sellable'. At the end of the presentation he asked to go back to the slide showing the master plan. With a laser pen he pointed to the diagrammatic representation of a commercial block, two storeys tall as was prescribed, at the corner of two streets.

'Is this a hotel?' he asked.

'That can become a hotel,' my colleague responded.

'Is this a hotel?' he repeated.

'That is a hotel,' confirmed my colleague.

The presentation took place in a traditional Chinese courtyard villa, which wasn't fitted out for a presentation with a laptop and beamer. The windows had been covered in a makeshift fashion with tablecloths borrowed from an adjoining restaurant. Enough light filtered through to be able to see the client sitting in an enormous easy chair. He was wearing a dark blue suit with thin pinstripes. His red tie had a subtly woven pattern of dragons. His hair had an indestructible parting and he wore large silver-framed spectacles, typical of older Chinese men of standing. On either side of him sat several assistants who were similarly, but slightly less perfectly dressed. Next to them were the external specialists. One of them smoked relentlessly and stubbed one cigarette out while reaching for the next. A waitress continually poured hot water into porcelain cups filled with tea leaves. The tea must have been extraordinarily good as it cost, according to the client, 500 renminbi – more than 50 euros – per gram. That could be the monthly wage of the waitress, I thought to myself.

A blood-red carpet covered the floor and on the wall there was an enormous painting of the Great Wall of China which 'crept over the Chinese mountain ridges like a dragon'. A Chinese flag stood against another wall. All the tables bore fruit and nuts, which those present devoured enthusiastically. I sat opposite the client on a traditional Chinese wooden sofa that slowly proved to be very uncomfortable. While I sought a more agreeable position, Mr Chen nudged me and whispered: 'Eat, that's a sign of respect!' I leaned forward to take a mandarin orange.

My action had drawn attention and while I began to peel the mandarin, I heard the men opposite me.

'Where does he come from?' someone said in Chinese.

'Holland', answered Mr Chen.

'What is Holland famous for?' was the response.

'Architecture, trade and sport', replied Mr Chen resolutely.

I peeled the mandarin and waited to see if I would be involved in the conversation. But the theme of the discussion changed when one of the external specialists asked the client how many square metres of buildings he had already realized. The client sprang to life and began to calculate. Now and again he had some figures confirmed by one of the assistants. He concluded the sum with an estimate of his company's capital. I tried to make use of the moment by asking via Mr Chen what the common denominators were among the 'impressive number of projects'. With the answer I hoped to hear indirectly a possible philosophy upheld by the client, something that was not only endlessly fascinating to me personally but could also improve our project. But the answer was little more than: 'The social contribution to the demands of society and the good sales figures of the projects'. The theme of the discussion changed once more and, while I ate the mandarin, I considered that the overlap between socialism and capitalism was logically untenable to a Westerner like me. To the client, however, an ideal balance between yin and yang, the dialectic process of the continuously developing and never determinate truth, was probably in there somewhere.

With the statement that 'design is not expensive, materials are expensive', the client terminated the discussions for that afternoon. This conclusion was the closest thing to a potential philosophy that I heard from him.

Everyone nodded in agreement, except for myself. If 'design was not expensive', 'design' would not be of much value in Chinese thinking. And, to a Westerner like me, this was not only logically untenable, but fundamentally irreconcilable. Once again I had come with many questions and expectations, and was leaving with even more questions.

In the evening, I watched a documentary in which a mayor from Xiamen was quoted, in a flawless combination of Marxist rhetoric and capitalist values: 'Model workers represent the working class in this new era. They are an example to Party workers and Party members. The labouring masses must ride the tide of material civilization and build success on the battlefield of the city's economic construction.'

The unending quest for the combination of the right values continued. I hoped that this could also be found outside the seemingly inevitable domain of camouflaged hyper-commerciality.

THE ARCHITECT AS SEARCH ENGINE

J *(annoyed)*: Why do we always have to show two complete schemes at a first presentation, based on hardly any requirements? Why then does a client often choose one scheme, ask us to adjust it based on 'some suggestions' and then often ask us to make another scheme? And why do other architects work on the same project behind our backs?
C *(worried)*: Chinese clients are very demanding, John, the Chinese market is very hard. Chinese clients often don't know what they want until they see it. And things can change very quickly in China.
J: ...
C: Is Europe so different then?
J: Hard and demanding doesn't necessarily result in such working methods. In Holland, a client starts a process with one architect, after a selection process or a competition. The architect starts a dialogue with the client, after ideally analysing all aspects of the requirements. In our case, we often develop the design in workshops together with the client and users. That's almost the opposite of random design.
C: You have to understand, John, economy is very important in China now, people feel time is very limited and there's a lot of pressure from all sides, also from the market.
J: So again, you're saying architecture is primarily part of an economic process?
C: China is a developing country, economy is very probably most important.
J: And what you mentioned about clients not knowing what they want, do you really believe that is true?
C: Most of the clients have no professional real estate background. I had a client once who had earned a lot of money with building towers for pigs in Xinjiang [the most north-western province of China, bordering on Central Asia]. Because he had a construction company, he became a real estate developer, but he had no idea

about architecture. It was very difficult to work with him. There are so many examples. Do you remember that European-style project near the North East Third Ring Road? The empty residential buildings? That project was developed by the village that was once there. They found an investor, demolished their village and built the project on it. But they didn't have the building licences, that's why the buildings are still empty now.

J: I didn't know that. It's almost like your story of the villagers who built a tower on the edge of their village, all moved in there, and then sold their land. From rural to urban in a split second. But what about the meeting last week; that client had an assistant who spoke English very well, that client seemed pretty professional.

C *(smiling)*: He's not professional, he only looks professional. And his assistant doesn't know architecture. He speaks good English because he studied English.

J *(smiling)*: Nobody is allowed to have more knowledge than their boss?

C: At least not to show it.

J: But what about all these 'marketing' specialists who attend all our meetings?

C: The market is the most important thing in China now, but these marketing offices have hardly any experience. Marketing is a completely new kind of job in China.

J: I'm often quite annoyed with their input, it distracts from essential content and they can even be quite detrimental to a project.

C: What do you mean?

J: Like when we propose what you call 'special spaces', their reaction is most definitely: 'Maybe expensive?' And more simply, when we propose glass, their reaction will be: 'Maybe light pollution?' When we propose aluminium: 'Maybe too modern?' When we propose outside spaces: 'Maybe high management costs?'

C *(smiling)*: I see what you mean.

J: They also seem to lack a clear vision, aim to play safe and therefore seem to question anything out of the ordinary.

C: It's more complicated and everybody plays these games very well. Sometimes the client needs to negotiate designs with the government, sometimes with other leaders. Therefore they need choice. If the requirements are unclear, the more different schemes they'll get. The more different architects they ask, the more different

choice they get. The more different marketing specialists they ask, the more different opinions they get.
J: Chinese clients like to choose, not to judge! *(thinking:)* You know what I told an architecture journalist from Holland last week?
C: What?
J: The architect in China has evolved into a search engine. The client searches 'hotel', the architect pops up a range of possible hotels. The client clicks on a few thumbnails to see the larger image, and then often closes the windows. The architect, meanwhile, keeps producing different thumbnails of different hotels until the client clicks on one and says: 'I like this one!'
C *(smiling, nodding and thinking)*
J: But you're right, things in China can change very quickly.
C: What do you mean?
J: You know, what I said last week, I'm not so sure about it anymore.
C: What do you mean?
J: About architects being search engines.
C: Why did you change your mind?
J: Chinese clients are very 'lihai' [powerful].
C: Why do you think that? Because they're rich?
J: Not so much that.
C: So why? Because they're mighty?
J: Because they have the ability to balance a myriad of uncertainties.
C *(smiling, nodding and thinking)*

TIME AND SPACE

To my question to Mr Jiang about what was the most important thing in organizing a project, he answered in no uncertain terms: 'Relations!' I was surprised and asked: 'What about time?' We looked at one another questioningly. Incidents like this were interesting because they were pickets around which a bigger picture could be constructed.

It was perhaps vague, but I increasingly began to develop a feeling that a different perception of time and space applied in China. I had once discovered that theory somewhere on the internet and now I could imagine it in real-life practice. In the West, time seemed to be linear, as a sequence of moments to be experienced. In China, time appeared to be much more synchronous, or behave as a collection of recurring moments. My feeling for this difference had gradually grown from observing a distinction in the way things were organized and priorities established.

In Western perception, everything had a time and place; there was a chronological relationship between events. Everything was dealt with on this basis and a time schedule was specified. Time was money, in a manner of speaking, and one had to act as efficiently as possible. In China, relationships seemed to have greater value than the efficient use of time according to Western norms. Time was much more of a reference, relationships prevailed above everything and, as a consequence, the chronological structure – which we greatly esteemed – of time schedules and appointments was subordinate to these.

To a Westerner like myself, it was often exceptionally complicated to understand these different attitudes towards time and relationships, not least because they often remained below the surface. It touched on the different ways in which information was dealt with in China and in the West, and the issue of how much information was accessible. I had the idea that information in China was regarded much more as something that held a potential 'advantage'. Therefore, information was only shared when the maximum advantage of not sharing it had been exhausted or when the sharing of information could give a greater advantage. In comparison, Westerners seemed to treat information much less strategically and were much freer in sharing it.

It was interesting to see how these different perceptions of time and relationships were expressed in real-life practice, say in the way that a project was developed. Huan once told me that he had been engaged on his PhD for six years. My reaction showed that I was surprised that his study had taken so long.

I articulated my astonishment: 'Didn't things go ten times faster in China than in the West?'

'My research is complicated,' he responded euphemistically. And continued: 'For that reason, time is less important.'

I looked at him enquiringly.

Using a metaphor about crossing a river, he explained the difference between a Westerner and a Chinese person doing research.

The researcher stands on one bank of the river and the result is on the other bank. A Westerner will start by analysing the river, a Chinese will begin by crossing the river step by step, 'by feeling the stones'. At the slightest hint of the river becoming too deep or the stones unreliable, he will turn around and seek another potentially fordable spot.

I thought his comparison exceptionally evocative and I said to him with a smile: 'We call the Chinese method "looking for a needle in a haystack".' Huan only smiled.

Later I realized that he had been seeking the correct relationships between the stones to be able to reach the other bank. And later still, I discovered that 'crossing the river on stepping stones' referred to a celebrated quote by Deng Xiaoping who thus described the task of modernization facing China.

YOU CAN'T CHANGE CHINA, CHINA CHANGES YOU

A few weeks after this last discovery, I was on my way to a restaurant where I had agreed to meet Lao Qing. Lao Qing wanted to let me taste *real* Chinese cuisine, because he somehow had the notion that I, as a Westerner, had not yet discovered enough of all 'the good things' that China had to offer. I met him outside the restaurant where he had booked a table. It was a genuinely excellent restaurant, he confirmed again before we entered: he knew the owner well, it was hygienic and the food was good and inexpensive. I was smiling from the start of his little speech.

The waitress led us to the second floor where a table was already set and waiting for us. Lao Qing opened the bag he had brought with him and took out a knife and fork and a bottle of Chinese rice wine.

'Why did you bring cutlery?' I asked him provocatively, because I knew he had done it for me out of politeness. He smiled, but did not answer, because he knew I was aware of his motives. He took two empty glasses and filled them with rice wine. He brought out a toast and said he was happy with his Western friend. I responded by saying that I was happy with my Chinese friend.

We ordered too much food, again based on Lao Qing's sense of politeness. When we had tasted the final dish and I had appraised it positively, the small talk changed into a serious discussion.

LQ: What are you reading now, John?
J: I'm trying to understand Taoism better.
LQ: Why would you want to do that?
J: What do I always answer when you ask me such a question?
LQ: Because you want to understand Chinese culture better.
J: Right, Chinese culture, but also Chinese clients, colleagues and friends.
LQ: What's to understand better?
J: A lot. For instance: why is there almost always an aversion against absolute statements and why are there almost never absolute value judgements, especially in group meetings?
LQ: What more?
J: Why is there lack of specificity in communication and why the preference for diffuse responsibilities?
LQ: Why would you think the answers to your questions can be found in Taoism?
J: I'm not sure, I'm searching. A colleague explained me that all these questions relate back to Taoism and to the thinking of Lao Zi.
LQ *(eyes distended)*: Ah Lao Zi! A real smart man, a great thinker! So what do you think?
J: I think Taoism is a slippery philosophy, slippery because in itself it is diffuse and contradictory.
LQ: Do you know 'yin and yang'?
J: It symbolizes the existence of two fundamentally opposite but complementary tendencies.
LQ: And where do you encounter yin and yang in China?
J: In Chinese language and sayings, in the ease with which Chinese people deal with contradictions, in Chinese symbolism in ... many things.
LQ: You're starting to see things, John.
J: There's so much to see ... Do you have any advice for me?
LQ: If you keep seeing everything, you can't always go forward.
J: Thanks for your suggestion, Lao Qing.
LQ: Not at all, John.

After lunching for an hour, there was the question of the bill, which, of course, I didn't even get to see. The bottle of 'baijiu' was still half-full, Lao Qing inserted a cork, and the bottle went back into his bag, just like the unused knife and fork. We said our farewells outside, but not before I had invited him to a following lunch.

I began to value Lao Qing as a true friend. He was a very intelligent person and exceptionally outspoken for someone of his generation. He was only too pleased to share his intelligence. To reinforce his argumentation he often opened his eyes wide, straightened his spine and leaned his head a little to the right. Sometimes we made an appointment, but more often I simply met him by chance. He seemed to live according to a fixed pattern. For example, very early every morning he went to a nearby park in his flannel trousers and sports shoes, with his characteristic white hat, to do 'exercises for his health'. If he saw me, he moved swiftly in my direction calling 'John!' He then summarized in a few sentences the purely positive moments that he had had in the time since I last saw him, such as his small successes on the Chinese stock market or the discounts he had earned in negotiations.

I asked him many questions, questions I knew might not seem very intelligent or which could possibly be experienced as insulting. But Lao Qing appreciated every question because he realized that this was the only way we could 'learn more from one another'.

'You can't change China, China changes you', he once emphasized.

This statement was his personal mantra to overcome any setback or shortcoming. It harmonized perfectly with the concept of 'shenghuo shunli', or 'smooth life', which he had explained to me before. But, unintentionally, this statement touched upon what was an existential issue for me, something that not only concerned me but also NEXT collectively. Did we actually wish to be changed by China? Or, vice versa: how did we want to develop in China?

Our 'trial period' in China had elapsed a long time ago, and the reason to stay was the same as the reason to come to China in the first place: intuition. But an answer to the simple question of how we wished to evolve in China was not readily available. Definitive statements were meaningless in a context in which I could exert so little influence.

During a flight to Amsterdam I had once listed a number of possible scenarios:

'NEXT as a Dutch office that realizes Dutch architecture in China.' After which I wrote: 'Doubtful. Why should China gain any benefit from Dutch architecture? A Disney Park perhaps, or a Dutch embassy, but the context and the briefs are otherwise utterly dissimilar, so why should the answers be the same?'

'NEXT as a Western office that realizes Chinese architecture.' Followed by: 'Inconceivable, but tempting as an experiment. Inconceivable due to the opportunities we would miss to experiment with our Western thinking. Tempting as an experiment, if only to get to understand Chinese architecture better.'

'NEXT as a global office that realizes international architecture.' Comments: 'Stifling. In China, many global offices are building projects that could belong anywhere in the world. Many of these offices rely upon their reputation and portfolio, and are specifically asked on this basis. Fortunately, we are compelled to operate at the other end of the spectrum, where clients are feeling their way and where lack of experience in just about every project rules out repetition.'

Finally: 'NEXT as a Western office that realizes international architecture for China.' I later underlined what I had written behind this: 'Favourable. This is where most scope for development seems to lie. By exploring the limitations of our own cultural values as well as the Chinese restrictions in the broadest sense of the term, it must be possible to develop specific answers to current Chinese briefs.'

Months later, the last-mentioned scenario again came to mind, as did Lao Qing's 'you can't change China, China changes you'. I had been invited by a Chinese office to attend the presentation by a Spanish architectural office in Beijing. The Spanish office wished to initiate a collaborative venture with the Chinese office. The Spanish architect-owner held the presentation in Spanish. One interpreter translated everything into English and a second translated that into Chinese. When the Chinese asked how the Spaniards envisaged the collaboration, the answer was that the Spaniards would make the design in Spain and the Chinese would elaborate drawings in China. What if the client phoned for an immediate appointment with the Spaniards? There was no answer for the interpreters to pass on, just a clear statement of intent: 'Once we have finished the design in Spain, nothing about it will be changed and so there will be no need for meetings.'

The Chinese smiled. I knew by now that a Chinese smile could mean anything from total contentment to total dissatisfaction.

The situation called to mind three other occasions when I began to wonder if there was something like a cultural alchemy that could give rise to added value. The first was a discussion I had with a Chinese architect who had worked with a French office. The French office had detached a French architect to the Chinese partner, with the French partner being responsible for setting up the joint design department. Much time had been invested in teaching French to the Chinese architects. The collaboration was terminated after less than a year. When I asked the Chinese architect why the collaboration hadn't worked, although I knew the answer, he replied resolutely in Chinese: 'We are here in China, not in France.'

A second occasion was a discussion with another Chinese architect who had worked at an American office. The 'headquarters' in America had divided the world into three sectors: North America, Europe and Asia. Energy and quality of people and ideas were deployed according to this division. The American architect who led the office in China was insensitive to the risks, outlined by the Chinese architect, of implementing old, unmodified ideas from the US or Europe. Ultimately the Chinese architect began his own office, taking dozens of colleagues and a large share of the dissatisfied clients with him.

The third occasion was a discussion at a Chinese developer's where, much to my surprise, a Scottish partner was present in an otherwise totally Chinese environment. To my even greater surprise, he chaired the meeting and spoke fluent Chinese. I was spellbound. He seemed to enjoy an enormous advantage; with his fluent mastery of the language he had infinitely greater access to China than I did. This third occasion came the closest to a clear picture of how NEXT saw itself on the Chinese stage. But even from that position, the question of cultural alchemy and cultural added value would persist.

It was all too easy to state that, as a Western architect, one could combine 'the best of both worlds' in a design. The 'best' in one context was not necessarily the best in the other, and the 'best' in the one world was not necessarily the best when directly combined with the 'best' from the other world. It was a dilemma that had not been foreseen by NEXT or by myself personally. All the ingredients for cultural alchemy between China and the Netherlands, in our case and mine, were present. There was just the question of who was the alchemist and which ingredients predominated.

My thoughts were interrupted. The Spanish architects were thanked for coming and for their presentation, and were accompanied to the exit. The Chinese extended no invitation to lunch, which was not a good sign, I concluded.

'You can't change China, China changes you', resounded in my head.

EXISTENTIAL CHALLENGE

I noticed that I was becoming increasingly diplomatic in the discussions with NEXT Amsterdam. The enthusiasm with which I had articulated excellent prospects for our projects in China months ago had made way for 'perhaps' and 'looks good'. I relayed almost literally the information about developments that I received from Mr Chen. Nor was there any need to translate it into the Dutch context; until now everything he said was completely accurate, probably because everything he said about our projects had an open end.

However, a growing discrepancy arose whenever a sketch came in from the Netherlands that I knew would provoke outspoken objections in the Chinese context. In China many things could be interpreted in many ways, but that didn't mean that everything was accepted. How could I best communicate this to Amsterdam? The problem was that much of this accumulated insight came to Amsterdam as retrospective feedback, when the sketches had already been sent. This being the case, it scarcely functioned as input in the design process. Often it was impossible to underpin my assessments with concrete arguments or absolute truths when it was assimilated insight that was the deciding factor.

In the same way that I had subconsciously concluded, during the television interview about 'The Image of Metropolis', that the Chinese context was so different from the Dutch one that it could never influence our work in the Netherlands without being adapted, the reverse was also true. In its current undiluted form, Dutch thinking seemed to have very little chance of taking root in China.

In addition, it proved quite impossible to share the development and experiences of NEXT China in a direct correlation with NEXT Amsterdam.

Taken altogether, this seemed to be sufficient reason to make the necessary adjustments to our original strategy. Three quarters of the core of NEXT had Amsterdam as a home base and the fourth quarter was domiciled in Beijing. The original idea that the focal point of the development of our thinking about building in China ought to lie in Amsterdam had seemed self-evident. But to be able to actually build in China, the focal point had to come to lie in China. And this was also the case, as now, when the minority constituted the focal point. If the focal point of designing shifted to China, Amsterdam would have to function as a critical sounding board for Beijing, This would secure an integral and consistent NEXT factor.

Just as we had discovered an endless series of meanings behind a single image during 'The Image of Metropolis', the task was now to enable different meanings in the Netherlands and China with the same architectural themes. 'Made in China' had to become 'Created in China' and, to create in China, the 'windows' on China had to be set wide open. Even if, from a Dutch point of view, dust and mosquitoes entered along with the fresh air.

Here lay the existential challenge for NEXT: how could we develop ourselves synchronously in utterly different contexts? The real challenge lay in bridging the mental distance between Europe and China rather than the physical distance. In the worst case, Beijing would be a limiting factor in the development of NEXT Amsterdam, and vice versa.

In the best case, truly boundary-defying working and thinking could become a reality.

3. Freedom

SURRENDER

My train of thought, just like that of most Western architects, was based on an unconditional belief in the power of reason and a schooling in modernity. These were the basic values upon which projects were developed. Western architects, and certainly those from the Netherlands, tended to have a strong notion of right and wrong in such matters. I remember all too well the uncompromising truth that Aldo van Eyck seemed to have patented and the impression that this made upon me as a student.

But within the Chinese context, this frame of mind met with continual resistance. And not the kind of resistance that offered a designer scope to discover opportunities that had remained concealed up to that moment and which would eventually lead to an enrichment of the project. On the contrary, in most cases it led to an impasse and to consequential impoverishment.

It was this discrepancy that began to play an increasing role in my thoughts. I worked on the basis of a rational framework, but the more firmly I held on to this, the more it worked to my disadvantage. This realization was a first small step. The essential step I still had to take was to surrender to what was possible as soon as I began to operate beyond my own frame of reference.

What I needed was a new beginning.

'There's nothing there!' said Mr Guo resolutely. We were leaning over a map of China. My finger pointed to Yinchuan, the capital of the province of Ningxia. 'There must be at least a couple of million people living there, how can there be nothing there?' I asked him. He thought about it and repeated: 'There's nothing there.'

Two days later, on Friday evening, I was on my way to this nothingness. My Chinese colleagues didn't understand my urge to travel, they preferred to 'rest' in their scant leisure time. After a two-hour flight from Beijing, I arrived at Yinchuan airport at the heart of China in the middle of the night. A half-lit unofficial taxi brought me to my hotel along a brand-new highway. I concluded that with my Chinese gradually improving, my world in China was expanding considerably. The next day, I was up and out early. The hotel turned out to be situated on an enormous shopping street flanked by a series of large shopping malls. The shopping malls were all under construction and in the distance the contours of a Central Business District began to take shape. There was not so much nothingness here after all. Yinchuan, too, seemed to have succumbed to China's modernization.

In the afternoon, I happened to pass by a bus station and gazed in fascination at the huge numbers of people swarming around the small, old buses which seemed to transport anything and everything. Some buses were double their normal height because of the baggage tied together on the roof. I made a snap decision, chose a bus at random and boarded it. The driver, who was eating a carton of rice behind the wheel, looked up, startled. I smiled, said a friendly 'Good afternoon' to him in Chinese and sat down behind him.

Fifteen minutes later the bus was full and we drove off. A woman made her way expertly down the violently shaking bus, collecting money for the tickets. After three stops that seemed completely random to me, and where more people got in, we drove out of the city. Half an hour later, the asphalt turned into a sand track. An hour later the city was out of sight and we were driving across a large sand flat.

In a village, we stopped just in front of a waiting mother with two children. They climbed aboard and the mother told the two boys that they had to sit on the luggage between the driver and me. When we were on our way again, one of the boys sat looking at me intensely. To my surprise and fright, he began to cry. I turned to the mother and she told me, in broken standard Chinese, that he had never seen a foreigner in real life before.

After driving through the empty surroundings for an hour, the woman who had collected the ticket money asked cautiously what my destination might be. The further we were from Yinchuan, the more my presence in the bus seemed to unsettle her. 'The last stop', I said. My answer, or perhaps the fact that I answered in Chinese, seemed to calm her somewhat.

Half an hour later, she informed me that we had reached the terminus. The few people who were still in the bus got ready to disembark. The woman gave me a small piece of paper on which she had written a time. She explained that this was the time at which they would leave this spot to drive back to Yinchuan. It was the last and only bus back to Yinchuan, she emphasized. I thanked her cordially and got out.

Within a few minutes, all the remaining baggage had been removed from the roof of the bus and everyone had vanished in various directions. The bus drove off and I had a better look around. The bus stop consisted of no more than three old benches under a corrugated-iron roof. The village was no more than a road flanked by two-storey buildings, whose upper storeys were covered with advertising signs the entire length of the street. There was no traffic. A shepherd crossed the road with his sheep and looked at me warily.

I walked to the end of the street and, after the last building, headed straight on into the desert until I could no longer see any buildings or people in any direction.

I was in the middle of nowhere.

I turned around a few times, staring at the horizon. I was in the middle of China, I saw sand, dry grass, mountains and a hazy horizon. And nothing more, just total emptiness.

I took some photos and returned to the village to wait for the bus.

The woman who had sold the tickets on the outward-bound journey greeted me in a friendly way. I greeted her back. During the return journey it slowly began to grow dark. Yinchuan was brightly lit in all conceivable fluorescent colours when we arrived at the bus station. I walked back to the hotel and the next day I took an unofficial taxi to the airport. An hour after arriving there, I flew back to Beijing and an hour after landing in Beijing I was home again.

The following day I had an appointment with Huan in a restaurant. He asked me about my China experiences. After hearing my stories, he gave me some succinct advice: 'In China, sometimes you have to surrender before you can win.'

'Surrender in order to win', I repeated to myself. Wasn't that what I had hoped to achieve with my experience of two days earlier?

'MODERN AND INTERNATIONAL'

My experience in Yinchuan had instilled in me a kind of freedom. Instead of feverishly looking for answers, I increasingly seemed capable of working with uncertainties, and thus of developing the ability to operate beyond my own frame of reference.

Huanyang asked me if NEXT would be willing to design the new interior of our joint office floor. The brief was 'you can design freely'. The first time I had received a 'you can design freely' brief was for a design for a hotel in the mountains during my first visit to Huanyang. The result of this open-ended brief remained unknown for a long time. When I returned to Beijing and asked about the status of the project, I was told: 'No news yet, we're waiting'. After waiting for a considerable time I still hadn't heard anything about the design, so I concluded that the project hadn't got off the ground. The non-obligatory nature of the brief was far from ideal; it was a matter of hoping to hit a moving target. This being the case, the brief to 'design freely' had left me with an ambivalent feeling.

'Design freely?' I now asked myself out loud, after enthusiastically accepting the project. 'If everything is possible, nothing is possible,' I attempted to explain. 'Are there absolutely no preconditions?'

Questioning eyes and a straightforward answer: 'We like it to be modern and international.' 'Modern and international'; it sounded no less unsettling than 'design freely'.

I proposed a workshop in which a representative from each department would participate. These representatives could first inventory the wishes and demands of their own departments. On the basis of these preconditions, the architect could make a number of proposals and discuss these with all the representatives collectively. The representatives could then report the proposals back to their departments for more input for developing the ideas.

I wanted to give my proposal more emphasis, but the expression on various faces told me that the story wasn't getting across. So I held my peace and waited for their first reactions. My idea for a joint workshop was subtly rejected. The reason was simple: 'But *you* need to advise *us*!'

So I consented to the brief 'to design freely and advise'.

The Huanyang Group, consisting of three different but affiliated companies, would occupy the office floor along with NEXT. Based on an initial sketch sent to Amsterdam, we committed ourselves to a strong organizing element. We took the 'lang', the traditional landscape corridor, as the point of departure. Activities such as waiting, discussing, projecting and exhibiting were taken as a motive for transforming the typical corridor in both section and floor plan. By 'charging' it with such activities, the corridor aspired to become more than just a connecting element.

The first presentations were sketchy and I attempted to provoke reactions that would give me motives to develop the ideas further. The idea of an unified image for the upper storey was appraised positively. 'Very good, each smaller company looks bigger this way.' The envisaged atmosphere of semi-industrial and minimalist workspaces was less positively received however. 'Maybe it looks like a space for poor companies.' 'Maybe not suitable for the Chinese market.' And: 'Maybe not very creative.' I then realized that a more 'corporate' and more 'businesslike' ambience would go down better.

At the last presentation, the entire project was discussed, from the concept to the final details. When I explained the underlying central idea, the transformation of the traditional landscape corridor, the response was: 'No need to say that, we like your design because it is modern and international!'

A few weeks previously, my reaction to this would probably have been recalcitrant, something like: 'Modern and international, what is the value of these hollow concepts in China?' Then, my conclusion would probably have been: 'Total design freedom for the time being, without any kind of motive that might take root.'

Such an attitude had now lost its appeal. The design was to be realized; the interior of 1200 square metres was to be implemented in forty-five days. NEXT and Huanyang would jointly move in and occupy the storey. The executed design would give insight, better than any questionnaire, into the way our ideas could influence our practice and vice versa.

SEEING BETTER

'If you keep on seeing everything, you can't always go forward', Lao Qing had once remarked. I thought with a smile that I was beginning to become selectively blind, but paradoxically that I was also beginning to see better. During my first few months in China, it was almost impossible to estimate where and how I should divide my energy among the various projects. Each project and each component of each project seemed to demand maximum priority. And now, because of the increase in practical experience, I began to develop a better sense of reality. With each small practical step, I was increasingly able to invest energy, to assess priorities, and to apply these skills more specifically in projects.

Like many revelations, this one came spontaneously. It was prompted by a new project, and my awareness came on two different occasions. The first was when I became conscious of the hidden agenda of this new brief.

It seemed a very tempting brief: a country hotel, something we had never designed – with the exception of the 'fast-track' brief earlier in Beijing. And the location, with mountains in the background and a large lake in the foreground on the south side, was simply stunning. To my Chinese colleagues, this location embodied the perfect conditions for good feng shui. The potential of the surroundings was also underscored during a visit there with the client: 'It is only that it is too far from the Forbidden City, otherwise the Emperor would certainly have had an external palace here.'

We continued our walk and got to hear a 'detail' on the way: 'The local government doesn't want a hotel at this location yet.' With this remark, the project was downgraded from an architectural project to a politico-economic one within a fraction of a second. It became immediately apparent what the architect's role was: the client needed some designs to be able to negotiate with the government.

The brief was for a luxury five-star hotel, initially with conference areas, sports and spa facilities, and all other conceivable amenities for relaxing and doing business in a relaxed ambience. But with the remark about the local government, the brief became very transparent indeed. Many preconditions were initially less relevant. The surface area, for example, was as yet no more than a reference: 60,000 square metres would be a good estimate. The height of the building had been determined to a degree: it wasn't to exceed a certain number of storeys so that it wouldn't be too influential on the surroundings.

The client again stressed the importance of the project, and declared seriously: 'The architect represents the key role of diplomat in this project!' As usual, a broad offensive was then unleashed. NEXT would draw up a proposal, Huanyang several proposals, and 'other architects' would make 'even more proposals'.

In view of the minimal chance of seeing the design onto site, this type of brief was primarily interesting as a form of architectural mental exercise. The proposal had to be developed within a short time, and so was an excellent opportunity to refine the interaction between Amsterdam and Beijing. This interaction had given rise over time to a form of communication in which designs could be discussed in only a few sentences or in a single diagram. In doing so, we sought to develop designs with a degree of clarity.

Our offensive followed the strategy that Huanyang had mastered to perfection: first convince people with a sweeping gesture, then invest energy later in matters that were 'details for the time being', such as surface areas and internal organization.

Our proposal was architectural and diplomatic at the same time. We wished to intensify and accentuate the exceptional beauty that we encountered at the location. By repeating the typical stratification of the mountain ridges in the hotel we enabled it to blend naturally into the surroundings. This gave both an abstract relationship with the setting and a critical response to the 'political' desire for a 'non-hotel'.

The client showed the designs to the local government, which got us an invitation to present our design. In the car journey to the government office, the client was visibly tense. He emphasized that we had to accept every suggestion by the government with respect, and spoke once more of our role as diplomats. When the local government office came into view, I realized that this would be a case of diplomacy at the highest level. This feeling was reinforced when the gate opened and we advanced upon a Chinese copy of America's White House.

The bizarre aspect of this experience was not so much seeing a Chinese White House at a location far outside Beijing in a city that was largely unknown to the Western world, or the megalomanic ambitions this city seemed to radiate; the truly bizarre thing was that my surprise extended no further than a smile. Not even when a Chinese colleague told me that dozens of copies of the American White House could be found throughout China. In accepting this surreal situation, I had taken a second small step along the road to a greater sense of reality.

SMART GUY

That said, the quest for a greater sense of reality more often required diligent work rather than an unpremeditated experience. The conditions were good for one of our following projects because we could negotiate directly with the client. The process was arduous nonetheless: the client, a distinguished lady in her mid-forties, had already exhausted four marketing offices on us, and her ideas and opinions seemed subject to constant change.

The project was for a court of 2500 square metres surrounded by high-end serviced apartments. We wished to introduce a relationship with the building's exterior and had already made three different proposals. On Friday afternoon, a fourth idea was rejected. The client wanted two new proposals by Monday morning. This speed was necessary because the project was already under construction. However, we had no idea whatsoever of the direction the client wished to take with this building. The only information we had consisted of her reasons, which weren't clear to us at all, for rejecting our previous four suggestions. And we failed to understand why she didn't appreciate the quality of our theme – seeking a relationship with the exterior. Were there perhaps reference projects that resembled what she had in mind?

She thought hard for a while, sighed and gave no answer. One of the men from the marketing agency took the floor and repeated *their* concept for the building: 'The five elements'.

The client smiled and named a building that did please her: Hyatt Residences in Jianguomen. I knew that building. I had lived right next to it and I had to shudder: soft-yellow stone in the same surface as the glass. Corporate slickness in a nutshell. She mentioned another building, a government building adjoining Tiananmen Square, which I couldn't call to mind at the time. Then she apologized for the fact that she had to attend another appointment, and left the room.

We went directly to the Hyatt and to the government building. The government building had the same yellowish stone as the Hyatt building, but had protruding square windows (bay windows). The render company was called from the car and when we arrived back at the office, the boys were already waiting for us. Both façades were then drawn and given to them. It was late Friday evening by then.

A few hours later, I lay in bed feeling restless. We had invested so much energy in the first four proposals and were on the brink of losing this project. It was still dark when I crept out of bed and opened my laptop... *the five elements?*

I had begun to appreciate marketing in China as a complex professional area. It required an understanding of many subtleties. These seemed to be a paradoxical condition because advertising in China, compared to that in the Netherlands, was invariably characterized by an overdose of visual effects and very direct relationships between the form and the aim of the message.

I had to smile when I recalled a conversation with Mr Jiang. He told me doggedly that everything in China was malleable and adjustable, even the weather. I had heard the stories about 'rain-making' in Beijing. Rain was induced by firing rockets filled with chemicals into the air; the smog disappeared and blue skies were guaranteed on important days and for significant events. But Mr Jiang went further: prior to the start of the sale of a housing project, a developer had had gigantic snowmaking machines installed on the roofs of the high-rise blocks. In this way, the thousands of apartments could be sold in a romantic winter landscape in the middle of summer with Christmas music playing in the background.

However, the subtleties tended to reside in the things that were not to be seen, such as colours that ought to be avoided and numbers with bad connotations. Or in the impossible quest for the right slogans and texts that, despite identical characters, did not always have the same favourable meaning in all of the many dialects spoken in China. Many of these subtleties were lost on me. But evidently the marketing agency had touched a sensitive spot with its concept, even if it were only because it had managed to hold on to this project longer than the other marketing agencies had done.

What was the most magnificent scenic area in China where the five elements could be experienced? I asked myself that night, sitting at my laptop. It turned out to be Huangshan, the area with the yellow mountains to the west of Shanghai in the province of Anhui. In Chinese philosophy, literature, poetry and art, this region was endowed with a whole range of meanings. Annually, millions of Chinese tourists visited the mythical mountains. What if we were to project a panorama of Huangshan onto the façade of the court and attempt to suggest the stratification by varying the depths of the windowsills?

An hour later, everything was being further developed at the office. The panorama of the mountains, represented by the façade, was linked to a water landscape in the courtyard. The image was completed by adding a roof structure of louvres, the abstract pattern of the louvres depicting clouds in the sky. This way sky, panorama and landscape were unified.

On Monday morning I presented, with little enthusiasm, our bastardized version of the Hyatt and the government building. And then I informed the client enthusiastically that we had made another design ourselves based on the five elements.

The first slide of Huangshan filled the projection screen. This was followed by a diagram in which the view of the mountains was projected onto the four façades. Then came the renderings accompanied by explanations: a layered panorama of bay windows, the connection with the courtyard and the sky, stone for the façades, water for the landscape and louvres for clouds.

The marketers grinned.

The client responded enthusiastically. 'You're a smart guy!' she said laughing.

As I smiled modestly, I realized that the space for this project had not been found by critically examining the client's question, but by embracing it. To arrive at the design, we had taken a 'concept' that initially meant little to us and had abstracted it into an image, a façade.

It would be hard to imagine this happening in Amsterdam; besides, it was contrary to our way of working. But it made sense in China. Was that a loss of integrity, or an enrichment of working and thinking?

Whatever the case, it was an increase in relative architectural freedom.

DIFFERENTIATING

In the Netherlands it was our aim to work on as many aspects of a project as possible. And, in design processes, we worked from inside to outside. Form and image were the outcome of a process, of an idea, for example, about the intrinsic quality we were seeking for a building; form and image were certainly not an aim in themselves.

From this point of view, the design for the courtyard was less Dutch than, say, our design for the children's day care centre. The latter concentrated on an intervention that would enable an informal inner space. There the required collective space had been thrust, as it were, through the slab of facilities. The aim was an informal inner space; the consequence was a transformed exterior. In this way, interior and exterior were inextricably linked.

In contrast, the design for the courtyard harmonized much more with the way in which Chinese architects created their designs: from outside to inside. In doing so, they followed an agenda that was largely beyond the reach of the architect: first the client had to be convinced with an exterior, with form and image; only then could the interior be discussed along with a possible added value for the user or organization.

I had had my first acquaintance with this inverted design approach in Qingdao, in the project for the Olympic Games. Since then I had often been surprised by the situation. The mere thought of designing from the outside inwards was inconceivable in Western architectural discourse and at Western architecture schools: there the architect's primary task was to order space and functions; form and façade were of secondary importance in terms of time and meaning. This Western 'rule' was diametrically opposed to the Chinese approach, where architects seemed to regard the ordering of space and functions as subordinate to image and meaning.

However, the Chinese way of working appeared to be more of a strategy than a fundamental design approach. First of all, the programme was often unknown at the time of commissioning and therefore could not be taken as a starting point for a design. Furthermore, the most obvious argument from the Chinese viewpoint was that if you didn't have the brief for the exterior, why invest time in any follow-on briefs such as the ordering of space and functions in the interior?

The architectural risk of a possible later discrepancy between the exterior and the interior was often put firmly into perspective. 'I can fit any function in any rendering', Mr Jiang once said to me proudly. I could only affirm that he had proved this on several occasions in the past.

From the moment that this inversion of the design process became clear to me, we engaged in a number of ambivalent experiments with the Chinese style of designing. For example, we worked for almost two weeks on a housing block, 250 metres long and with a surface area of some 35,000 square metres. Due to the preconditions – loss of square metres was to be avoided – we couldn't divide the block into smaller pieces. Sunlight requirements made it impossible to introduce much variation in height. So how could we give this 250-metre-long building added value for both users and context?

Studies indicated that it was possible to give each apartment a rotated but nevertheless extremely economical head end, an intervention that was repeated on every other floor. In this way, the building could be accorded a smaller scale and a sculptural façade could be created using only two different forms.

Chinese colleagues saw a dragon's skin in the building. A dragon is a mythical figure in China and is strongly associated with power, prosperity and happiness. But the client was not enthusiastic, for reasons that were unclear.

'Good design, wrong project', was Mr Chen's reaction. 'We can use it for another project.'

I doubted whether the project could be called 'good'. After all, it had not been designed in terms of all aspects: we had no idea of the users or of the size and organization of the apartments behind the façade. But my doubts were not shared and even put into perspective by my Chinese colleagues. They pointed out, by way of example, that Vanke, the largest residential project developer in China, had its own research department for floor plans. 'Units', the English translation of 'huxing', were therefore not necessarily a part of the architect's design brief.

My question as to what *was* the domain of the architect evoked a simple response: 'The concept, the big feeling for the landscape' and, not least, the 'building elevations'. I could not fully convince myself of this limited definition of the design brief, but did discern a slight change in my attitude. Increasingly, I began to see in it a design brief in its own right.

This discovery was partly nourished by experiences with a new project on former factory grounds in the north-east of Beijing. It bordered on '798', a factory area built in the 1950s in Bauhaus style with help from the East German Republic. Huan had shown me around there in the first few weeks of my stay in Beijing, and I had returned regularly since then. Before visiting the site of our new project, we were first shown around the '798' area by the client's project manager. It was a fascinating place. The former factories had been partly taken over by the creative industry and increasingly by commerce. The atmosphere that prevailed there had no precedent in Beijing. The area was traffic-calmed, whereas cars seemed to dominate everything elsewhere in Beijing. The zone was also exceptionally green and the scale of the buildings was smaller than in the rest of Beijing, which was characterized by a politico-urban scale.

The former factory grounds next to '798', the site of our own project, had been built in that same decade largely by the Russians in classic Russian style. That area had a human scale and atmosphere comparable to those of '798', except that it had been allocated as a 'business garden'.

Along with my colleagues from Huanyang, I looked at a hollow measuring 260 by 60 metres where foundations had already been laid. Grass grew between the beam floor and it was obvious that construction had ground to a halt some time ago. The client's project manager told us that the project had once been designed as a factory, but that the factory function had been viewed as obsolete while the foundations were being laid. An office building now had to be realized on these existing foundations.

Bound by these conditions, we designed a building consisting of various parts connected by bridges. In this way, urban routes became a self-evident part of the building. Half-open courtyards in every direction were included in the complex. Accordingly, the green environment in which the building stood would form a smooth transition into the courtyards.

The mass studies were appreciated by the client: to him, the ideas seemed to dovetail with the future 'business garden concept' of the area. But he was more critical of the various façade concepts, which had been developed in conjunction with the mass studies. He concluded: 'Make it more simple, if necessary we can change the elevation in six or eight years.'

It was again an example of the dilemma of 'differentiated architecture', in which 'inside' and 'outside' were less mutually dependent in China than we in the West were accustomed. This time it was not specifically related to segregated design briefs or to a working method that ran counter to what was customary in the Netherlands. The dilemma was more intriguing than that: if 'parts' of a project were exchangeable in the course of time, if relationships were lost or could simply be replaced, how could an architect come up with a proposal that would retain its quality with the passage of time?

YIELDING

The idea of 'differentiated architecture' melded seamlessly with the way Chinese building practice worked. This type of architecture 'could be realized to good effect' within a 'minimum of time'. No unnecessary design effort was invested in the interior as long as the client failed to issue a follow-on commission centred on a design for the exterior. Chinese architects seemed to have no problem whatsoever with designing in the absence of a programme. If differentiated architecture was the unwritten agenda of real-life practice, many Chinese architectural offices were fully fitted out for the job.

The last part of the full Chinese name of Huanyang, translated into English, was 'architecture service company'. The idea that a commercial company would provide service was obvious, but the fact that an architectural office characterized its work primarily as 'service' was less familiar to me with my Dutch background. In the Dutch approach, architecture was linked much more closely with its cultural significance, and for that reason was rarely defined as a service-providing industry.

In China, the concept of providing service seemed to have only advantages. Service was a magic word and was directly linked to a good relationship with a client. Working on a good relationship was the first and most important task of the architect, since only an established relationship would make it possible to build up trust. It was only with trust that it became possible to convince a client, and it was only if a client was convinced that designs took on meaning and there was a possibility of getting them built.

An architect who had worked in a reputable Dutch architectural office once told me that, despite the architecture for which the office was responsible and which was held in high esteem in professional circles, no client had ever given that office a follow-on commission. The office was simply too uncompromising, which was good for the architecture perhaps but didn't enhance the relationship with the clients. I told this anecdote to Mrs Hu, who reacted uncomprehendingly: 'Why? In China, our clients are our best friends and we hope to have long-term relationships with them!'

Establishing and maintaining relationships were tasks that plainly could not be ignored by an architectural office in China. And one of the common ways to enable this was to provide service.

One form of service would be to use personal relationships, for example to get approvals for building permits pushed through quickly. Or, in an urban planning framework, to make master plans for land acquisition. A successful pitch by a client for a piece of land on the basis of the design and a suggested land price could earn an architect a commission to build. But service could also be of an architectural nature, say by 'helping' with façade designs. To many clients, help with a façade design was the most natural request and to many architectural offices it was the most natural service to provide. The benefits were twofold: the architect received the chance to show off his qualities and forge and maintain relationships, while the client had a greater choice.

The production in 'assisted façade designs' had to be vast, many times greater than the market itself, I estimated. This type of 'architectural shadow market' was utterly unknown to me in the Netherlands. Any comparison could at most be made with the culture in the Netherlands of open architectural competitions where dozens of offices often competed for commissions on a non-obligatory and unpaid basis.

But in the Netherlands, taking part in competitions was done voluntarily choice. 'Assisting with façades' was hardly a voluntary matter for an architectural office in China. It was perhaps the most concrete form of service provision and one of the few opportunities to invest in a relationship with a potential client. It was also the reason that clients in China regularly involved external architects in projects. Often a client was only looking for 'more feedback'. It could also be the case that external architects were being 'tested' for other projects. Sometimes they were deployed indirectly to 'stimulate creativity'. A brief could fall apart due to the fact that external architects were awarded sub-contracts. Occasionally an entire project was lost in this way. But it also worked inversely: sometimes you acquired a sub-contract yourself or other architects lost their projects to you.

The concept of 'service' as an investment in a relationship with a client brought with it the real risk of the architectural limitations of differentiated architecture and a discrepancy between the façades selected from the many alternatives on the one hand and the necessary internal organization of a building on the other.

Up to the design for the courtyard, the building with the dragon skin and the office building on the factory foundations, we had only had indirect experience with this type of differentiated architectural brief. And we had had equally little experience with the involuntary practice of 'providing service'. But all that was about to change.

Mrs Hu had transferred control of her office temporarily to Mr Yang. On Wednesday morning I bumped into him in the corridor. He told me, disconcertedly, that one of his most important clients had phoned him that morning: 'He's not really satisfied with the elevation design of his most important project'. Mr Yang asked if I had time that afternoon to look at the design and perhaps make some 'suggestions'.

That afternoon I heard that Huanyang had been involved in this project for years. It was an important project of about 200,000 square metres and consisted of a five-storey podium atop which were five towers of up to a hundred metres in height. Those towers had once been designed as offices, later they became offices with a hotel, and now they had to be realized as apartments with a hotel.

I looked at the design and saw the contours of the 'Big One' that Mr Chen had shown me during one of the first guided tours of the office. I looked at Mr Chen and asked: 'Is this ...' Before I could finish my sentence, he reacted excitedly: 'Yes, yes, it's the Big One ...'

Huanyang had been involved with the project right from the outset and was responsible for the mass studies, the permits and the working drawings. An American architectural office had designed the elevations. When the programme changed, the client had asked Huanyang if the elevations could be altered. Dozens of different proposals were created over a period of weeks. And now an alternative elevation by a different architectural office had suddenly appeared. 'The client likes their elevation a lot', Mr Chen said, looking grim and playing nervously with a laser pointer.

That afternoon, unmistakable tension reigned in the meeting room. It was Wednesday and the client had given Mr Yang until Friday to come up with an alternative proposal. It was an important project, already under construction, and there was a real chance that

Huanyang could include it in its portfolio of realized work. But the request from the client for an alternative proposal could also be seen as a motion of no confidence. If the results of the test were unsatisfactory, the future relationship with the client could be under threat, in the worst possible scenario.

The new elevation produced by the other architectural office was analysed feverishly, as were the previously rejected designs. Due to the fact that we lacked criteria, we got no further than denouncing the alternative plan on the basis of too much glass, too-high 'management costs' and the excessive use of 'too-expensive' materials. Fascinated, I watched the discussion and had the feeling that I could contribute very little of essential use.

Suddenly the decision fell without a clear, preceding conclusion: 'Architects, get to work. Friday is the deadline!'

My jaw dropped. The Chinese architects ran to the bookshelves to look for references. I went back to my office and wanted to press on with an as-yet uncertain project of two towers eighty metres tall. Then Mr Yang entered and asked if I could 'assist' him with this project. Counting back from the deadline, there was less than an hour to make a design. The rest of the time was needed for elaborating and processing renderings and drawings.

How could I design an elevation for a building of 200,000 square metres in less than an hour?

I said I would do my best and he left my office visibly relieved.

I gazed in front of me, through the glass wall, at the architects who were rampaging through the architecture books like madmen. Then I looked at my screen, which displayed the first ideas for the uncertain project with the two towers. Without scruples, I pasted the design for the elevation of the two towers on the project with the five towers.

Two nights later, everything was finished and we drove to the client's office. Completely exhausted and running purely on adrenalin, I presented the ideas behind the elevation. It had to be a cross between an office and an apartment building elevation, so that in the event of a future modification in the programme the permits wouldn't need altering. I continued: In the design, the stone and glass had a gradual relationship. The lower part of the towers had more stone, which would give the complex a solid foundation. Moving upward, more glass was introduced into the façades, so that the towers seemed to dissolve into the sky. The higher up an apartment, the better the view and the light. And the better the view and light, the greater the apartment's potential market value.

It was probably the first time in my life as an architect that I had used a marketing argument.

'That's what I want', said the client.

In China it's called 'instant success'. And instant success was addictive.

From the meeting I raced to the airport to catch a last-minute flight to Dalian, a metropolis in the north-east of China. I needed the distance for reflection, in view of the fact that I was increasingly allowing myself to be led by the magic that Huanyang not only promised me but also seemed to deliver.

At the airport I phoned NEXT Amsterdam, which had received little notion of the project due to the extreme pressure of time. None of the partners was present, and I shared my thoughts with Joost Lemmens, one of the office stalwarts. While I recounted the story to him, I also told it to myself: the words made their way both to Amsterdam and to my own consciousness. Not only had we worked on 'the Big One' without for a moment asking ourselves what we were doing, but, with the pressure of time as an excuse, I had unscrupulously pasted an elevation from another project onto this one.

This contradicted all my original values as well as our train of thought and way of working in Amsterdam, in which context, programme and wishes of both client and users ideally were together translated into an architecture that harmonized perfectly with the streetscape and the interior. In this way of thinking, there was no leeway for an elevation as a separate design brief, let alone for elevations that could be projected from Project A onto project B within an hour.

On the mental bridge between Beijing and Amsterdam, I began more and more to gravitate towards Beijing. As I entered the plane, I concluded that I had been aware of this and had gravitated there of my own free will.

WESTERN CONSCIENCE

Since our arrival in Beijing, the number of Western architects at the office had gradually increased. The idea behind this was that the interaction between various kinds of 'design intelligence' would benefit the quality of the projects, as was the case with many architectural offices in the West.

But the situation also helped us to maintain a critical 'Western conscience' in China.

I thought back to the French architect who had designed the braille pattern of stars on a square in Hangzhou. He had recently admitted that, with that project, he had surrendered unconditionally. Since then, he 'had accepted the inevitable architectural fate in China', as he himself described it. He used the Chinese term 'meiyou banfa' to reinforce his declaration. Freely translated this means 'there is no alternative' or 'it is simply so'. It is a frequently used concept in China and one of the first to be taught to me in Chinese.

I felt strong resistance to the idea of 'meiyou banfa'. In my opinion, the acceptance of fate harboured much less potential than a quest for new critical equilibrium. And it was in that quest that the Westerners at the office in Beijing were important.

Wopke Schaafstal, in collaboration with NEXT Amsterdam and the Faculty of Architecture in Delft, was responsible for a study of the development of housing in Beijing. With his intractable character, probably connected to his Frisian roots, he was often unpredictable to his Chinese colleagues. Schaafstal was sporadically critical of our work and thinking in China and, as such, represented the dynamic boundary between value judgements in the Netherlands and in China.

Bob de Graaf was part of the team for a time. His typical tranquillity was constantly tried by the Chinese pressure of work and the inherent deadlines. 'Bobby, is that part finished?' 'Not yet, almost.' 'No need to finish it, we need to start working on a next project.' De Graaf let himself be fully immersed in China, and he appeared happy to share the energy he ostensibly gained from this.

Then there was Melle Pama, who enjoyed a high position in the retail department of Huanyang for a year. His initiatives to raise the quality of the designs to a higher level were greatly appreciated by the Chinese. But it was primarily his business instinct that cast a new light – for me as well – on our practice.

And there were Laz Çilingir and Thijs Klinkhamer. They represented unbridled enthusiasm. Their stories of China and Beijing made me realize that my admiration had begun to level out. This was a dangerous development, because it might cause me to see things less clearly.

But above all there was Lao Mi, as our Chinese colleagues called him. Phonetically, Mi referred to Michel. They used 'Lao', the Chinese form of address expressing respect for older people, because he was already forty-five years old. With his shock of grey hair and huge frame, Michel van Tilborg towered above the Chinese. Lao Mi was doing a design course in the Netherlands and had come to Beijing for six months. He had my special respect; not many people were able to reinvent themselves at that age and start on this type of adventure.

With the arrival of several Western architects, I deliberately confronted myself with my 'new self-evident insights' and the critical attitude of Lao Mi in particular was beneficial to many projects. Like every Western architect in China, he also underwent a process of resistance and powerlessness, while the resilience of his own values was tested. But where I tended to accept a new layer of values, he appeared to opt resolutely for a defensive policy. There were many conflicts: designs were not understood by the Chinese, the deadlines for projects were unrealistic, everything was oriented towards quantity and speed rather than to quality and content. What seemed to unsettle him most was the 'subservient, almost humble attitude towards the client'.

'You shouldn't go along with that kind of thing!' he once sneered when I told him about an impossible deadline without clear preconditions. When he strode out of my office he repeated 'You shouldn't go along with that kind of thing!' But I did go along with it, I did so deliberately. To explore the limits of my Dutch frame of reference. And to broaden my value system.

At one point, I came up against a particularly hard boundary. The telephone rang. Someone introduced himself and asked what kind of architectural office we were. Then came the question of whether we were a *real Dutch* office. In my office an hour later, I was looking at photos of two artificial islands of sand in the Yellow Sea between China and Japan. These 'islands' would be accessible from Beijing within five hours due to the construction of a new highway. In view of the location – islands and sea – the decision had been taken to give the entire project a 'typically Dutch' theme. Thousands of houses, hotels, conference rooms, business centres and shopping malls, a yachting marina and a Holland Museum were to be built there.

In reply to my question as to what we could mean for this project, I was looked at in surprise and told that they were looking for an architect, preferably with Dutch origins. There would be an important meeting the next day. If I was interested, I was most welcome to give advice as a Dutch specialist.

The following day I attended a meeting with a team of developers and investors. The latest imported luxury cars were lined up outside. A group of Chinese architects entered in a chaotic fashion. Within a few minutes, the projection screen was filled with a master plan of one of the islands. To my surprise, a part had already been completed: I saw Volendam-style houses and the pier of the Dutch resort of Scheveningen. The houses were on stilts so that it was possible to look out to sea over the dike.

Then came the question: could I design a five-star hotel? During a visit to the Netherlands, they had seen a building that would fit impeccably into the plan. A picture of the Palace on the Dam in Amsterdam, the perfect example of Dutch classicism from the 17th century, was pushed across the table in my direction. Somewhat surprised, I said that our expertise lay more in 'modern projects'. A moment of silence followed. The general manager of the client looked at me and repeated that this style would harmonize very well with the project. Everyone at the table was acutely aware of what was going on here: the client had made an explicit request and I didn't wish to meet it.

I repeated in a friendly way that our expertise lay in modern projects. Then I made an attempt to explain my position and said that the Netherlands was more than only history. Just a few words later, the general manager thanked me for coming. Without articulating it in so many words, we had both concluded that we could not mean much to one another. After a friendly farewell, I went back to the office.

That afternoon, Mr Jiang asked me why I wasn't interested in this project. He didn't understand Western architects, he said. For instance, a Western architect had once told him that he 'couldn't design architecture with sloping roofs'. 'Why not?' Mr Jiang had asked him. He received no answer. 'Didn't we live under sloping roofs for centuries?' he asked me, in an attempt to obtain a response.

I didn't let myself be drawn into a discussion about sloping roofs and declared that this brief was not interesting to us because we had to implement literally what the client wished. As a result, there was no leeway for interpretation and development.

My answer was scarcely understood, going by Mr Jiang's questioning look and his pregnant conclusion: 'Western architects need a lot of leeway to design'.

CHINESE CONDITIONS

Lao Mi mentioned, in passing, that our projects in China appeared to have gone into the fast lane. Measured against the increasing quantity of projects designed by NEXT that were being implemented, I had to agree with his observation. But, more importantly, the development of *ideas* behind our projects also seemed to have moved into the fast lane. Nevertheless, there was absolutely no euphoria: this acceleration was not accompanied by greater control over the way projects developed.

One of the most substantial obstacles to control over a project or process was 'new information'. And 'new information' was an everyday occurrence in Beijing's architectural practice. I had reached a second limit of my Dutch frame of reference but – in contrast to the restriction that I had encountered in 'the Dutch project' – this new limit also brought new scope.

We had worked for ten days on end on 'M13', a competition entry for three office buildings, totalling 50,000 square metres. The site bordered on an enormous park and we sought a possibility to exploit the relationship between the site and the park. The buildings were elaborated in the ground plan and with regard to their volume so that as much frontage as possible could be oriented towards the park. Green roofs were proposed as gardens and terraces. The elevation was designed as an abstract tree pattern. Everything seemed to fit together, the project appeared to be sound.

A telephone call came the day prior to the deadline. New information: the client wanted six buildings instead of three. The message was brought to me by Mr Chen. He entered my office, saw me working conscientiously on the project and asked me nonchalantly how it was going. I suspected that he had again come to examine and refine the project with me. After he had told me the news, I looked at the ceiling. I turned to the computer screen and then looked out of the window.

I shut my laptop: 'That's it, I'm off!'

Mr Chen was visibly startled.

I pulled the cables out of the laptop and looked for my bag.

Mr Chen began to stare at me uncomfortably.

'How can we work like this? It's impossible to make good designs this way!'

Colleagues outside my glass workplace looked at us. It became quiet in the office.

I propped my computer into my bag and went to get my coat. I grabbed it, but then hung it up again. I sat down and asked Mr Chen to sit down too. Then I stared at the draft scale model of the three buildings.

'I just heard it too. I know, this is very bad', he said.

I didn't respond and just stared at the scale model. This was the moment when bending turned into breaking – this was the limit.

'We can change the design, there's still time.'

If I responded, he would convince me and I would opt for China, not for the Netherlands. I said nothing.

'There are three buildings here, it's easy to make six out of them.'

I continued to stare at the draft scale model. 'Nice project ...' is what Amsterdam had said about the first sketches.

Then it happened, I reacted. 'Why?' I asked loudly. 'Why?!'

'I don't know,' he said, 'the client phoned just a minute ago ...'

I looked at him, seeking answers that I knew I wouldn't find.

'There are three buildings here, it's easy to make six out of them,' he said once more. I laughed sceptically and sneered: 'How would you like to do that?'

'There are three buildings', he repeated, while he looked at the draft scale model. 'We cut all of them in two and then we have six buildings'.

It was the Chinese logic that I had grown fond of: if a solution to a problem could not be described in a few sentences, it wasn't a good solution. I placed a Stanley knife in front of him and looked at him. He picked up the knife and cut the model of the first building in two. A few moments later, we had six buildings.

I stared at the scale model with the six buildings. The only good thing that still remained of the project was the glaring visibility of the operation with which we had doubled the number of buildings. Once more I could reproduce the smile that was so important in China. Then I looked at Mr Chen: 'We'll make two schemes, one with three and one with six buildings. I'll present the proposal with the three buildings first and we'll show the scheme with the six buildings as a second option.'

Mr Chen smiled and agreed. The oppressive atmosphere cleared and sounds could be heard again on the office floor. Everybody was informed of the situation and without asking a single question, the Chinese colleagues began to adapt the drawings, renderings and scale models.

I had stood at the limits of my own values and had surrendered. This project was lost, the strategy with two different options was hopeless. The mutilated plan had lost all of its original qualities; it had even become totally 'strange', as Chinese colleagues who didn't know the original plan later described it. Why did I accept? Why did I give in?

Not yielding was not an option, but yielding too much resulted in equally hopeless projects. It had to be possible to produce designs that were so powerful that the unexpected adjustments impossible to avoid in China could be made without diminishing the genuine architectural quality of the proposal. This was where the challenge lay: not in an unwinnable struggle against the Chinese conditions but in developing a strategic acceptance that not only took Chinese conditions as its starting point but would include them in the design as an added value.

4. Synergy

'SLEEPING IN ONE BED, DREAMING TWO DREAMS'

We had founded our decision to collaborate with Huanyang largely on intuition. And, in view of the portfolio with which we came to China, Huanyang probably had a similar motivation. Together we had begun on 'crossing a river by feeling the stones', as it were. And we had left the shore behind: the first building projects had been realized and a number of others were in preparation.

This being the case, NEXT was on its way to giving substance to the original agenda of our stay in China: to find possibilities to realize Western conceptual thinking in real-life practice there. Since our arrival in China, however, this agenda had become filled with an increasing number of substantive ambitions. For example, there was the quest for architecture 'Created in China' rather than 'Made in China', but there was also the quest for an architecture that was robust enough to retain its quality regardless of any imposed modifications. And, not least, there was my personal quest for space beyond my own frame of reference.

To pursue these ambitions, it was necessary to generate more interaction between NEXT and Huanyang. And it seemed that this was increasingly the case.

At first, there appeared to be only one 'we', and that was NEXT. But a new 'we' arose in the course of time: 'we' as NEXT Beijing. And now a third 'we' was forming: a sense of community between NEXT Beijing and Huanyang. My world began to oscillate continuously between all these 'we's'.

The most exemplary occurrence so far of the third 'we' presented itself on the occasion of a visit I made with Chinese Huanyang colleagues to an Australian architectural office in Beijing. We were there along with a Dutch-Hong Kong company that was pitching for the project of an American company, whose commissioning principal was also present.

Huanyang was interested in the project due to the role of 'local design institute', the Chinese office responsible for construction drawings in accordance with Chinese construction law. Huanyang had asked me if I would represent them, with the idea that it would be easier for me to communicate with the Westerners. Without hesitating for a moment, and completely in line with Chinese customs, I had agreed. In the discussion I represented Huanyang and I began unconsciously with the we-form that was normal when someone introduced a company in China.

The moment in Qingdao at which I had assumed the temporary identity of a Canadian architect seemed to belong to a very distant past. And the remarkable thing was that double identity was no longer an issue. I was NEXT, but was here as Huanyang: sincerely, without problems, without friction.

Potentially, there was optimum interaction between NEXT and Huanyang, interaction free of misunderstanding. It seemed possible to simply synchronize ambitions; true synergy would become a possibility. But, as so often in China, apparent certainties, just like apparent uncertainties, were continually subject to change.

All Huanyang employees had gathered in an exuberant mood to celebrate the Chinese New Year, which occurs in February according to the lunar calendar. A large reception room in a hotel was invariably hired for the occasion; there was an abundant banquet, a number of light-hearted performances and various prize bestowals. Prior to the festivities there was always a serious introduction by the 'laoban', the boss.

Mr Yang entered the room in an impeccable suit, mounted the stage confidently and made his way to the lectern. The hundreds of people present fell silent. A spotlight caught him and a beamer flashed on. A first slide appeared, with the word 'Welcome' in Chinese. I looked around me in the semi-darkened room and thought about the unprecedented achievement he and his wife had managed to realize. Within a period of eleven years, they had built up an empire with hundreds of employees. They were the new elite of China – thanks to an unbounded ambition, they were the ones who 'had become rich first'.

After a cordial word of welcome, Mr Yang assumed a serious expression. The first slide made way for the second: a large diagram in which years were set against square metres of construction drawings. His voice was deep, resonant and extremely self-assured: 'In the past year, 1.3 million square metres of construction drawings have been produced, 12% more than last year.'

I calculated that, by now, around 125,000 families must live in projects created by Huanyang. At the same time, I wondered why those accursed square metres were always seen as more significant than something such as *quality*.

Mr Yang's voice rang resolutely through the speakers; a well-known credo echoed through the hall: 'Everyone should continuously ask himself: what does the client want?'

I had recently had a discussion with him on this topic. I argued that the primacy of the wishes of the client was probably the right policy for China at this moment but, in the longer term, the demand for architectural offices with vision would almost certainly increase. Competition was growing; according to the stipulations of the World Trade Organization, foreign architectural offices could now settle in China without having to have an obligatory local partner. The youngest generation of developers had travelled a great deal, and many had studied abroad. The world was expanding and offices with vision would be able to offer added value to the client through innovation and creativity. Mr Yang agreed, but subsequently insisted that, in his view, there were only two types of architect: artists and businessmen, and he was a businessman. For this reason, a development towards greater architectural vision at this moment was 'maybe not necessary'. Vision as form was fine, vision as content was as yet not really essential. With this, of course, he was himself expressing a vision: a commercial vision that was diametrically opposed to my idea of the added value of an architectural vision. The discussion demonstrated that, in their doing, thinking and acting, NEXT and Huanyang represented the two extremes of the 'vision spectrum', at least for the time being.

After ten minutes, Mr Yang's speech on the aims for the coming year reached its climax, the champagne was uncorked and the first performances began. There were sketches, song and dance acts, and parodies. And there was food, an abundance of food.

The highlight of the evening was the prize-giving ceremony: prizes for the best section manager, best junior, best assistant, best English speaker, etc. The prizes consisted of a refrigerator, toys, flowers, video cameras and mobile phones. The main prize for the best project of the past year was a sum of money.

The results of this competition had been determined democratically: everyone had been able to submit a vote. It fascinated me because it could provide an interesting picture of the Chinese meaning of 'best', down through all layers of the office.

Of course, the older managers were inundated with flowers and prizes.

Then: there was a roll on the drums for the bestowal of the prize for the best project of the past year. There was cheering in the hall, a housing project had been chosen as the best project and the team that had worked on it had won the main prize. I could not really imagine why this was regarded as an exemplary project, let alone the *best* project. Until I realized that it was the *largest* project of the past year. A Chinese colleague next to me confirmed that most of the people in the office had worked on this project. 'Of course they voted for their own project', he added, 'so that they could share the financial prize.'

The staff was totally oriented to the policy of the larger the project, the better. Again the power of numbers had triumphed. Again I realized that NEXT and Huanyang represented one another's opposites.

In my head I drew up a list of contrasts:
NEXT was small, Huanyang was big.
NEXT was non-commercial, Huanyang was hyper-commercial.
NEXT sought quality, Huanyang sought quantity.
NEXT sought innovation, Huanyang did what the client wanted.

I wondered why our collaboration was successful despite their different circumstances and I could only think that the Chinese were masters of uniting the ununitable.

'Sleeping in one bed, dreaming two different dreams', as the old Chinese saying goes.

LEAST COMMON MULTIPLE

My realization that NEXT and Huanyang represented each other's extremes was linked to the conviction that input from various perspectives could actually be very productive. In fact, the field of tension that accompanied this could be exceptionally fruitful for the development of a project. But sometimes the tension morphed into something that could only be described as exceptionally unproductive.

'We really appreciate your scientific working methods, and we hope to learn a lot from you!' This 'compliment' and this 'desire' to learn were articulated with some regularity. I found it difficult to gauge the value of this statement. I even had difficulty with it because it referred to a superior position ascribed to me, which I regarded as both thoroughly untrue and undesirable. Initially I had invariably tried to neutralize the compliment. But, due to its consistent repetition, I no longer really knew what to say about it. Accordingly, I accepted it each time, smilingly, silently. In retrospect, this proved to be a fatal assessment.

The 'assignment' to learn from us was not a new one; it was actually as old as one of our first joint discussions. But now the powers that be were putting more and more pressure on Chinese architects: 'You still talk about emotion and feeling; John is talking about the advantages of his design, his design method is more scientific!' They seemed to be encouraged to seek scope for development primarily in the form: 'Look at his drawings, they are really very good indeed!'

The last remark had the consequence that our 'form' of working – the typical Dutch way of creating schemas and diagrams – was adopted by Huanyang. To the outside world, it made NEXT and Huanyang perhaps a bit more equivocal, but internally, the 'assignment to learn' tended to put personal relationships under stress. The 'more successful' our designs were, the more criticism the Chinese architects could expect, and the worse the mutual relationships would become. 'More successful' projects by NEXT led irrevocably to a more unproductive collaboration with our Chinese colleagues.

A former senior architect once sneered: 'Thousands of years ago Chinese architects travelled all over the world to teach foreign architects how to build!' Another colleague remarked: 'If you guys present something, a client accepts it a hundred times faster than when the same thing is presented by a Chinese architect!'

These were comments that issued from a deep-rooted pride. I could imagine that pride: China had a culture more than 5000 years old, it was one of the oldest surviving civilizations in the world. Why should Chinese architects now have to 'learn' from Western architects, especially in a cultural profession such as architecture?

This tension generally remained subliminal – harmony was everything – but sometimes there was a minor flare-up.

A client approached us about a new project. They explicitly wanted a foreign architectural office, they wanted two different designs and they had two weeks to spare. It was a very promising project, but we had too many ongoing projects to make two well-considered proposals. This hesitation was seized upon rather too quickly by one of the Chinese architects. He suggested that NEXT should produce one proposal and he would make the other, and I would present both.

His face betrayed the hidden agenda: the possibility of a competition in which the client would opt for a Western or a Chinese architect purely on the basis of the designs themselves. I agreed, without seriously assessing the possible consequences in advance.

However, the ongoing projects demanded more time than planned and, in my case, the new project visibly suffered. In contrast, the proposal by the Chinese architect was completed two days prior to the deadline. And there had been no need for overtime – a good sign of control and efficiency. The last two days before the presentation, the full-colour A0 panels stood against his desk and people came by regularly to compliment him on his design.

Our proposal was only completed on the morning of the presentation and had been realized with endless overtime. In the run-up to this moment, it seemed as if we had been repeatedly and structurally impeded. The Chinese staff pretended to be working on our proposal, but in the meantime worked on the other one. Without being informed, we worked with the wrong data on, for example, building boundaries and the results of sunlight studies. All previously developed personal relationships appeared to have dissolved into thin air. The project had gradually evolved into a titanic struggle, and I had the feeling that for my Chinese colleagues, it had become a competition between China and the rest of the world.

On the day of the presentation, around twenty people were waiting for us in a presentation hall. When everything was presentable, the 'big chief' arrived. An hour later we left the hall. The client had opted for our proposal without a moment's hesitation; the project had to be completed by the beginning of 2010. In the car back to the office, I kept quiet and listened to the conversation between my Chinese colleagues. They expressed their admiration for the fact that we had developed in such a short time the capability to estimate what Chinese clients wanted. I had become Chinese, someone said. Everybody laughed at that remark.

I kept out of it, and looked out of the window, watching Beijing speed past. It would only be a question of time before there was another such competition. I thought about how extremely unproductive this kind of collaboration actually was, with no shared intrinsic goals beyond that of getting buildings on site.

Back at the office, nothing more was said about the run-up to the project and the feeling I was left with was how 'thin' synergy could be. It was only a few days later that I realized that it was the 'assignment to learn' that seemed to exclude mutual interaction as a shared intrinsic goal. And, in retrospect, I realized that it was not just the assignment to learn that was exceptionally unproductive, but that my own attitude was not helping things. With my persistent silence and smiling acceptance of all the compliments, I had apparently secured what I had always regarded as undesirable: a position of superiority. I became conscious of this when, in passing, I asked Ms Jia for her opinion about a design. She reacted uneasily, and suggested I present it to the senior architects. The argument that she used was revealing: 'They will appreciate it: they can show their knowledge, and will feel you respect their opinions.'

Although I had opened the 'window' on China, I had never wondered how far that window could actually be opened. To enable more interaction with my Chinese colleagues, it would have to be opened further. In the first few months in China, I had sought – unsuccessfully – the opinions of colleagues. Now it was our contribution that was being appreciated. With that experience, it would be possible to take the first steps towards a truly collective agenda.

I subsequently developed the following insight gradually over a period of a few weeks.

Ideally, NEXT drew upon analyses and research as the basis of its design interventions. In principle, analyses involved the direct context of a project, and research might deal with the broader context of a brief, such as typological innovation. This strategy had the advantage that a project could be developed integrally, from various scale levels and angles of approach.

Chinese architects tended to work much more with images and analogies as the basis of their inspiration. The image was generally found in the form of international reference projects and the analogies in the cultural associations of a specific image. Finding inspiration outside the context of a project meant that projects could be developed not as a single entity but in a differentiated way: parts could be replaced relatively simply, or 'adapted'.

It became interesting when I compared these different approaches to the way in which projects were evaluated in China. In a Chinese evaluation, the key issue was not whether something worked – a pre-eminent Western criterion – but the associations it evoked. Projects seemed to be assessed primarily in terms of the visual concept, the renderings and the possible market potential. A second assessment seemed to be a more practical one related to usefulness and feasibility. In the West, the evaluation was more three-dimensional and, beyond the temptations of image and market potential, there were, for instance, also criteria in the realms of use, technique and sustainability. In the West, the evaluation of a project appeared to be more objective, in China more subjective. In fact, if the associations were negative in China, the image and therefore often the entire scheme were rejected.

But was the brief to apply 'more scientific working methods', which had been imposed from above, genuinely desirable in such a case? If the above observation contained a hint of the truth, which 'working method' was better? Not necessarily ours. What could we 'learn' from our Chinese colleagues and add to our Western 'working method', if we examined it in the light of Chinese value appreciation?

We had come a long way since the moment when Mr Chen had subtly suggested that there was 'maybe a problem' with our renderings. Our original aim with these images was to communicate information as clearly as possible. For this reason, the images were made as abstract as possible. In the meantime, our images had the objective of representing a desired feeling. And to communicate a feeling, realism and detailing were essential, as well as a tangible setting and, for example, dramatic cloud-filled skies.

A second, more substantive aspect with which we had increasingly begun to experiment was the opposite of integral designing: differentiated designing.

In many projects, as a result of China's extremely rapid urbanization, there was often little information available on the context outside the site boundaries of the project. And the site itself generally offered little concrete information, in view of the fact that every existing structure had simply been erased from it. Accordingly, every project embraced so many unknown factors – unknown to the clients too – that a systematic, integral approach seemed almost by definition to be hindered by an unbridgeable series of pitfalls. With differentiated design, priorities could be restored and freedom for future additions and adaptations built in.

But experiments with this way of working were consistently faced with dilemmas. Western architects found integrity in a linear and rational design process, in which a certain logical succession of motives was evident. In this type of thinking, it was impossible to change or leave out 'parts'. It challenged the consistency of a project and led to arbitrariness, which was undesirable in our work and thinking, certainly in Europe. In combination with the more limited role that architects in China seemed to have, this made the risk of 'two-dimensional architecture', as it was called in Amsterdam, very real.

Mr Chen seemed to be following our development closely. Casually, he pointed out the limitations of my rational frame of thinking: 'It's the battle between your brain and your heart. We Chinese people think more with our heart, Western people think more with their brain. There's a big difference. The heart is delicate and sensitive, not like the brain, logical and rigid.' He continued, 'Thinking with our heart is rooted deeply in our culture and is reflected in our language, art, poetry and literature. It explains what you said earlier, that things in China are more descriptive than precise.' With this remark, he shed a great deal of light on the way in which Chinese architects designed their projects and on how projects were evaluated.

Simultaneously with our development in China, the architects at Huanyang seemed increasingly to be experimenting with more analytical design methods. To my surprise, Mr Guo came into my office one day and showed me a design on which he was working. He asked my opinion, not about a rendering but about the design steps he had taken.

In the joint projects, this mutual 'learning process' led us time and again to the discovery of space outside our own conceptual framework. And with every discovery we found still more space, an endless quantity, if only we took the risk of relinquishing our own dogmas. The challenge lay in the creation of designs that reflected contemporary Chinese conditions and which simultaneously took their meaning from what was of value in China. The ideal Dutch building was not necessarily ideal for China, so why should the ideal

Dutch design process be ideal in China either? The combination of the mental baggage we had brought with us to China and continually added insights was the basis for the development of our 'design method' in China. It was a matter of working from the least common multiple and a quest for the correct balance between objectivity and subjectivity.

While the powers that be at Huanyang continued to emphasize the potential of the 'form' of our 'working method', a much greater potential gradually made its presence felt. This was embedded in a shift in the nature of our working method. Here, interaction with Chinese colleagues had a fundamental role to play.

A MOUSE THAT EATS GOLD

Mr Guo showed me a rendering. It was a design by a foreign architect for a building somewhere in China. The façades consisted of enormous overlapping Chinese characters. He looked at me and appraised my reaction. I found the interference of the façade pattern most intriguing. Then he warned me: 'Chinese people don't like this; foreigners like this.'

In the meantime, we had done various experiments with subjectivity, in which we attempted to integrate Chinese concepts into designs. The reaction by Chinese colleagues was often an unequivocal 'No need!' After repeated attempts, the responses were even more explicit: 'Don't do it!' Accordingly, concepts such as 'yin and yang' and 'bagua' and references to mythical figures such as dragons vanished from our designs. The risk of such literal interpretations was that they could conflict painfully with 'the deepness of the Chinese mind', as Mr Chen described it. As such, it became for us a complicated quest that could widen our understanding but little else at first.

After a guided tour organized for a delegation from the Dutch Ministry of Housing, Spatial Planning and the Environment, I introduced some of our projects in a meeting room. When we arrived at the design for the Waterstone Sales Center, I stated that everything that involved finance seemed a more sensitive issue in China than it was in the Netherlands. The Sales Center had been designed as a place where financial contracts were concluded for the hundreds of high-end serviced apartments that were being sold. I emphasized the fact that buying an apartment meant investing in one of the three 'Chinese mountains': education, health care and housing. I quoted Mr Chen and described it as an ultimate private experience. But besides offering the desired privacy to purchasers, the building also had to tempt people in the street to find out more about the project. This ambiguity between public and private, between temptation and protection, had been worked into the design.

I was interrupted by a question: 'Have you told this story to the client in this way?' I smiled and said that the client recognized 'a mouse that ate gold' in the building's appearance.

There were questioning eyes.

Ms Qin, who had translated the client's remark during the presentation, had then added her own opinion. Visibly touched, she had confirmed what I had suspected: the client's remark was a great compliment. A mouse was a mythical animal and represented a special form of intelligence. 'Eating gold' stood for the acquisition of wealth. Buying an apartment in this building meant making an exceptionally intelligent investment.

People still looked at me questioningly.

I made a second effort to explain: the agendas of the architect and the client need not be mutually exclusive. The potential layering of meanings could even enhance a project. In the best instance it threw up associations, but this seemed consistently to occur beyond the reach of the architect – in our case, the Western architect.

I concluded: an architect didn't give meaning to a building, not even in China. Then I realized that in China, in contrast to the Netherlands, the client still seemed to enjoy a monopoly position in this domain.

REASONABLE FENG SHUI

'In China, everything is possible, but nothing is easy.' Mr Chen's remark was difficult to assess: it was neutral, positive and negative all at the same time.

We were looking together at a sketch in which two buildings were oriented east-west in a zigzag configuration. I looked at my computer screen and zoomed out with Google Earth. All apartment buildings in the vicinity of the site were oriented north-south. I zoomed out further. Practically all apartment buildings in Beijing were oriented north-south.

Mr Chen looked with me at the screen and explained: 'Feng shui'. The sketch investigated the possibilities for a live-work complex of 55,000 square metres. The client required that all units in the complex should be some fifty square metres in size and able to be linked together. But in combination with a north-south orientation, this requirement would mean that at least half the office apartments would be oriented to the north and thus would be subjected to bad feng shui.

I thought back to my first attempts to delve deeper into the world of feng shui. It was during the site visit with the 'feng shui expert' when it was impossible to get a dialogue going. Afterwards, I shared my experience with various colleagues at the office. Ms Wang dismissed it smilingly as Chinese superstition but at the same time declared that the rules of feng shui were there to be followed. And Mr Chen underlined the indubitable importance of feng shui when he announced: 'We must always take it into consideration!'

He seemed to be a passionate advocate of feng shui, but not in its classical form where, for example, a small fountain needs placing near the entrance to a building. When I asked him why that should be necessary, he smiled and confined his answer to: 'That's old China'. His conviction was expressed much more explicitly in, for example, his almost ritualistic behaviour in meeting rooms, where he invariably sought out and sat at the spot with the 'best feng shui'. I once realized, with a smile, that I had adopted his habit. Without sufficiently understanding the classical Chinese argumentation, I also found it 'more comfortable' not to sit with my back to a door or a glass wall.

We looked at the sketch again.

Within the boundaries of the site, there were now the beginnings of two buildings whose zigzag structure would enable an optimum view and daylight incidence, but they were oriented east-west. I had discussed the sketch with a number of other Chinese colleagues and they were all sceptical. Challenging the north-south orientation? That was challenging the unwritten law of feng shui. A colleague had explained to me that the centuries-old philosophy behind this was as follows: Everything good, like the gold of the sun, comes from the south. Everything bad, like the cold wind from Siberia and Genghis Khan, comes from the north.'

I looked at Mr Chen, in the hope of discovering more.

J: Can you recommend any good books about feng shui?

C: Many, but they're not in English, only Chinese. A professor from South-East University wrote a good book about the relation between 'feng shui' and architecture. It's all reasonable, for example: 'Why will a restaurant under the bridge never win?' Because nobody visits it, it's hard to see the sign. So if you open a restaurant under a bridge it means 'da tian tian shang', like a beam in a room, just like a knife: it will cut off your career. I think this way of thinking is reasonable because it's about the effect something has on the surroundings.

J: The effect on the surroundings?

C: Like a T junction: at the end of the T, there must be a very powerful building. Like the main building of Tsinghua University. It can never be a small building. A small building there will be 'crushed', it will always lose.

J: Crushed, always lose?

C: Yes, everybody at night will point their car lights at you. It's not comfortable, not for a restaurant, not for housing. V-shaped streets aren't good either, they are shaped like scissors. It must be hard to make a profit from a building on a V-shaped street because it's too busy and no-one wants to stay there. And I think that's reasonable.

J: That's urban planning, what about architecture?

C: 'Feng shui' for architecture is also reasonable, just like the large building at Xizhimen (three office towers on a podium above a metro station). The feng shui master said the site was not good and I believed him. The traffic is unreasonable there: people using the metro won't use the building and the people using the building always travel there by car, they won't use the metro.

J: So it's too busy?

C: You know, Xizhimen was built for the emperor. In old Beijing it was a gate from which water entered the city. Its planning was very narrow, there was no need for broad views, only for space for water carriages. Because the original gate was narrow, the feng shui now is not good. Even today, with the traffic there, there's not enough space for all the roads. Bad feng shui, it's reasonable: that building has been empty for over six years now. Nobody wants to rent it!

J: Why is a mountain in the north and water in the south good feng shui?
C: Because of the sunshine! The back of the mountain has no sunshine! Everybody knows this, the emperor also knew this. And in China, the main direction of the wind is from the north, very cold, which is why the south of the mountain is good. It's reasonable.
J: Why isn't it good to sit with your back to a door?
C: If somebody comes into the room, they can make you jump, that's not good. It's true – not only the ghosts, real people can make you jump too. You know, I think feng shui is a custom of people from thousands of years ago, about what they thought was good for the surroundings. And I think many things are still reasonable.
J: Do you believe feng shui masters who walk around with a 'luopan' (feng shui compass) saying that something should be here and another thing should be there?
C *(laughing)*: That's 'mixin', not feng shui.
J: That's what?
C: 'Mixin' – 'confused trust' – it's unreasonable feng shui.
J: Unreasonable feng shui?
C: Maybe yes. The feng shui master has to do this, because he needs to be an expert. And he wants to show knowledge other people don't have. In old China, feng shui masters always danced with a sword and sprayed water to kill ghosts. And they used little yellow papers to stick on bad places. Then the ghosts wouldn't come near that place again. And eventually the feng shui master would find one direction that had no ghosts and that's the direction he would recommend you to use.
J: You're sceptical? But many people believe it, don't they?
C *(smiling)*: They're professional cheats and they earn a lot of money. It's easy to cheat. You know, if you buy a high-tech machine for let's say, a hundred dollars, you can think: 'So cheap, maybe it's fake.' But if you pay one million dollars you will think: 'It's a good one!' They always do this, it's easy.
J *(smiling)*: So what should I believe in?
C *(smiling):* Believe in 'reasonable feng shui', it's Chinese culture. 'Mixin' is also Chinese culture but don't believe in it; it's unreasonable.

We looked again at the sketch of two buildings whose zigzag layout would enable optimum views and maximum daylight incidence but which were oriented east-west. The advantages were, in the words of Mr Chen, more than 'reasonable'. But the advantages were not enough.

In the following few days, I began to realize that a great degree of flexibility would be needed to facilitate the many as yet unknown wishes and requirements regarding this live-work complex. On the basis of that thought, I divided the zigzag ground plan into six building parts that could vary in height independently of one another and even could be adjusted independently quite late in the building process. I proposed that the façade should be horizontally articulated only, so that its units would be relatively easy to connect and there would be no influence from the internal organization.

After the presentation, it turned out that the argument of 'share all good things fairly' had not been decisive on its own. It was this in combination with the flexibility that we had built into the design that appealed to the client. When the project entered the building preparations phase, this flexibility was called upon: the height of the various building parts changed several times when 'new information' became available, contradictions in outcomes of sunlight studies had to be 'resolved', and the surface areas had to be 'optimized'.

Six months later, when I zoomed in on the location with Google Earth, I was surprised to see a new photo of it online. The first contours of the two east-west-oriented buildings were visible. I proudly showed the images to Mr Chen, and several colleagues crowded round my computer.

'In China everything is possible, but nothing is easy', I said with a smile.

Familiar faces smiled back at me.

GREEN BUILDING

Perhaps the greatest opportunity for developing a common agenda lay in the projects in which both NEXT and Huanyang had relatively little experience. It was when we trod mutually unknown territory that we both benefitted more from interaction.

One such opportunity arose when a Chinese client explained that ABB wished to set up a 'demo centre'. It had to be a green building, to underline ABB's 'green corporate philosophy'. It was the first request made to us to design a green building. Before then, the topic of sustainability had only played a limited role in our projects. It seemed a difficult theme, a 'luxury', as colleagues called it, although the theme was gaining in urgency. Until that time, the green elements in many of our joint projects had been confined to additions. For instance, there was the selective use of sustainable materials such as low-e glass to reduce emissions, and the application of solar panels to make use of sustainable energy resources. But there had never been mention of an integral 'green building'.

During our first briefing, the client, who was to lease the project to ABB, explained with a smile that the green in this building had a double significance: 'A green building, but we have to count the "greenbacks": the dollars and cents!'

When I heard him utter this desire, I envisaged the inevitable generic Chinese office block: the plan with a matrix of 800 × 800 mm-thick concrete columns on a grid of 8.4 metres, the floor limit exactly adhering to the field of columns and only the core of lifts, staircases and wet cells having been defined. How often had I stared at such multi-storey car-park-like ground plans?

The majority of the buildings in Beijing had been built in accordance with this standard grid of 8.4 metres. This grid measure was ideal: columns ended in the basement car park and left room for exactly three cars. It was excellent for implementing in concrete, and concrete was cheap, many times cheaper than steel. Form followed economics: clients did not accept deviation from the standard measure of 8.4 metres because ground plans would then become illogical and 'difficult to use'.

As a consequence of these laws, architectural freedom had often been reduced to the design brief of a fashionable skin 30 centimetres thick around identical concrete frames. How was architectural freedom to be regained under such circumstances?

We sat with a number of architects around a table and discussed the problem. One way of varying the standard office block would be to use setbacks from the street. These were relatively easy to implement structurally, but came at the cost of a reduction in leasable floor area, and therefore income, so they were difficult to defend. Cantilevers were another possible means of variation, but these could be no greater than 4.2 metres. Anything in excess of this would have to be executed in steel and then costs would increase substantially.

Corners were often the most attractive places in a floor plan. In Beijing, the corners were often occupied by a column, not because a column-free corner was impossible, but rather because it was an ingrained habit as a result of the column-copying trend that had been unleashed on the 8.4 metre grid. Cantilevers of up to 4.2 metres and column-free corners were possible at almost no extra cost, and to me the advantages were evident: 8.4 metre grid + maximum of 4.2 metre cantilever + columnless corners = architectural freedom!

In a certain sense, ABB illustrated the boundaries of architectural freedom in the Chinese building economy today. In the design, our introduction of green terraces or green roofs on the storeys prompted us to stretch the standard building envelope to the furthest extremes of Chinese 'economic building'. The terraces were the most prominent part of a series of green interventions and they reduced heat emission, visualized ABB's green philosophy to passers-by and enabled the growth of vegetation close to the employees on the upper storeys.

The demo centre for ABB had the potential to become one of our better joint China projects. It was the first project in which we could apply the irrefutable importance of a green architectural agenda throughout. And by uniting this with other agendas, we had found architectural freedom beyond the standard office block.

The project moved into the fast lane. We received the approval of the client, ABB, and the government. The final design and working drawings were completed within a month of the first presentation. But just as construction was scheduled to begin, the project fell victim to the worldwide financial crisis. ABB had to reconsider its development in China and the necessity of a demo centre perished in a 'new strategic vision'. The design's strength turned out to be a weakness when the developer simply stated: 'I can't use your design for another client. It's too specific.'

TERRA INCOGNITA

NEXT, together with the Delft Faculty of Architecture in the person of professor Rudy Uytenhaak, had been invited to contribute to the first Moscow Architecture Biennale. This was on the strength of the results of a NEXT study carried out in conjunction with Delft architecture students. The request from Moscow was to combine the research results with a presentation on how academic research was reflected in our practice, both in Europe and in China.

For the exhibition, NEXT Amsterdam had selected two projects, one developed in the Netherlands, the other in China. The Dutch project was the design for a villa for five families. This had combined the requirements of its occupants with maximum exploitation of the qualities on site. The Chinese project was the design for student accommodation at the Normal University, the project in which we had sought out and exploited the tension between individual and collective. Each project had a presentation scale model made for it in Beijing.

As the two models took shape, Ms Jia began to look increasingly puzzled. She knew the student accommodation, but what was that other building? The project was a puzzle for the scale-model builders too. The company had made many models but they had clearly never come across anything like this before. When it was sprayed orange in the last week, it elicited the obvious answer: it wasn't a building, it was an oil rig!

'Why did you design the building that way?' asked Ms Jia: 'And why is it orange? Dutch people like orange, right?'

The more intriguing question that she failed to ask was: 'What is the relationship between these two projects?'

In the Netherlands, we had brought up the question of the relationship between our projects years ago. Our conclusion was that, ideally, a NEXT project was not recognizable as such. It was our collective conviction that a fixed style or signature had no permanent value. In fact, more of the same led to loss of value. We had concluded that if any correspondence could be found in the projects, it should be sought not in the results but in the process leading up to them.

The issue was again exceedingly topical, particularly due to the increase in Chinese projects in our joint portfolio. To what extent was our original conclusion still tenable?

The week prior to Ms Jia's remark, I had been in the Netherlands for a short stay. In the plane, I had a short article with me that we had once sent to a common friend in Buenos Aires for publication in an Argentinian architecture magazine.

Dear Max,
[...]
Our quest does not result in a series of substitute paradigms, but offers a possibility to develop a practice in which the boundaries of the architectural domain are constantly questioned and stretched. The possibility to create a practice without style, nor dogma or utopia.
[...]
Our work is not about formal positions. We believe that classical architectural parameters such as proportion, order and harmony could be used as tools, but never in a dogmatic sense. We work with an open sight and without prepossessed propositions. It enables us to take a mobile position, to circle around the subject and to take a look at it from different perspectives. We are driven by the potentials that arise from contemporary cultural, social and urban developments, and we see it as evidence that the built environment should reflect the changing society that evolves daily. That does not mean that we have to reinvent architecture every time, rather it is the slight shift of the existing, that expresses innovation. This subtle shift of our daily environment is an important issue in our work.
[...]
The understanding of the city as a system of layers is the motive for the search for an equilibrium in the hierarchy between the fixed and the temporary; between permanence and changeability. This permanence could be found in the introduction of the framework, a robust structure which both fixes and determines specific use, but simultaneously creates a maximum capacity of transformation.
[...]
This opposition, or maybe even better, equilibrium, between the very specified and the open (and undefined) is an important characteristic of our work. You could state that consequently we make our design subservient to the user. Our architecture facilitates, not only in the supply of a new perspective, but also in the sense that it enables the user a continuous possibility to make it his/her own.

Our very best and warmest regards,

Bart Reuser, Marijn Schenk, Michel Schreinemachers, John van de Water

When I reread the article I was surprised by the resilience of the ideas. At the same time, I became aware that our arrival in China could be compared to setting foot in an endless *terra incognita*. After a stay of several years, that *terra incognita* paradoxically seemed to have become both larger and smaller. It was larger in the sense that more could always be discovered, and smaller in the sense that we increasingly seemed to be a part of Chinese reality.

I LOVE CHINA

I returned to the Netherlands less and less regularly and my stays there were short and intensive. But one permanent component of the programme was the dinners with friends. These were the yardsticks against which I measured the development of my personal orientation between the Netherlands and China. To an increasing degree I realized that my personal Chinese *terra incognita* was not identical to that of my friends in the Netherlands. However, it was precisely these stories and discussions that enabled more mutual insight.

To one of these dinners I had brought a stack of images of renderings and project drawings, the size of picture postcards. While other topics were discussed, the stack passed from hand to hand. When it arrived at the opposite side of the table, a friend reacted with disappointment: 'I thought I was going to see travel photos!' She was not the only one; several friends seemed to have had this expectation.

'Tell us about China, not about work or projects', she said.

It was a straightforward request that on reflection proved exceptionally complex due to the magnitude of the subject.

'Where shall I begin?' I asked.

'The Olympic Games', said someone else.

Our development in China was related to the Olympic Games in several ways. First of all, there was the e-mail that Huan once sent asking us to collaborate on a competition design for a stadium. When we finally had our own office in Beijing, we surfed along on the building frenzy that preceded the Games, as many architectural offices did. But I interrupted this train of thought. I had received the request not to talk about work or projects.

I began a narrative about how, in the run-up to the Olympic Games, the mood in Beijing tangibly changed. This change was fed by many factors, and certainly by the Western media which concentrated on topics such as human rights, freedom of expression, Xinjiang and Tibet: matters that China regarded as internal affairs.

Someone enquired about the way this Western focus was regarded in China.

It was seen as criticism, and that was poorly understood in China. China had spared neither cost nor effort, it aspired to be host to the world and had been treated with contempt. This collective feeling was nourished by a national media offensive, initiated by the Chinese government. In the process, discrepancy between Chinese reality and image-forming in the Western media was magnified and nourished the assault on Chinese national pride.

Where was this reflected?

The sentiment towards foreigners changed, friendliness made way for mistrust. A taxi driver would only allow me admission to his vehicle if I was not French, because 'France supported the Dalai Lama'. And all relationships that had been built up seemed to be undergoing re-evaluation, such as that with the security guards in the lobby of the building in which our office had its seat. Although we had greeted one another in a friendly manner day in day out, and had often exchanged a few words, all at once I had to show my passport on entering the lobby.

So, what was my idea of human rights in China?

It was important to see the development in perspective. And I hoped that this development would continue, that there would be an increase in public participation, especially in political processes.

And what did people in China think about it?

Many Chinese friends and colleagues held the idea that you had to see developments in perspective, and I increasingly began to realize the value of this. The hope that there would be more participation so far seemed to be my own Dutch contribution.

What did I base this hope on?

I began an answer with a short dialogue I had had with Lao Qing, in an attempt to approach hope from a broader context.

J: Can foreigners ever understand Chinese culture, Lao Qing?
LQ: Maybe.
J: Can Chinese ever understand Western culture?
LQ: Maybe.
J: Not very hopeful!
LQ: They can at least try to understand each other better.

I was interrupted by healthy Dutch sceptical laughter.
'That was a pretty bland answer', was one reaction.
I smiled and wondered how I could underpin my intuition. But I was interrupted by two new questions: 'How do the Chinese regard the West, and what issues are important to them?'
I thought about a discussion with Mr Hong, a colleague in his late twenties, at a building site a few weeks ago. I had written down the discussion afterwards, but it was too long to reproduce in the restaurant. Then I thought about what is called 'zhong ti xi yong' in China. The four characters could be translated as 'Chinese core, Western form', but I was still too unfamiliar with the subject to raise the topic in the restaurant.
People were waiting for answers. 'Give us a one-liner', someone said impatiently.
Without thinking too long, I responded 'One step at a time is good walking'.
This was met by silence and frowns.
'Do you have the idea that they fully understand you in China?' someone else asked.
I repeated the Chinese saying: 'One step at the time is good walking'. More frowns.
The food arrived and the topic of conversation changed. Later, I couldn't escape the idea that I had missed an opportunity to provide more insight into China.

Almost a week later, I was back in China and I looked out the notes I had made of my conversation with Mr Hong.
H *(annoyed)*: Why are most foreign countries against China?
J *(surprised)*: Why would you think that?
H: China is a very friendly country. We have never sent one soldier to another country to conquer it!
J: I'm sure there are foreigners who like China, it's just that many foreigners have different ideas about China.
H *(annoyed)*: Right, ideas about Tibet, Taiwan, Falun Gong....
J: Among other things. Why would you think foreign countries are against China?
H *(thinking)*: Because they are afraid.
J: Afraid?
H: Yes, afraid for two reasons: economically and politically. They

are afraid of losing power because China is becoming an economic world power again, and two, because they are afraid of our socialist system.

J: I think there's truth in both, there is certainly some kind of fear among people.

H *(thinking)*

J: But don't you think there's something good in foreign opinion?

H: I think giving suggestions is good, but criticizing is not. Sometimes I think it's too difficult for foreigners to understand China.

J *(smiling)*: So help me understand China better.

H: You know, China is a developing country with a large population. We believe in unity and stability. Therefore, we consider many questions from foreigners not as isolated questions but as questions that touch on the very foundation of the stability of our country. Moreover, our population is simply too large: more than 1.3 billion people! We have no other choice than to solve problems slowly, step by step, no other choice than to modernize step by step.

J: Many foreigners think China is modernizing economically and technically, but lacks political modernization.

H: What do they mean by this?

J: Some foreigners believe the Chinese government, more specifically the Communist Party, is not willing to solve 'political problems' but wants to keep 'some things the way they are now'.

H: You have to put this in perspective, John. Look how many people have a better life since China became more open. Isn't that problem-solving? Since China's opening, millions of people have come out of poverty, China can launch space rockets now!

J: These foreigners are not talking about economic or technological development but about social development, things like human rights.

H *(thinking)*: Human rights are still a problem in China. But look at other countries like the United States, who invade countries without a reason. And look at what countries that now talk about human rights did to China when they invaded us. My grandfather talked about signs at parks: 'No dogs or Chinese allowed!' *(annoyed)*

J *(unsettled)*: I know the story about the dog sign, Hong, but some Chinese people now say it never existed, that it was made up for educational purposes. Let's not talk about the dog sign, Hong, let's talk about the idea of ultimate human rights.

H: I see where you're going with this conversation: you want to talk about democracy again. I already told you, the Chinese government tells Chinese people we don't need elections. They tell us: look at the United States and see how much money elections cost. It's much better to spend all this money on the people.

J: But wouldn't you like to be able to choose your own leaders?

H *(worried)*: Yes and no. We have free elections in some villages, people there can choose their own leaders. But, you know, I studied in Denmark for many years, I graduated from two universities: why am I not allowed to vote? I am an educated person! But still, the danger I see is much larger than the desire: if everybody is allowed to vote, what will the vote of 800 million illiterate peasants do? It will bring a new Mao Zedong and chaos to our country.

J: Why do Chinese people have such a fear of chaos?

H: Why do you think?

J: History and education: chaos leads to division and that's why unity needs to prevail over everything. It's what you said earlier: it touches on the very foundation of the stability in China.

H: You're right, but why did you mention education?

J: Isn't that what every Chinese child learns at school: unity needs to prevail over everything? At least, that's what my Chinese teacher told me.

H: It's something history taught us.

J *(thinking)* ...

H: You know, president Hu Jingtao called democracy a dead-end road for China and maybe it's true: most people in China are just not interested in politics. They are too busy caring for their family as it's difficult to rely always on the government. (...) You know, the Communist Party promised peasants a better life during the revolution in exchange for their help. And what's happening now? There's a huge gap between rich and poor and this gap is only getting wider. *(looking worried)* People are becoming afraid that poor peasants who have nothing will come to the cities and take what they were promised sixty years ago. Stability and safety for the future. That's what's on Chinese people's minds, not democracy.

J *(surprised)*: Are you afraid?

H: You know, almost every fifty years in Chinese history there has

been a revolution, a big change. Now it has been almost sixty years since the last revolution. I'm not afraid, I think, but I am worried.
J: What's your biggest concern then, besides a possible revolution?
H *(laughing)*: Like all men of my age: I need to save money for my marriage, I need money for an apartment and a car. It's a lot of money, more than 'yibaiwan', one million renminbi (more than 100,000 euros).
J *(smiling)*: You know, Ms Jia told me Shanghai girls were the most expensive to marry in China; as a guy you need to save at least 'liangbaiwan' (more than 200,000 euros).
H *(laughing)*: Yes, I'm happy that I'm going to get married in Beijing.

Half an hour later, while we were still walking around the building site.
H: You know, I think Western democracy, as I saw it in Denmark, is not suitable in China right now. Our population is just too big!
J: Why not? Just because of the large population?
H: There's another thing: China is a country with a long history in which people always lived in very hierarchic societies. People are not used to having rights the way European people do. Even when our feudal system changed and Chairman Mao became our leader, everything was determined by the Communist Party; from the moment we were born until the moment we died. We have come a long way from there. We are much more liberated now.
J: Mr Chen told me that ten years ago, during his first job at a company with hundreds of architects, he and his girlfriend planned to get married. But according to the law then, he had to ask his boss for approval. His boss didn't even know him, let alone his girlfriend. He uses the example often, when he talks about the development of human rights in China.
H: Can you imagine something like this in Holland?
J *(laughing)*: Ten years ago asking your boss for approval to marry? Unthinkable. There would probably have been a revolution.
H *(smiling)*: So what's Mr Chen's opinion about human rights in China?
J: Nothing is allowed but everything is possible.
H: Many people in Denmark asked me about human rights in China. I agree with Mr Chen: slowly our rights are improving but

the gap between rich and poor, we call this 'pinfu chaju' in Chinese, seems to be becoming bigger.
J: Is there a relationship between having more money and having more rights?
H *(smiling)*: Money is power, power is having rights. Money gives rights.
J *(smiling)*: Is that the reason why so many Chinese love money?
H *(smiling)*: Sure, everybody wants a smooth life.

An hour later, on the way back to the office.
J: Did you get the idea that your friends in Denmark could understand the transition China is going through?'
H: It's difficult to explain and it's also difficult to understand. So many things are uncertain, there are many problems and uncertainties and everything can change so quickly.
J: Do you think China can solve these problems only internally?
H: You're asking if Western countries can help? How could they possibly do that? With their opinion? We know we don't see everything Western people see in the media, we know the Chinese government controls the news and the internet, but with what we see, Western countries are not really helping. Maybe it's also what the government wants us to see, but we see so many misunderstandings that it's difficult to believe they can really contribute.
J: So what effect do they have, the Western media you see in China?
H: It makes us love China more! Do you know Chinese people now have 'Love China' behind their MSN and QQ [Chinese internet chat program]?
J: I saw it on my MSN buddy list when I chatted with a Chinese friend who now studies in Delft, Holland.
H: So what are your friend's ideas about foreign opinion on China?
J: More or less the same as yours, she also has the idea that most foreigners are against China.
H: Do you love China, John?
J *(surprised)*: That's a difficult question, Hong.
H: It's a simple question.
J: It's difficult to answer.
H: Why is it difficult, why are you in so much doubt?
J *(thinking)*: There are several Chinas I love...
H: Chinas?

I closed the notebook and reflected. I received so much energy from China, so much energy from daily experiences, from moments like these. And this energy didn't come from slowly being able to appreciate the elusive cultural foundations of the country, but rather from the effect of those foundations in the present, in the people I met, people with whom I worked on joints projects and whom I was slowly getting to know better and better.

I had boundless admiration for the self-made capacities of Mrs Hu and Mr Yang. I had boundless admiration for the speed and flexibility with which Mr Chen manoeuvred through uncertainties. I had boundless admiration for Mr Jiang who, out of millions of people in his province, was one of the eighty people who had been able to enter one of China's top universities, and explained that simply with 'because my family supported me'. I had boundless admiration for the Chinese hyper-effectiveness of Mr Guo. And also for Huan, who sought room for improvement, whereas he knew that so little room was there to be found. And for friends such as Lao Qing, Victoria, Ms Wang and Mr Hong. And for the unparalleled stamina of the guys who always produced our renderings: Xiao Liu and Mr Huang. For the engineers, the draughtsmen, the scale-model builders and the dozens of other immediate colleagues. And for all those many others impossible to name but more than worthy of being named.

I had boundless admiration for the collective resilience and quintessential inventiveness with which a possibility was found for everything. And for the eagerness, patience and strategic power of thought.

I loved China, I genuinely did, the China of my Chinese colleagues and friends who lived in such a different cultural context, on such a different scale, at such a different speed and in such a different concept of time and space.

5. Vision

FROM THE INSIDE

A German architect friend who was working for a German architectural office in Beijing, described their work as 'Sinicized'. The portfolio in China had very little in common with the portfolio in Germany; he concluded regretfully that their designs had become 'pure Chinese'. The fact that they, as Western architects, would make true Chinese projects seemed extremely hypothetical to me. He reinforced his standpoint: 'Don't you ever accept any influence that you would not have accepted in the Netherlands?' I had to agree with him, but remarked that it was through that influence that something new could arise, something that wasn't Dutch but wasn't purely Chinese either. We sought an exchange between the two spheres of influence, something that could be both Dutch and Chinese.

My reaction called to mind the alchemist and the question as to which elements predominated over others. It was a comparison that arose within me during the presentation by the Spanish architectural office in Beijing. Then, in a bar in an alleyway in East Beijing late at night, I had concluded out loud that in our case no one was the alchemist other than myself. It had become my own personal quest, rather than that of NEXT as a collective.

It was now mid-summer and the air-conditioning made a feeble impression on the sultry heat. I looked fleetingly around the bar and lapsed into metaphors, as I increasingly did in China. It was too restrictive for an alchemist to attempt to develop insight into all the various ingredients before starting the mixing process. Perhaps the science of mixing itself ought to be critically investigated. My own position as an alchemist until then had only studied the 'elements' of Dutch and Chinese would also have to be reconsidered. Only then, when I had understood the 'science of mixing', could I exercise any influence on the genesis of something new that contained both elements.

I leaned over the table, took a gulp of Tsingtao and asked my German table-companion if he too had found himself in a process of shift. He looked at me in surprise and asked if I was asking about whether or not he had adapted as an architect.

'Adapting is no more than unilaterally adjusting the direction in which you are moving. A shift goes further, it is about a turnaround in mentality.'

'A turnaround?' he asked laconically.

'A turnaround in awareness of what is "good" and "bad".'

'You said "too". So how about you?' he responded.

I began thinking aloud about the turnaround in my own attitude as an architect. In the Netherlands there was an acute need for control over the entire building process, from concept to detail. Usually there was a proactive dialogue in which we, as architects, sought 'the conflict in the brief'. This was the means par excellence to chart the limits of our possibilities. The goal was architectural quality. For instance, an e-mail that we had sent to the client for a new office interior in Amsterdam had as its subject 'Design Matters'. The mail we received in reply was entitled 'Finance Matters'. The project was realized within that field of tension.

In China, however, the induction of this type of force field between the architect and client often led almost by definition to the failure of a project. For example, I remembered all too well Mr Ma's irritation at my repeated 'suggestions' to alter the boundaries of his 'Liuming' compound. In China, an architect seemed to have more benefit from a reactive attitude than from our Dutch proactive approach.

The fact that a turnaround in my thinking and acting was slowly taking place became obvious to me from the difference in the way I used to communicate with Dutch clients and now communicated with Chinese clients. In contrast to the situation in Europe, in China most information was communicated in dialogues by the things that were not said.

My German conversation partner smiled and nodded. A Western architect with China experience required no further explanation. He wrote on a beer mat: *proactive versus reactive.*

Then he sprang up and told me that he had had difficulty in China right from the very first project because one's role as an architect in China was so different from what it was in Germany. He looked at me sternly. In Germany he had been relentless during projects, during their development and implementation. In China, an architect has much less influence and he found it difficult to assume the necessary subservient attitude. In Europe he had much more control over a project as a guiding player – and wasn't it precisely this that was so essential?

I agreed. In the Netherlands, we also had a guiding role in the processes. In order to unite all the different requirements and to test ideas, we regularly organized large workshops in which all clients could participate. We made use of participation and public consultation to arrive at a design, but nevertheless it was we who guided the process towards the desired final result. This had to be innovative and could not simply lead to something that already existed.

In China, at a presentation for the 'green building' for ABB, an Austrian manager mentioned having had a bad experience with a new ABB building in Europe. The architect had proposed a certain colour that ABB had been dissatisfied with after the building had been delivered. But the architect refused to change the colour and a magistrate was called upon to give a judgement. The manager ended the anecdote with the question as to how dominant 'an architect in a Chinese project' would be. Our client had followed the story with increasing surprise and responded imperturbably: 'Change is no problem, this is China, the client is always most important!'

My own turnaround lay in the fact that I no longer regarded it as an obvious loss of integrity if design decisions were passed on to others. With that, I seemed to have come to terms once and for all with the notion that I, as an architect, had a patent on 'objective truth' with regard to design decisions. In China, to a greater extent than in the Netherlands, I had benefitted from looking for 'values', in interpreting, considering and accepting subjectivity. Without looking at my table companion I picked up the pen and wrote on the beer mat: *guiding versus serving*.

My response met with incomprehension. Dutch and German thinking seemed to be diametrically opposed at this moment.

'Subjectivity leads to trendy interventions,' came the resolute opinion from across the table, 'and architecture should stay away from that as much as possible.'

'That is your truth,' I said, smiling.

'But not yours?' was the indignant reply. I was in doubt. How could I answer this question in the negative? It reflected everything I had learned as a student and everything I had represented as an architect in the Netherlands. Fashionable interventions represented temporary value, meaning had to be sought in permanent value. But how could you find 'permanent value' in a rapidly changing world like China?

Without reaching a decision, we moved on, via a detour, to a discussion about the different processes within which architecture was realized. In the Netherlands, our projects were based on extensive analyses and 'visions' – perspectives on the brief and also broader perspectives that transcended the brief, perspectives on the discipline and on society. Design processes were organized linearly: a perspective on the brief was developed, preferably with several parties involved, on the basis of analysis. This vision defined a design ambition and ensured that decisions could be continually assessed against the departure-points. NEXT developed a number of visions, including 'Holland layer by layer' and 'The future landscape of labour', visions that later were made material in the practice of projects. In contrast, the final image of a project seemed to be the directive element in China, much more than analyses or visions. Projects were organized synchronously, and alterations were the rule rather than the exception. I wished to illustrate this claim with an example of a project on which we were working, a 'multi-use' building of more than 180,000 square metres. Before we were actually involved in the project – it was already at the implementation stage – dozens of different architectural offices had worked on it. And even now, the functions and the organization of the building were continually changing.

My table companion had nodded during my first sentences. The story seemed to make little impression because it was so typical of China. He concluded that the process within which architecture was generated in China was opposite to that in the Netherlands. I continued by saying that processes in China were organized synchronously, whereas those in the Netherlands were structured in a linear manner. My turnaround had led to an appreciation of 'differentiated architecture'. And to the recognition of a new architectural brief: the development of a design strategy that guaranteed the retention of architectural quality despite all change.

My table companion had listened attentively and shared my conclusion. In the meantime, he had jotted down the new antithesis on the beer mat: *linear versus synchronous.*

In a lull in the conversation, I realized that outside, dawn was breaking. I intended to call it a day, but I was too late. A new round was brought to our table. While we toasted, my companion wished me good morning in German.

We looked at the summary on the beer mat: proactive versus reactive, guiding versus serving, linear versus synchronous. The first antithesis referred to one's attitude as an architect, the second to the architect's role and the third to the process that gave rise to architecture. From the other side of the table came the statement: 'We've left out the *agenda* of architecture.'

I nodded and thought for a moment. In the Netherlands, architecture was generally regarded, even from the client's perspective, as the cultural added value of building and, in that sense, as a cultural investment. Architecture cost money and was allowed to cost money. Research, quality and sustainability were highly appreciated values. To achieve this, time, space and budget were made available in order to test intentions and to experiment with ideas and materials. For instance, in the early days of NEXT we invested a number of years, in conjunction with a client, in realizing a new type of villa.

My discussion partner smiled and seemed to predict mentally what was coming.

In China, architecture appeared much more to serve an economic goal. Practically every architectural decision had to justify that goal. And for that there was a minimum of time, space and budget available, just as there was a minimum amount of leeway to experiment with ideas and materials. For example, a new type of facing concrete was proposed for one of our projects. The Chinese developer eventually allowed me to choose from three types of stone: 'Time is limited' was the familiar argument.

'Time is limited,' repeated my table companion with a smile. 'When I hear that remark, I always look at the client with a comprehending air and bow my head slightly.'

'Me too,' I laughed in return, while I showed him how.

Then he said judiciously: 'In China, the objective of contemporary architecture seems to be to generate economic value, in both the short and the long term.'

He was right. The fact that architecture in the Netherlands could also serve this kind of economic agenda was well known to me, but

I was not always conscious of the fact when I was there. In China, I was permanently aware of it.

He wrote the fourth antithesis on the beer mat: *investment versus generating*. While he was writing, I responded: 'The fourth antithesis is closest to an explanation of the first three.'

We looked at one another in agreement while we appraised our summary in a way that can only be done with discoveries that are made in a bar early in the morning. The sun was shining when we took our leave of one another outside.

On my way home I thought about a famous Chinese saying: 'Ru xiang sui su.' It means something like: 'Anyone approaching a village follows the customs there.' I approached China from the inside as much as possible and worked from the world in which I was standing. I learned from those customs and I found space beyond my own frame of reference. But, despite this turnaround, I was convinced that this didn't necessarily make me a 'villager'.

CROSSING BOUNDARIES

Another 'village' in which I was active was Huanyang. In the past few years the office had enjoyed unprecedented growth, which I had been able to follow from close by. Now it was on the verge of its next big step: it had bought five storeys of a new office block on Beijing's West Third Ring Road. The new office, covering 8000 square metres, was envisioned as the head office and, despite the fact that the building was a slab, it was to be called 'Huanyang Tower'. Although no initiative had yet been taken to consult me about a design, I had already started planning the new interior in my mind. There was no single company I was more familiar with and as a result there were, alongside Huanyang's boundless ambitions, unparalleled opportunities to realize a joint project from the inside outwards, from concept to detail.

A week earlier, I had been in Shanghai for a meeting and afterwards I walked back to my hotel. The pavement bordered on a green strip that had been partly laid out with pebbles. Two different companies had been involved in the construction: one for the pavement, the other for the green strip. The company that laid the green strip was ahead of the company laying the pavement.

My eye alighted on a detail, a fragment of the boundary between a paving stone and the pebbles.

The worker who had laid the paving stones had been confronted with a pebble laid by the company that had installed the green strip. The pebble was not quite in line with the other pebbles and protruded a little. A dilemma must have arisen, consciously or unconsciously. There were two options: to move the pebble or to adapt the paving stone to it.

The paver had gone for the second option and had cut a small piece out of the tile to allow space for the pebble. From a Dutch perspective, this was not the most obvious solution. I was quite certain that a Dutch worker would, almost without thinking, have made a different choice: he would have shifted the pebble a little towards the green strip and laid down a complete tile.

What did I think I'd discovered in this image?

The way the paving stones and the pebbles were related was the result of differing responsibilities. The paver's responsibility was to lay the paving stones. His only relationship with the pebbles was that his paving stones had to fit tightly against them. And in view of the fact that the pebbles were there first, it was clearly self-evident to him that the paving stone had to be modified.

In the most abstract interpretation, the paving stones and the pebbles represented the story of different boundaries. They depicted the hierarchy of boundaries at different scales, that of different responsibilities and of different relationships. When I projected this onto the various boundaries I encountered in everyday life, it gave an intriguing picture in which the modified paving stone seems to clarify a great deal.

When I attempted to place NEXT and Huanyang in this image, NEXT represented the pebbles. NEXT is a shared collection of ideas and people, organized seemingly at random into surprising combinations and mutual overlaps. For example, in Amsterdam we worked at huge tables. The partners sat literally in among the trainees, with the result that information was disseminated in all directions. Although the office and the projects had their own clear responsibilities, these were organized in a non-hierarchical way as much as possible. The idea behind this was self-evident to us: maximum capitalization on the potential was only possible with maximum interaction between people and ideas. Instead of there being internal boundaries, there was an overlap of responsibilities. From a Chinese perspective, I estimated, NEXT would be characterized as a chaotically organized office.

Using the same metaphor, Huanyang could be regarded as the strictly organized pattern of paving stones, with clearly legible and sharply defined boundaries between the stones. Huanyang had a strong hierarchy. Everyone who worked there was thoroughly aware of their role and position in the greater whole. And every individual confined themselves to the relevant responsibilities, without deviating from these to any major extent. The horizontal boundaries in Huanyang between the various departments as well as the vertical boundaries between hierarchical levels were particularly dominant when compared to NEXT. Seen from a Dutch perspective, it gave a relatively segregated office probably with great potential but with little scope for developing creativity and talent.

By regarding NEXT as the pebbles and Huanyang as the paving pattern, both the relationship and the boundary between the two offices became clearly visible.

The image of the borderline between pebbles and paving stones immediately exposed the weakness of the collaboration. The ideas and working methods of NEXT and Huanyang were merely co-existing.

The two offices failed to mix well and collaboration between them was marked by a limited exchange of ideas, at least from a Dutch perspective. Nevertheless, there was something very promising in the image: the boundary had been dented. And if I projected that image onto myself, then I was that one pebble stone that had made inroads on the boundary. At the same time, I realized that there was another scenario in which this cautious erosion of the border was the most we could expect. In that case, perhaps we were fated to never actually mix.

I took the pebble-paving stone image with me on my flight back to Beijing. During the landing I concluded that the project for the new interior had the potential to cross boundaries: the boundaries between Chinese colleagues among themselves, the boundaries between NEXT and Huanyang and – probably the most ambitious of all – the boundaries between China and myself. So NEXT should and would submit a proposal for the new office.

Huanyang and NEXT were creative offices. So clearly this project would be about the conditions for creativity: the enabling of an exchange of ideas and interaction between people. On the basis of these starting points, we began uninvited on a proposal in which the link between the five new floors would be the central feature. Connection was added as a third condition of creativity and had to ensure the necessary cohesion in the explosively growing organization.

The core of the design proposal consisted of two stacked forum stairways that connected the five floors literally as stairways and figuratively as forums. The forums could be used for a whole range of formal and informal activities such as presentations, discussions and exhibitions. The stairways were round, which symbolized harmony and unity in China, and were positioned centrally in the floor plans, where the vacuity of a lobby normally presided.

From a Chinese perspective, the plan was radical. First of all, this was because it sacrificed the void of the lobby. Emptiness represented size and therefore the power and with it the 'face' of a company. The design additionally was intended to undermine the Chinese hierarchy. From a Dutch perspective, however, the plan held great promise. Due to the fact that the stairways were round, anybody using them would automatically end up at the centre of the forum. For us, it was a subtle but critical reference to the fact that not only did everyone have the right to speak but they also had the right to be heard.

When developing the design I engaged as many Chinese colleagues as possible, from both NEXT and Huanyang. Mr Chen expressed exactly what was going on in my mind: 'Usually the lobby of a Chinese company is big and empty. Our design is very interesting: we put people in the centre!'

We presented the unsolicited design unannounced. The result was an uncomfortable situation in which it was made clear to me, subtly but explicitly, that other agendas prevailed. Connection, exchange and interaction were very important but the 'world-renowned' Korean architect who would make the design and who belonged among the 'top ten in the world of commercial interiors' was more important. We 'could learn a lot' – after all, he was 'a master', I was told. Mr Chen tried to put things into perspective: 'We're clients now, that's much easier than being the architect!' I understood even less of the 'commercial' goal than of the necessity to tender the project to an external architect.

The process with the Korean architect lasted about three months, after which the collaboration was silently terminated. The proposed ideas weren't catching on and there was no feeling of mutual trust. At that moment Huanyang approached me for the job. It was emphasized how important the new interior was. 'We can best realize what's best for us!' Mr Chen now contradicted himself. I smiled and recognized an opportunity.

While I accepted the brief without hesitation, I thought back to the three previous months in which I had watched the process with the Korean architect from a distance. It seemed as if I had experienced something new in that period: patience. I had always regarded patience as one of China's indestructible strategic properties. And now that I seemed able to share that capacity, I had the feeling that I had come closer to my Chinese colleagues than ever before.

Full of renewed energy, we returned to our first ideas for the dual use of the stairways as forums. We worked out a series of meeting places, including the forum stairs and a 'meeting plaza', fully fitted out with a coffee bar. Each employee would receive an electronic card enabling them to enjoy a number of free consumptions every month. Using encounter to dissolve boundaries could make a real and positive contribution to the way we worked together. However, at the first presentation much doubt was expressed about the radical idea of sacrificing the lobby. At the second presentation, it was explicitly stipulated that there should be as large a void as possible between all the floors: 'More open space is better.' At the third presentation, doubts were raised as to whether the forum would ever actually be used. At the fourth presentation we were asked if we perhaps had any other ideas. These were scarcely veiled words that confirmed that the design had been rejected.

In the subsequent months we presented a myriad of new and adapted proposals. The process had disintegrated, every discussion seemed to have become a kind of lottery, everyone began to collect images and to announce: 'I like this picture...'

After a long patient wait, a new opportunity arose.

We still had the idea of a stairway connecting the different floors. It was only that during the 'process' the forums had made way for a gaping, empty well. And the stairway that seemed most likely to be accepted could have belonged in a shopping mall or luxury hotel. An engineer had been asked to calculate the loads and the outcome was clear: the well and stairway were possible if we reinforced the floors locally with joists 800 millimetres thick, which would lie on the topside of the floors as enormous obstacles.

During a lunch with Mr Chen I sketched the original forum stairs on a napkin, without thinking much about it. He looked at the sketch and reacted spontaneously: 'Let's try one more time.'

I nodded and grinned. Back at the office, the original design was worked up further with a new scale model and new animations, renderings, drawings and calculations. The collective stamina among colleagues was simply astonishing.

The meeting was scheduled for two days after the lunch. Was the 'design' of the well feasible without the joists on the floor?

'Very difficult', was the engineer's answer. The scale model of the forum stair had pride of place on the table and had attracted attention right from the start of the discussion. The meeting room was full of colleagues of all ages and departments, all having committed themselves to the design in their own way.

'Can this really be built easily?' someone asked, while the scale model was being rotated.

'Yes', was the resolute response from the engineer.

A brief moment of silence followed. All eyes were still fixed on the scale model.

'This design is really good. Everything has to be finished in four months' time. Are we going to manage it?' asked Mrs Hu, pre-empting the opinion of the other directors.

Almost a year after the first sketch, we were back at square one. But from that moment on, everything happened at lightning speed. The project was completed and in place within four months. In the first week after moving into the new office, I was summoned by Ms Jia.

'John, come quick, they're using the stairs!'

I hurried to the forum and saw young and old, engineers, architects and people from all departments jostling round an enormous cake: someone was celebrating their birthday. The sound of talking and laughter rang through the office storeys.

A grinning Mr Chen came and stood next to me. Together we looked at the spectacle. A small revolution had taken place in the relationship between the architect and user on the one side, and the client on the other. There was also a small but promising revolution taking place in the border zone between the Chinese colleagues individually. And, not least, there were now the conditions for a new revolution, namely in the border zone between NEXT and Huanyang.

I looked at Mr Chen as he observed the spectacle, still smiling broadly. Suddenly it seemed as if I was feeling something that transcended my own euphoria: collective euphoria. Achieving 'instant success' was addictive, but this was better, much better.

ZHONG TI XI YONG

In the new office I had exchanged my glass room for a place on the open-plan floor. In doing so, I was deliberately challenging the hierarchy.

'You're a leader, so you should have your own office!' was a much-heard reaction. My response – 'Business people need boxes to work in: architects don't!' – was scarcely understood.

From my new workstation, I gazed out across the work floor and thought back on the old office. I once had a discussion with Mr Jiang about our then minimalist principles.

'Why do Western architects like simple, empty spaces?' he asked. 'And why always white? That colour is so difficult to use!' He looked at me and without waiting for a reply continued: 'I know, you always say: It's pure! But I just think it's uncomfortable.'

'It's about searching for essence,' I tried.
'But what if you're searching for the wrong essence?'
'It's about undefined space, leaving space for things to happen,' I tried via another route. Mr Jiang looked at me in incomprehension.
'I think spaces like that are art, not architecture.'
At the time, such opinions mocked the self-evidence of my 'modern thinking'. But now something new seemed to have arisen: a mutual conciliation. With this design we had succeeded in realizing together with Huanyang a project beyond form but with substance. It was a project that could bring additional benefits to an organization, beyond the superficiality of 'face'. The project distinguished itself primarily because we, in conjunction with Huanyang, had been successful in further developing our Western ideas regarding the context within which creativity could unfold.

I recalled the trip to North Korea, where my quest for answers to the existential question of the possible influence of Western ideas upon a totally different ideology had once begun. That question had never been answered. Just as with so many other subjects where China was involved, every attempt to define an absolute answer seemed to exclude more truths than it included. Perhaps this search for truth, 'absolute truth' at all events, was itself typically Western. Mr Jiang characterized these attempts as 'blue eyes staring at China'. As a consequence, the quest itself probably had more potential that any conclusion. And this quest was nurtured by the daily practice of projects, discussions with colleagues, travel experiences, contact with friends such as Lao Qing, and also by surprising incidents such as a conversation with Ms Wang, my Chinese teacher.

When I entered the classroom, she was just rounding off a telephone conversation. With a smile, she looked at her mobile phone and told me that she could go to her tailor that afternoon. I asked what she had had made.

'A qipao,' she said, while picking up a felt-tip pen to make a drawing on the glass partition. A 'qipao' is a traditional Chinese dress. I had never regarded her as someone for a qipao, in view of the fact that she had once made a parachute jump – 'absolutely amazing!' – liked to go wild camping on the Great Wall of China – 'watch out for scorpions and snakes' – and primarily because she was on the brink of leaving China to take a Master's Degree programme in Australia.

She drew a qipao and told me that traditionally this dress had a high closure around the neck. But because this was not very comfortable she had adapted the form of the neck to that of a Western dress, which closed quite a bit lower. She grabbed a brush, erased the upper, Chinese part of the qipao and drew the Western part in its place. She further explained that she didn't really like qipaos but her studies in Australia offered her a golden opportunity to present herself as a Chinese person. It seemed one could earn quite a lot on the side there teaching Chinese. I smiled broadly and grabbed a second pen.

Next to the drawing of the qipao I wrote the four Chinese characters 中体西用. The four characters, 'zhong ti xi yong', could be literally translated as 'Chinese core, Western form'. I had picked up the concept from a book promisingly called *De Chinacode ontcijferd* (The China Code Deciphered). According to the author, a Dutch friend who had lived in China for more than twenty years, the concept originated sometime in the 19th century, at the time when the West overwhelmed China with its superiority in weapons and technology. To save the ancient empire from decline, reformers had decided to study and imitate everything Western. But there was one strict condition: the 'essential nature of the Heavenly Empire' must not be lost.

After encountering this concept, I had read the whole book in one go. What was the 'core', what was the essence of the 'Heavenly Empire' that should not be eroded? It could not be outlined in simple terms, but had something to do with the uniqueness of the country: the mystical beauty of the calligraphy, the Confucian system of values that takes social harmony as its point of departure, the timeless tone of the Tang poetry, the sacred mountains, and socially unifying celebrations such as the Spring Festival and the Moon Festival.

I myself had subsequently compiled a much more extensive list. But I observed that it was subject to continuous re-evaluation and adjustment. As such, the upkeep of the list had become a permanent project. A fundamental project, moreover, because the four characters 'zhong ti xi yong' could give me an answer to the question of 'fresh air, dust and mosquitoes' in present-day modern Chinese architecture.

I looked at the drawing of the qipao and at the rough boundary between the Chinese and the Western part.

'Is your qipao an example of "zhong ti xi yong"?' I asked.

'Dangran', she said. 'Dangran' means 'naturally'.

I latched on immediately and a conversation in Chinese followed.

J: 中体西用，'中体'是什么意思？(Chinese core, Western form, what is the significance of the core?)
w: 这个问题非常的难阿！(This question is very complicated!)
J: 是的，对我是一个外国人是很难，但你是一个中国女孩阿！(That's right, to me, because I am a foreigner, but you are Chinese!)
w: 但是这个对我来说也很难啊！(It is also difficult for me.)
J: 试试解释给我听听！(Try!)
w: 从文化，历史上解释么。。。(Culture, history …)
J: 对，但是告诉我，关于中国文化的独特之处是什么？(Good, but tell me: what are the exceptional aspects of Chinese culture?)
w: 在风俗，语言字符,传统和节日中有很多特别之处。。。(There are many customs and symbols in language, tradition, festivals …)
J: 我们在欧洲也有这些，可为什这些在中国这么地特别？(But we have all of that in Europe too, why are they so extraordinary in China?)
w: 因为意义是不同的！(The meanings are not the same!)
J: 给我讲讲。。。(Tell me …)
w: 在中国，有很多特殊的含义。(In China there are very many special meanings.)
J: 多得让外国人不理解么？(Too many for a foreigner to grasp?)
w: 我给你讲一个古老的中国故事，是关于一群盲人和一头大象的故事。一群盲人不知道大象究竟是长什么样子的，于是他们决定去摸摸大象找出答案。第一个人摸到了鼻子，第二个人摸到了尾巴，第三个人摸到了耳朵，第四个人摸到了肚子，第五个人摸到了腿。他们摸同一只大象，但当他们互相告诉对方大象长什么样子的时候，每个人的答案竟然是完全的不同！(In China there is an old story about a group of blind people and an elephant. The blind people have no idea of what the elephant looks like and try to construct a form by feeling the elephant. One feels a trunk, the other a tail, still another person feels an ear, a belly, a leg. It is the same elephant but when they tell one another what they think the elephant looks like, their ideas are completely different!)
J *(in English)*: Chinese culture is so comprehensive that there's a danger in selective emphasis?
w *(in Chinese)*: 你太聪明了！(You're a smart guy!)
J *(smiling)*: 没有啦！(Far from it!)
w: 你觉得中国文化的特别之处是什么呢？(What do you think is exceptional about Chinese culture?)
J: 与荷兰文化相比有很大差异。(The essential differences with Dutch culture.)

w: 解释给我听听。(So tell me.)
J: 好比咱们刚刚的对话，就是如何扭转一个谈话主题的独特例子。(This conversation, in fact ... it's an exceptional example of tiptoeing around a topic.)
w: 那在荷兰人们是怎么对话的呢？(How would you do that in the Netherlands?)
J: 我们是直奔主题，不兜圈子说话。(Straight to the point, without beating around the bush.)
w *(smiling)*: 什么意思？(What is your aim then?)
J: 理解中体西用，什么是'中体'，什么是'西用'，两者的界限在那里？(Insight into 'Western form, Chinese core': what is the core, what is the form, where is the boundary?)
w: 你的问题就像一头大象。(Your question is like a big elephant.)
J *(smiling)*: 没有可能的答案么？(No possible answer?)
w *(smiles)*
J: ...
w: 好，让我来给你上一课吧！(Good, let's begin the lesson!)
J *(smiling)*: 哈哈，咱们已经开始了！(We had already begun!)

I looked one last time at the drawing of the qipao and imagined that the elegant lines of the traditional Chinese dress would transform fluently into a more revealing Western dress. East and West would blend perfectly without the seam being perceptible. It would be a dress beyond Chinese core and Western form, beyond 'zhong ti xi yong'.

Still sunk in thought, I gazed out across the office floor and realized that the boundary between 'Chinese core' and 'Western form' had become a part of an elementary quest in every project to which I had contributed. It was a deliberate but hazardous quest. With each brief there was the risk of the threadbare scenario of an East-West balance required by the client. And for me this scenario was represented in the most exemplary terms by the combination of the indestructible laws of Chinese building economics and a façade designed by a Western architect.

OVERLAP

'The input for the quest for the boundaries between "Chinese core and Western form" is multiple and varied, but comes mainly from the world of practice. In China, theory is primarily nurtured by practice, unlike in the Netherlands, where practice is fed by theory.'

The lady journalist looked at me interestedly, but didn't seem really to understand me. We were in a taxi on our way through a desolate area towards a newly realized project: a lobby for a new office building. This stood in an area that aspired to become the Chinese Silicon Valley. As its users would be both Chinese and international software companies, the design had to embrace 'Chinese tradition' and 'modern Western ideas'.

'Years ago, I would have regarded such a requirement as a risk to a project, now I see it as an opportunity,' I stated resolutely.

'What is meant by "Chinese tradition"?'

'The laws of feng shui, among other things. But tradition also entails the Chinese ideal of receiving. Receiving takes place in the lobby and, after the façade, it is the lobby that gives the second impression of a company. Size is a quality in itself: the larger the lobby, the greater respect a company will enjoy.'

Driving through the emptiness I explained the design steps: in order to make the relatively small lobby in this project look as large as possible, it was kept as empty as possible by integrating all the typical elements of a lobby – reception desk, art, seating – in the walls.

Not long after, we stopped in front of a building and walked through the lobby. I tried to appraise a first reaction. My description of the design didn't seem to correspond with the way the journalist envisaged it.

'How did you conceive these forms?'

I told her that we had invited a 'feng shui master' on the basis of a draft design. Taking his advice into account, we allowed a range of traditional Chinese meanings to influence the design. For example, he advised us to divide the wall into eight elements and to subdivide these into 88 smaller elements. And our proposal to colour the walls as an abstraction of a sunset had been enthusiastically received by the feng shui master.

The journalist pulled a microphone out of her bag and the recordings began.

J: The feng shui master stood here with his 'luopan', a feng shui compass. We jointly determined that the first six metres of the walls should run parallel and that beyond that height the forms could turn inward more freely. The feng shui master said: 'We must have a painting of the sea here, a red lamp there, a bamboo garden over there.' That was the extent of the preconditions with which we could work.

JOURNALIST: Was it pleasant to work like that, with such strict guidelines?

J: It was great to work that way. It made it possible to create something new on the basis of an overlap between Western and Chinese culture. The new element this gives rise to is not something you recognize directly, but it does get you thinking.

JOURNALIST: There are some people coming out of the lift... *(goes over to them and asks:)* Do you like this design?

CHINESE GIRL: I like it very much.

JOURNALIST: This is a feng shui lobby, do you recognize it?

CHINESE GIRL: Feng shui? I don't know.

JOURNALIST TO OTHER CHINESE: Excuse me, do you like this design?

TWO SIMULTANEOUSLY: I like it!

JOURNALIST, NEXT TO THE PAINTING OF THE SEA WITH ANOTHER CHINESE PERSON: Do you recognize feng shui here?

CHINESE MAN: Feng shui? I don't know, I just think it looks good.

JOURNALIST TO J: No-one can say anything about the influence of feng shui in this lobby, so how traditional is it?

J: Normally, 'qi' is stimulated by a small fountain with running water at the entrance or by a wall that screens off an entrance. This is very direct feng shui in Chinese architecture. There are no such literal feng shui references to be seen in this design and the feng shui concept accords much more with Western interpretations.

JOURNALIST: Chinese identity, is that something the Chinese look for in architecture?

J: Yes, and I think they do so for various reasons. In the thirty-plus years that China has been open to foreign influence, there have been various stages in this quest. In the beginning, everything that came from outside was accepted wholesale. In the meantime, we seem to have landed in a phase in which people are searching for a modern identity of their own. China is exceptionally interested in international things, but these must be suited to China and the Chinese context.

JOURNALIST: And you introduce the international component?

J: The combination of the international with the interpretation of

Chinese values. This creates something new for China, where the overlap between the international and the Chinese can be found.

The interview proceeded further, but not on the topic of the lobby. So there was no mention of the fact that not all advice given by the feng shui master had necessarily paid dividends. For example, there was the dilemma which arose when he criticized the floor plan. His argument ran counter to my design logic. The walls of the lobby were at right angles to the curved façade, which produced a funnel-shaped plan. This form followed the movement of people streaming in from outside towards a focal point, and then back outside again, fanning out toward the city. But according to the feng shui master, this form meant bad feng shui. 'Qi' could indeed freely 'enter' the lobby, but it could also freely 'escape'. Following his advice to place the walls parallel to one another would have produced a less transparent floor plan.

After the consultation I visited a Chinese colleague at the office. He was known internally as a connoisseur of feng shui. I explained the design and asked his opinion of it. A part of his advice agreed with that of the feng shui master. But to my surprise, he denied that the floor plan would have a negative effect on the feng shui. It would even have had a positive effect on the 'influx of qi'. Enthusiastically, I made my way to Mr Chen's desk.

Mr Chen had followed the whole experiment with the feng shui master with little enthusiasm. He had categorized many of the suggestions as 'mixin'. 'But "mixin" is also Chinese culture?' I asked in an attempt to convince him of the possible added value. My argument did not seem to have much effect. When I told him that I wished to present the dilemma between 'qi' and the lucidity of the floor plan to the client, he looked at me numbly. Then came the revelation that feng shui had a second agenda, that of alleviating responsibility. 'Imagine that the building is difficult to sell, then that could very well be due to the feng shui advice of our colleague.'

The entire situation remained uncomfortable but eventually he suggested presenting a new floor plan to the feng shui master. In that plan, the walls of the twelve-metre-high lobby were parallel to one another for the first six metres from the ground level and perpendicular to the curved façade for the six metres above this. A response from the feng shui expert quickly followed: 'No negative effect on positive qi.'

'So, you see,' Mr Chen reacted enthusiastically, 'a mouse has two lips!' I repeated his remark questioningly.

'In China you can always explain everything completely differently. For the same story you can always use the other lip!' he explained.

I smiled and revelled in the moment and in his enthusiasm.

IN SPITE OF – OR BECAUSE OF...

While reading through some old notebooks, I again came across the diagram drawn by the manager of DHV. The sword of Damocles that had hung above our heads a few years ago, the minimum chance of one per cent of getting anything built in the Netherlands, had perhaps been the reason to leave for China but it was certainly not the reason to stay there. The motivating force had to have been the alluring combination of architectural risks and opportunities. Once, during an exhibition at ARCAM, the Amsterdam architecture centre, on Western architects in China, it had been assessed that 'more than thirty Dutch practices' were active there. Most of these were in China for a single event, an architectural competition or a project. Many of these architects gave two reasons for being in China. First of all, there was the temptation of the greater number of architectural opportunities that China seemed to offer in comparison to the West. And then there was the curiosity about building in a foreign country like China. But, if anything was actually built, they invariably gave an apology for the quality of the realized work.

In the reality of Chinese building construction, programme and organization were often unattainable aspects of an architect's brief. In the most distressing scenario, there was only the frontage left to design. And when a design was realized, after an often none too controllable design process, the risk of further 'Sinicization' lurked just around the corner. The list of hazards threatening the construction was endless: extreme scheduling, minimum budgets, changing requirements on the part of the client, changing regulations on the part of the government, obligatory collaboration with certain suppliers of materials, the 'professionalism' of Chinese construction firms, so on and so forth.

These were the irrefutable clichés of the Western architect with experience in China. They were the risks of architecture *in spite of* Chinese conditions. But the question that increasingly interested me was the opportunity to create architecture *because of* Chinese conditions. And then a possible answer presented itself.

Mr Chen and I were having lunch in a new restaurant. While he studied the menu, the waitress asked him where I came from.

'From Europe', he replied quickly.

'Is Europe a country?' asked the waitress.

'Many countries', said Mr Chen without looking up.

'How can he come from many countries?' asked the waitress in surprise. Without waiting for an answer, she continued: 'Is Europe like China?'

Mr Chen squirmed in his chair, knowing that I was enjoying the situation. He consulted me fleetingly about some dishes, communicated this to the waitress and concluded with the remark that our order should be served quickly because we were very busy. He then looked at me uneasily, while I kept on smiling. Then his telephone rang and a conversation followed lasting no more than ten seconds.

'Is Europe like China?' I repeated the question with a smile. He sighed and seemed to have little enthusiasm for a discussion. I asked the same waitress – in Chinese, much to her surprise – for some napkins. On one of these I drew a diagram in which the horizontal axis represented time and the vertical axis surface area. The time went back 5000 years and the surface area ranged from zero to a million square metres.

Then I drew a line that started at year zero and rose on the vertical axis from a few hundred square metres to several tens of thousands. Above that line I wrote 'Europe'. Then I drew a line that began at hundreds of square metres 5000 years ago and at 1978 rocketed upwards to a million square metres. Above that line I wrote 'China'.

The diagram had aroused Mr Chen's interest.

'China has a long history, much longer than that of Europe!' he immediately remarked, with some pride.

A long history – what could that possibly mean? I was aware of the complexity of the question. China was a vast country with enormous geographical, climatological and cultural diversity. It was a country full of paradoxes and could not be easily described in simple terms. But I was curious about a Chinese answer to this question.

While Mr Chen considered the matter, I reflected that many Westerners thought they could write a book about China after spending one week there. But after a month, their insight had declined to the format of an article and, after a year, the complexity had in their view increased to the extent that they doubted whether it was possible to even produce one lucid sentence on the subject. It was more sensible to keep silent, as a German doctor friend who lived in Beijing once confided in me.

Those who did attempt to put into words the phenomenon of China ran a real risk of embarking on a story without end. I had once read somewhere that when Marco Polo returned to Venice after a stay in China of around seventeen years, he was referred to as the 'man of a thousand lies'. His stories of China were simply regarded as impossible. On his deathbed he was encouraged by a priest to alleviate his conscience by admitting his lies. His last words were allegedly: 'I have not told half of what I saw.'

During his own moment of reflection, Mr Chen had begun to look more and more unsettled. Then he snapped to with a spontaneous smile. He declared that I might grasp the significance of China's lengthy history if I tried to envisage what Europe would have been like if the Roman Empire had never declined.

I was surprised by his suggestion. Europe would then have enjoyed relative cultural and political continuity, and the most important traditions would have been largely handed down from the founding of the Empire to the 21st century. But present-day Europe had had a turbulent history and was still a puzzle of cultural, social, economic and political diversity, despite determined efforts to create unity. Traces of Roman traditions might have been evident in modern Europe in some instances, but this was not comparable with the situation in China where age-old values and traditions were still omnipresent thanks to the relative continuity.

Mr Chen smiled while I tried to sum up the facts: Chinese writing from a thousand years ago could still be read by students today. Confucius, a contemporary of Socrates, still had an influence upon our day-to-day dealings. Mr Chen continued enthusiastically: art forms such as Chinese opera, tai chi and the art of papercutting (jian zhi), all thousands of years old, were carried out in exactly the same way now as they had been long before the beginning of our era. I thought about Lao Qing, who was always boasting about present-day Chinese strategic thinking, which was apparently the consequence of an evolution of 'thousands of years of scheming and fighting'.

Mr Chen began to enjoy the conversation. He had travelled extensively outside China, and had visited a number of European countries. He wondered what European cities would have looked like if the Roman Empire had survived.

I parried the question with an attempt to compare Europe with modern China. Both had had a turbulent history in the past 150 years but in the last few decades the changes in China had taken place at an unprecedented rate. Nevertheless, some old Chinese values still seemed extremely relevant today.

'That is my answer!' he replied. His eyes flashed. I smiled while I reflected on how the question had rebounded on me.

The food arrived. I pointed out a second difference that the diagram made obvious. Unlike China, Europe had witnessed a gradual development in architectural scale. Although Europe and China had had rapidly expanding cities in the past, such as London and Amsterdam in the 17th century and Luoyang and Xi'an in the 8th century during the Tang Dynasty, the size of the buildings in Europe had only increased gradually. I summarized: In the Middle Ages, buildings in Europe were of hundreds of square metres, during the Renaissance thousands of square metres, in the 19th century tens of thousands of square metres and nowadays complexes were being built that occasionally exceeded 100,000 square metres. This scaling-up had been initiated by a series of technological discoveries and inventions that enabled social and cultural advances as well as advances in architecture.

Mr Chen confirmed that up until 1978 architecture in China had been characterized by its small scale, partly due to the building methods available. The first foreign building techniques had been introduced at the beginning of the 20th century, in the period of foreign occupation. It was 'new architecture imposed on China', particularly in the concession zones in various Chinese coastal towns. And after the foundation of the People's Republic of China in 1949, Russian and East-German architects had introduced new building techniques for industry and social housing.

While I pondered the fact that the essential difference between China and Europe was perhaps that China had experienced the modernization of its building techniques and architecture through influences from outside whereas Europe had experienced this from the inside, Mr Chen continued his discourse.

'Do you know Chairman Mao?' Without waiting for a reply to this rhetorical question, he went on to explain that although Mao's ambition to create a malleable society smacked of megalomania, its reflection was in fact visible in small-scale architecture. Mao detested the city and urbanity as symbols of bourgeois decadence. When he looked out over Tiananmen Square in 1949 and proclaimed the People's Republic of China, he predicted: 'In the future we'll see a forest of chimneys from here!' I responded stoically that the forest had since become a reality, but not of chimneys but rather of high-rise blocks, produced after the 'opening of the borders' by Deng Xiaoping in 1978. From that moment on, the availability of materials and construction techniques and a seemingly endless demand from the market had initiated an ad hoc development in architectural scale.

'China has a huge market, and there's a need for Big Ones everywhere', Mr Chen confirmed. This time, he placed the accent on 'everywhere'.

I recalled a conversation with my old colleague Mr Wang. He had made a different comparison between the development of architecture in China and that in Europe: in Europe, people built in stone, churches for example, for eternity and for God. In China, people built in wood, primarily for people to live in, for transience and for the emperor. Traditionally, the Chinese built from wooden scale models – volumes – made by craftsmen, not from drawings – spaces – made by architects, as in Europe. This, combined with the limitations of building with wood, imposed restrictions on the scale of the architecture. 'Even the 700,000-square-metre Forbidden City was a complex of smaller buildings', he had declared, and then: 'As a result of the building methods and the available construction materials, but also because of the idea that no-one should to rise above the emperor, China has never had a tradition of building upwards. That is why there is such a demand nowadays for modern Chinese façade designs for large buildings.'

Mr Chen's telephone rang. In fact, his telephone rang constantly. In China, there was as yet no market for voice mail – everyone answered the phone directly, whatever the time and place.

After a few clipped sentences, he looked again at the diagram. He picked up the pen next to the napkin and added a second layer to the diagram. Below the vertical axis he wrote 'months' and above the axis 'years'. Then he drew two new lines, first of all a line that represented construction time in China. The line began at the top of the diagram, ran horizontally until 1978 and took a sharp downward turn. He began a second line for Europe just below the line for China and allowed it to descend gradually. He put down the pen and looked at me proudly. Then he picked up his chopsticks to eat a while.

Besides history and the development in the scale of architecture, the sketch revealed a third difference. In China, they built much more quickly than in Europe.

Without speaking I added a third layer to the diagram. At the vertical axis I wrote 'budget' and then I drew a line for China, which ran more or less evenly for almost 5000 years. The line for Europe made a gradual but increasingly sharp ascent. Mr Chen leaned over to examine the new lines. A fourth difference loomed into view: in China, building construction was significantly cheaper than in Europe.

Besides the fact that China had a much longer history than Europe, we had discovered another three substantial differences during this lunch. Together we concluded that present-day projects in China differed radically in scale, construction time and budget from projects in Europe. I wished to emphasize the last two using statistics but Mr Chen would not be tempted: 'Statistics are politics. No use. And when used, then only for reference!' He was right; although construction time and budget differed to an extreme degree, they were also accompanied by great differences in quality. It was impossible to compare the two.

That said, present-day building briefs in China were of a far greater size than anything Europe had ever experienced. This wasn't a statistic, it was reality. For this reason, I tried to entice him into urban myths.

'It seems that there was more building done in Beijing last year than in the whole of Europe.' Without waiting for a reply, I continued: 'There's a story doing the rounds about a discussion between the new mayors of Berlin and Shanghai. The one proudly announced that ten new skyscrapers were to be built in Berlin. The other responded that hundreds were then under construction in Shanghai. A new skyscraper was completed every few days!'

[216]

Mr Chen repeated what he often said on such occasions: 'Speed is everything in China.' I agreed by saying that building construction in China took place as quickly as 'concrete can dry' or 'as quick as companies can build'. I was quoting Mr Mo, an engineer who once told me this with a smile when I asked him about the planning of a project. I thought about the speed with which our own projects were implemented. Working seven days a week, 24 hours a day in shifts was more the rule here than the exception. Some projects were being worked on by thousands of construction workers simultaneously. This meant that construction time was much shorter than in the Netherlands, where to compound matters application and public inquiry procedures could greatly delay the run-up to a project.

We calmly continued our meal. Mr Chen's interest in the topic seemed to have vanished. I could guess why: he had heard little that was new to him. To keep the discussion going, I asked: 'What about the budget for architecture?' He looked at me questioningly.

Budget was a subject difficult to fathom for a Western architect in China, because this aspect seemed to lie beyond his reach. Often only a rough budget per square metre was given as a guideline, but it was more common not to mention a figure at all. The idea behind this was that you first had to have a design before you could weigh the costs against the benefits. This weighing-up continued all the way to the project's completion and sat uncomfortably with architectural quality.

'Money is everything', was Mr Chen's simple conclusion. 'The emperor's daughter doesn't need to be pretty', he continued. The project would be sold whatever happened, because of demand from the market – that was his message.

Mr Chen's phone rang again. After a few sentences he looked at me and said: 'We have to go to a meeting.' I took the sketch with me and we made our way back to the office.

At home that evening, I looked at the napkin once again. Scale, construction time and budget in China differed greatly from those in Europe, and these three in combination gave rise to a major paradox in China's development model. The Chinese government prescribed that the reforms should take place gradually, in accordance with the mantra of 'crossing the river by feeling the stones'. But, on the other hand, the cities were changing at an enormous rate because of government policy, the drive of the property developers and market demands. As a consequence, the conditions for the development of modern Chinese architecture were subject to continuous change and, moreover, there was little time for reflection.

In the meantime, I had moved to Jianwai Soho, one of the more interesting housing projects in Beijing. The entire area was open to the public. The enormous density of public life generated a huge amount of energy – unprecedented for Beijing – in the project, which was organized across three storeys linked by courtyards and bridges. From the thirtieth floor I had a view out across the Central Business District, then under construction. A new tower block was being built in front of mine. I watched the builders at work there.

Then I thought about the chaotic life at the office. 'Everything is always an emergency', as Mr Chen described the everyday situation. The preconditions for planning were every bit as unstable. For example, during a lunch, my Chinese colleagues once discussed an adjustment to the regulations by central government. Almost overnight, 70% of residential projects throughout China had to consist of apartments of 90 square metres or less. This change was socially motivated: due to the increasing imbalance between high-end supply and low-end demand, millions of urban dwellers were still unable to afford their own house.

'How could this be implemented so quickly?' I asked my colleagues although I actually already knew the answer: 'In China everything can change very quickly.' Constantly changing circumstances and spontaneously shifting preconditions and regulations as they existed in China were difficult to imagine in the Netherlands. But Chinese architectural practice was entirely oriented to this situation.

As I looked out across the skyline, I recalled something that made me smile. 'In the Netherlands we have been talking about extending a motorway for the past fifty years.' It was the kind of remark that made a table of lunching Chinese look up in surprise. I made it after the story of a Chinese colleague who had received a letter from the government three weeks previously. It said that a stack interchange was to be constructed behind his apartment block three weeks later. Nothing had happened in the first week but in the next two weeks thousands of soldiers built the intersection.

I looked at the napkin again and realized that the list of differences between China and Europe was endless, and therefore probably less interesting than two other observations.

The first was that modernization, represented by gleaming façades and high-speed trains, was only a very recent phenomenon in the overall spectrum of Chinese cultural development. The previous week I had been a casual witness to another 'magic number': it was estimated that 120 individual cities in China had an 'urban exhibition centre' or were engaged in building one. I had visited such centres in a number of cities. Their urban intentions were invariably exhibited in enormous scale models often measuring as much as several hundred square metres. Two aspects were always uppermost in these models: high-quality infrastructure – airports, motorways, train stations, underground railways – and high-rise buildings in the form of Central Business Districts.

Infrastructure and high-rise were, without exception, the symbols of the modernization and progress of Chinese cities. I kept finding evidence of this during my travels. In Yinchuan it was the endless series of billboards with bird's-eye views of new traffic junctions with a backdrop of high rises as far as the eye could see. On a flight to Shenyang, a metropolis in north-east China, each passenger was greeted with a PR magazine full of similar bird's-eye views below which were the words 'Shenyang, our new beautiful modern city'. In Shenzhen, in south China, it was still customary to pose in front of the famous billboard with the picture of Deng Xiaoping. Behind his smiling portrait, in his wake so to speak, was a depiction of the new skyline of Shenzhen. But even less well-known metropolises I had visited, such as Urumqi, Hohhot, Chongqing, Chengdu, Changsha, Wuhan, Zhengzhou, Hefei, Jinan, Xiamen, Harbin and Changchun, seemed to aspire to such ideals.

Gleaming façades and high-grade infrastructure were often the first impressions Westerners had when visiting China for the first time. And it was tempting for them to associate these urban images with modern cities in the West. But in my experience there was a degree of friction here: the same construction materials and the often interchangeable images all too frequently had different meanings.

I looked out across the skyline again and concluded that my thoughts were not new. They were just difficult to capture in an all-embracing example. Then I remembered a discussion I'd had with a Chinese friend, Ms Xia, who once told me about the extreme differences between generations to be found in Chinese families. For example, the imperial era, the revolution and the modern age could all be represented within a single family. I asked her about the similarities between the generations. She knew what I was looking for: old values that were still current in present-day China. Without referring to the story about families, she told me about the complex construction history of the 'The Nine Dragon Crossing', the stack interchange in the centre of Shanghai.

A number of construction companies had been unsuccessful in laying foundations for the central pillar, which was to be more than six metres in diameter and almost forty metres tall. It took a visit to a temple to resolve it. A monk there knew the secret of the location: it was impossible to lay foundations because there was a dragon sleeping under the ground. The monk knew the solution, but stated that revealing it would cost him his life. On his advice, a new attempt was made to lay the foundations, at a moment determined to the nearest second. This time it worked. The monk warned that to keep the dragon happy the pillar had to be covered with a copper dragon pattern, which was subsequently done. Then he died.

I asked Ms Xia whether this was faith or superstition. She just said: 'It's true! It really happened!'

This example was no isolated incident. Lao Qing once referred to the late Qing Dynasty and the complex relationship between old values and the modernization process: 'The construction of railways, telegraph lines, factories and mines met with stiff opposition.' He suggested that the reason for this, held by large sections of the Chinese population, was that 'the souls of buried forefathers would be disturbed.'

Lao Qing traced the origins of Chinese 'superstition' to the influences of Taoism and a belief in the unavoidable acceptance of fate. 'Your thinking is much more influenced by the old Greeks', he said. When I asked him to illustrate what characterized our thinking, he replied: 'I have studied you as people: you are rational and level-headed, you live in the conviction that your fate is in your own hands.' I could only smile and confirm that, whatever the case, he was getting to know me better.

I had spoken about my second observation to colleagues and clients on several occasions. I even used this observation regularly to emphasize the necessity of collaboration. There was no precedent in world history for the hyper accelerated urban development taking place in China at the moment. The absence of a precedent implied a lack of references for all parties, including the government and clients as well as spatial planners, urban designers and architects. And this in turn implied an inherent share of uncertainties on whose basis China was developing. Concepts such as 'modern', 'international', and 'landmark' – to name just three – were easy to translate into Chinese and back into English. But the interpretation, the ideals, the conditions under which plans were realized and the way players acted seemed not to harmonize at all with the Western idiom.

China was an age-old existence that was modernizing at an unprecedented rate on the back of many uncertainties. Nevertheless, China seemed to know and respect deeply rooted cultural values under its extremely volatile modern surface. These were values that were not easily brushed aside and were interwoven with the modernization process in all kinds of ways.

Certain values and uncertain conditions: I had never been as close as this to a definition of China. I went to my desk and made an attempt to construct an image of 'architecture in spite of' and 'architecture because of' Chinese values and traditions.

In my view, the way in which Chinese modern architecture was developing could best be understood by abstracting the two observations – modernization as an extremely recent phenomenon in Chinese cultural development and the inherent welter of uncertainties on whose basis China was developing – into two domains. The first domain covered the certain values of Chinese culture in the broadest sense. The second comprised the uncertain conditions of present-day designing and building in China resulting from the Chinese intentions to modernize: the uncertain domain of the Chinese Architect's Brief.

Modern Chinese architecture seemed to evolve out of the overlap of these two domains. This overlap formed the operational reach of Chinese architects who worked within the 'uncertain' domain from their basis in their own 'certain' cultural domain.

A third domain was conceivable, shaped by the 'perspective' of the Western architect. This 'perspective' gave a basis, the Western position, from which Chinese values and conditions could be interpreted and projects in China could be developed.

This put a number of scenarios within the reach of Western architects by relating the three domains in various ways.

One scenario was to give a Western interpretation of the certain Chinese values, with a poorly understood 'Sinicized' project as a consequence; another was to take the uncertain conditions, resulting in a generic project. This scenario represented 'zhong ti xi yong', a Chinese core with a Western form at most, architecture created *in spite of* Chinese values and conditions.

The opportunities for Western architects lay beyond the imaginary boundary that 'zhong ti xi yong' presented between the three domains of Chinese values, Chinese conditions and Western interpretation. It was here that the chances lay for a possible architectural contribution beyond the skin of a building, giving rise to a third type of brief. By penetrating the Chinese domains, it was possible to realize projects for China from the Chinese position.

Here, then, were opportunities for an architecture *because of* Chinese values and conditions.

FACILITATING UNCERTAINTY

J: Thanks for inviting me! What should the lecture be about?
OTHER PERSON: No theme, you can talk freely, maybe about your projects.
J: But isn't there something like a common theme?
OTHER PERSON: It's a high-end forum on urban architectural design.

Giving a lecture is an obligatory moment of reflection, was what I thought when I put down the phone. And moments of reflection should be seized whenever possible. But, what should I do with an unrestricted lecture at a high-end forum on urban architectural design? It would be much more interesting to chart the strategy behind our projects than to simply explain them. Two weeks later I held my lecture and a first picture displaying a matrix of projects filled the projection screen.

When we arrived in China we had a well-filled portfolio of projects, ranging from concepts to product designs. But it was uncertain whether or not many of these projects would ever be implemented. In retrospect, this restriction had worked to our advantage. The lack of experience supplied the energy for the quest for knowledge on how we could build in China. And the findings from this quest led to our current architectural train of thought. Exactly how this train of thought would further develop was difficult to predict, but it was at least possible to trace where it originated from.

In retrospect, we had been confronted in China by multiple challenges. First of all, concepts had to be created in China and then developed there. Second, we were not equipped for the type of brief we worked on in China. Third, we were faced with an architectural scale virtually unknown to us before then. Fourth, we had to find a direct link with building practice. And fifth, there were the obvious necessities of speed and flexibility.

As a result of these challenges, our architectural strategy could be seen to develop over time.

In developing our small projects, from dozens to thousands of square metres, we sought added value in the idea of combinations. These combinations could arise from something that had already existed but was yet to be experienced. Or from an unexpected incident which made the sum of the parts worth more than the parts themselves. For example, the programme and volume of the sales centre for Liuming were combined with an internal and external route so that the quality of the surroundings could be experienced. And in the 'creative office', the combination of five typical office floors with forum stairways as a connecting element stimulated the conditions for interaction, exchange and creativity. The origins of these architectural combinations were strongly allied to our Dutch projects, where our portfolio largely consisted of projects at this scale. An architect in China had a degree of control over the process and architectural result at this scale, although to a lesser degree than in Europe.

When we began work on our first projects of tens of thousands of square metres and larger in China, it brought a shift in our architectural strategy. Projects at this scale sought their added value primarily through confrontation. This could be confrontation between details and the larger whole, or confrontation with the inevitable by taking what was required to its limit. For example, we could use a minor reworking of the loggias in the student accommodation at the Normal University to confront individuality with uniformity. And at ABB we confronted the rationale of the typical office block with the outermost limits of its structural possibilities, transforming it into a green demo centre.

Experience had taught us that, with projects of this magnitude in China, an architect had less control over the process and the architectural quality than with projects at a lesser scale. It was a general paradox: the larger a project, the smaller the architect's influence. I had only known of this paradox in theory, but with architectural briefs for hundreds of thousands of square metres, it became an integral part of our practice. In projects of this scale we increasingly began to experiment with concepts that sought added value in the idea of facilitating uncertainty. In the project with the east-west orientation, we enabled the different building segments to vary in height. As a result, it was possible to optimize the floor area and programme at a later date. We had incorporated urban routes in the volume of the building to be erected upon the former factory's foundations. At the same time, the design allowed maximum freedom for the façade, which would probably have a lifespan of six to eight years at the most.

The idea of facilitating uncertainty bore a strong relationship to our Dutch way of thinking, which saw us acting against over-designing in many projects. But whereas we had developed the idea of 'terra incognita' primarily in urban design and spatial planning projects in the Netherlands, the opportunities for terra incognita in China seemed to be at the architectural scale.

The lights went up and there was applause. A number of questions came from the auditorium. Then there was an extensive lunch, a meeting with various people and the usual expressions of the desire to collaborate. But a more interesting aspect was that the lecture had given me the opportunity to listen to myself. And precisely because of this I had discovered a new challenge: to develop further the strategy of 'facilitating uncertainty'.

SPECIFIED VERSUS UNSPECIFIED

For weeks, the diagram showing the opportunities for architecture *because of* Chinese conditions hung on the presentation wall at the office. As I looked at it, I realized that the architectural strategy of 'facilitating uncertainty' held out at least two basic challenges. How could architectural quality be guaranteed? And how to prevent a project from becoming purely generic?

As an answer to both points, a common denominator seemed to have developed in our projects, typified by a radical separation between what we specified in a design and what we left unspecified.

The *specified* aspect of a project seemed to develop from the overlap of the three domains: certain Chinese cultural values, uncertain Chinese conditions, and our architectural interpretation. The *unspecified* aspect comprised the uncertainties inherent in the Chinese conditions. In a project, the *specified* functioned, as it were, as the fixed framework that allowed maximum flexibility for the *unspecified*. The objective here was to allow for alteration without being detrimental to the essential qualities of the proposal.

I considered the possible origin of this way of working and soon reached the conclusion that it probably derived from the two-week design period stipulated in a competition for a project for IBM.

The IBM brief was limited to a building line, a maximum building height and a surface area of 'about 35,000 square metres'. After a briefing with this information by the Chinese developer, we visited the site where we found a 'lunar landscape'. Everything had been razed; nothing was left of the old structures. So, we were faced with a brief for a site with no context and four preconditions: IBM as the user, the building line, the maximum building height and a surface area of 'about 35,000 square metres'. While we deliberated on this back at the office, the client phoned with new information: the negotiations with IBM were still ongoing so we could not assume that the building would be for IBM alone. A little later we received still more information: each building for IBM should not only meet local and American building regulations but had to have an efficiency ratio of more than 85%.

Recapitulating, we recognized that the project so far lacked a user, a clear brief and a context. In terms of usable preconditions we had a building line, a maximum building height, a guideline for surface area, both Chinese and American building regulations, and an efficiency ratio of at least 85%. Instead of regarding all the unknown factors as limitations, we saw them as an opportunity to develop a design that was sufficiently flexible to accommodate any future change from unknown to known factor.

The given site was elliptical. To remain within its boundaries and to meet the surface area requirement, we envisaged a three-storey elliptical volume. We cut some of it away to guarantee sufficient daylight incidence. This excision referred to the courts of the *siheyuan*, Beijing's age-old courtyard houses. In this design, the courtyards were not to be used in a residential context but rather in a work setting and would act as 'places of silence' within this volume with its footprint of 100 by 200 metres.

We proposed four courtyards. The upper two layers of the elliptical volume were placed upon the four smaller ellipses at grade. In this way, we opened up the ground level, emphasized the entrances and enabled relationships between the courtyards and the surroundings. Ideally, collective functions would be concentrated in the four ellipses at ground level, and all public spaces found in the residual space between these ellipses.

The spatial proportions of the courtyards were optimized within the limits of Chinese and American building regulations. Internal circulation in the design was concentrated along an inner circuit and would pass along all four courtyards. So there was nowhere in the huge building volume where you felt you were situated in a large internal space. This earned the design an efficiency ratio of 87%.

When I evaluated the thought process, the strength of the proposal proved to be in its radical division between specified and unspecified. The only specified component of the project was the quartet of courtyards inside the volume, derived from the traditional *siheyuan*. Around the courtyards, everything else was unspecified all the way to the site's limits: the organization, surface area and height could be easily changed without compromising the design's spatial quality, namely the four courtyards around which the volume was organized.

The design won first prize and the limits of this strategy were explored during the construction when the building's surface area had to be enlarged from 35,000 to 50,000 square metres.

MODERN INTERNATIONAL LANDMARK

'Congratulations!'

Mr Chen stood excitedly at my desk. Grinning, he shook my hand: 'It's a Big One!' His eyes shone: 'Around 220,000 square metres!'

The project was a complex consisting of a podium with three slabs and two towers on top. It was exemplary in several ways, first of all because of the preconditions for projects of this scale. The complex had to be 'around' 220,000 square metres in surface area and was already under construction. Nevertheless, the programme was still largely unknown: it had still not been decided whether the towers and slabs were to accommodate offices, apartments, hotel apartments or a combination of these. As for the podium, it was not yet known whether it would contain a department store, a shopping mall or both.

The history of the project was itself exemplary: many architects, both Chinese or Asian and Western, had been involved in it. This is how it had been 'developed', step by step. After the envelope had been specified, a whole range of façades was designed, once again by a great many different architects.

And lastly, the task was exemplary to every architect who had ever worked on the project, namely to make this generic container of space a 'Modern International Landmark'.

Now that challenge lay at our doorstep. I looked at Mr Chen. He was still grinning. I had an ambivalent feeling about the project: it was a project for a façade. Mr Chen had sat down and was busy drawing a schematic plan of Beijing. He explained that the site was 'golden land'. I knew the site because I passed it every day on my way home. He began to outline what I already knew, but nonetheless I was taken by his enthusiasm. The site directly adjoined the former city wall and one of the nine original entrances to old Beijing. The old city wall had largely vanished by now. In Mao's time, the wall had made way for the Second Ring Road, a semi-highway with eight lanes around the old city. In a sense, the Second Ring Road functioned as the boundary between old Beijing and new Beijing; within that ring road, the Chinese urban structure enjoyed more protection than beyond it, where clients had much more freedom to realize 'modern buildings'.

The project embraced a theme I had not yet come across: 'local context versus Modern International Landmark'. I weighed up the opportunity against the two weeks we had been given by the client. The project offered leeway for an intervention; it was minimal, admittedly, but it was there. And, this being the case, 'My heart went completely into the project', to literally translate my reaction in Chinese to Mr Chen.

The quest to embed the project in a Chinese context, and to enable Chinese identity to extend beyond the boundary of the Second Ring Road, gathered momentum during a taxi ride to the site. During a discussion about old Beijing, the taxi driver told me that hundreds of years ago, at the time of the Ming Dynasty, a renowned silk market had existed at the site in question. I took this discovery, the site's particular history, as the motive for the design: hundreds of years of history were translated into an aluminium weave for the façade. The design was flexible: the pattern was adjustable to an extreme degree for when programme components became more specific at a later stage. So the design was also strategic: by making 'weaving flaws', it was possible to guide and facilitate a programmatic diversity. In Chinese building processes as opposed to those in the Netherlands, structural alterations were possible until an exceptionally late stage, enabling a variety of spaces that could include even such special functions as gardens on the upper floors.

The client was visibly convinced: 'This design is very, very creative!' The marketing specialists present spontaneously brainstormed about slogans such as 'Silk comfort in an international landmark'. After the meeting, in the car back to the office, Mr Chen grinned again: 'It *is* a Big One!' I grinned back: 'And a Modern International Landmark!'

But my agenda went beyond what had been described in the presentation. By rendering the history of the site in abstract terms and imperiously projecting it onto the surroundings, the project attempted to enable a certain continuity between the site and the surrounding city, and thus offer an alternative to the characteristic radical fault lines in the evolution of Chinese cities.

Despite my enthusiasm, Amsterdam was reserved about the project. They didn't hold it in the same high regard as I held it in Beijing. And from a Dutch perspective, they were perfectly right: after all, it was 'just a façade'.

So why did this project intrigue me the way it did?

It was because, from a combined Dutch-Chinese perspective, it was such a topical project in Chinese building practice. And because there was space, unlike in the case of the project with the Royal Palace of Amsterdam as a five-star hotel on an artificial island in the Yellow Sea. There was space and that space had to be explored, even if it was only to experience in practice what was possible and what was not.

But I also realized that through my way of assessing the project, I had never been as remote from the Netherlands as I was now.

6. Reflection

BEING COPIED IS BEING A MASTER
Beijing, 2008, a month prior to the Olympic Games

Work had stopped and laughter resounded through the office. From behind various desks, my colleagues looked at me with wide eyes. It was the pinnacle of what, at the very least, could be called a surreal day.

That morning, Ms Jia and I had been to a scale-model company to examine the progress being made on a model for a presentation. The principal of the project in question had recommended the company to us. After asking around, we found the appropriate building and as we approached the entrance, I looked up. The building was old and anonymous, similar to thousands of others in Beijing. We took the lift to the fifth floor and on exiting the lift, I had an eye-rubbing experience.

We had arrived in a cheap copy of our old office. More or less everything was recognizable: the floor, the shape of the reception desk and the lines of illumination in the ceiling! I shared my excitement with Ms Jia, took out my camera and asked the girl behind the desk whether her boss was around. She was visibly shocked by my agitation and answered that no one was there. Then she turned to Ms Jia to ask her what was going on. Ms Jia told her candidly that the design of their lobby was a copy of our old lobby. And that had been a NEXT design.

The receptionist became nervous. She asked which company we were from and with whom we had an appointment. After Ms Jia's explanation, in an ultimate attempt to divert our attention, she immediately phoned the project leader dealing with our scale model. While I took several photos of the lobby, the project leader hastened toward us, looking first at me, then at Ms Jia and then at the receptionist. All three then looked earnestly at me, with pursed lips, waiting for what was going to happen.

The whole scene was surreal, too improbable to put into words. So I just smiled.

When the project leader saw my smile, a smile spread across his face too. We greeted one another amicably and after a brief conversation in which he subtly fathomed my objectives he reached the conclusion that I had no evil intentions. Once his distrust had disappeared completely, the story behind the copied design became clear. Six months previously, the scale-model company had moved into this building. They had asked a number of construction companies to give a quote for the interior including, as it happened, the company that had built ours. The foreman of our construction company had shown a book with reference projects, and from that book the head of the scale-model company had 'chosen' our interior. 'He liked it very much!' Ms Jia translated the information for me. She repeated: 'He liked it very much!' as if we should be proud that the design had been so widely appreciated as a product.

Back at the office I tried to find out from our works foreman if other instances of this kind of copying had occurred. 'Maybe ...', he joked, but silence reigned when I asked where these copies could be found and what kind of companies were involved.

Still in a strange form of ecstasy, I showed the photos of the copied interior to my Chinese colleagues. Most of them just smiled. Mr Jiang didn't restrict himself to a smile and concluded out loud in English: 'Being copied is being a master!' After my bow of gratitude, the entire office floor resounded with laughter.

CHANGE

It was impossible to describe it in any other way: it had been a disastrous day. To start with, a crucial discussion of 'Xidan 110' had been planned. 'Xidan 110' was one of our long-running projects, a multi-use shopping mall of more than 180,000 square metres. The discussion was crucial because we were about to meet the new developer.

Xidan and Wangfujing have been the major shopping streets in Beijing for centuries. A Chinese colleague once typified Wangfujing as a destination for national and international tourists. Xidan is one of the most popular areas for young people in Beijing. 'We're building in the heart of China', our client had remarked. Only a few hundred metres away lay Zhongnanhai, the headquarters of the Communist Party and the residence of president Hu Jintao.

Our first sketch for the project was more than three years old. When I visited the site for the first time, an enormous hole had been dug for the subterranean car park. Various architectural offices, including Chinese, Japanese and American ones, had worked on the project. After construction had commenced, the client had begun to doubt the most recent proposal and had asked us to make two new ones.

Because the project was already under way, our input was largely limited to a design for the façade. But instead of taking the exhortation to 'make it beautiful' as our stepping-off point, our proposals concentrated on facilitating possible changes to the programme and organization. The starting point was a façade design that could guide such changes. In addition, there was the strong intention on our part to respond to the immediate environment, which was a mass of commercial buildings and a cacophony of forms and advertising.

Despite these intentions, during the presentation we had placed the emphasis on argumentation that is more appreciated in China. I presented the proposal chosen by the client as 'a crystal volume over which a curtain of façade columns had been draped'. The idea of draping was reinforced by the elliptical excisions in the 'curtain of façade columns'. Where the glass volume was visible, It was possible to design special-function spaces such as sky lobbies, lofts and LED frontages at places where the glass volume was visible. And the design was flexible: the ultimate form of the ellipses could be decided at an extremely late stage in the building process.

In the next three years, the design proved to be sufficiently robust to survive the switch from shopping mall to department store, back to shopping mall and then to a combination of both. It was also capable of facilitating the changes from office to hotel apartments and back to offices. The design combined various suggestions made by the client based on national and international trips she had made 'to gather ideas'. It was solid enough to meet the specific conditions of a potential Japanese buyer who wished to give the frontage of the first five storeys colours customary in Japan for 'this kind of building'. The design had been positively appraised by a feng shui master and was compatible with the ideas of a Taiwanese interior architect. The design was also strong enough to 'resist' four marketing offices, each of which, with the best of intentions, wished to 'improve' it in marketing terms. And the design had survived countless 'other ideas' advanced by other architectural offices. It had outlived delays brought on by negotiations with local residents who were due to occupy a new housing block a stone's throw away. It had survived the run-up to and building shutdown during the Olympic Games, as well as the first signs of the global financial crisis.

Exactly half the building had been completed. But that seemed to be the limit. The client's liquid assets had evaporated. The work in progress was sold as it was to a different developer.

And we were on our way to that new developer earlier that day.

I looked out of the car window as Beijing glided past us. We had received no agenda for the meeting and we had no idea what news we could expect.

Half an hour later, we were received in a vast meeting room. The project manager of the new client was surprised by our arrival – surprised in a way that smacked of miscommunication. He told us that some thirty marketing specialists would be brainstorming about 'positioning this project in the market'. But we were 'welcome too'. It was a subtle indication that no input was expected from us. Mr Chen said, in a friendly way, that we were very busy and would keenly await the outcome. 'We don't sit second rows in meetings', he said with conviction as we stepped into the lift once more.

Back in the car, I challenged a Chinese colleague to let his intuition speak on this new development. 'Maybe this will be difficult', was his reaction. 'These specialists have to show their work, effort and knowledge to their bosses. *So they have to change the design*'. That remark echoed through my head as I reviewed his sentence word by word.

By coincidence, we drove past the building site of the 'Big One', the project with the aluminium weave façade. The sale of apartments would commence shortly. Three weeks previously, we had approved a mock-up of the façade and construction was scheduled to begin in two months. While I was still deliberating on the possible impact of a necessary 'change' to Xidan, I stared at the building site. Workmen were busy installing renderings on enormous billboards. I jumped a mile when I saw a rendering that had already been installed: without informing us, they had modified the façade! The weave pattern had disappeared to make way for a grey stone front.

'Jiude bu qu, xinde bu lai', mumbled the Chinese colleague who had seen the same thing. 'If the old doesn't go, the new won't come', I translated into Dutch out loud. 'It doesn't matter', Mr Chen offered in English; he had observed my agitation while driving.

He had made increasing use of this argument in more and more projects under construction. Invariably a second sentence followed, to reinforce the perspective: 'Nobody will care about it!'

Just as in so much of what Mr Chen said, there was probably a core of truth to it. But this didn't weigh up against another truth: that *I* certainly cared about it. Mr Chen was undoubtedly aware of this, but he also knew that by now I had realized that the architect's reach had its limits.

'The Big One' was a lost project and, to my astonishment, we were on the brink of losing Xidan as well.

'What can we do?' I asked Mr Chen out loud.

'We wait patiently...', came the familiar answer.

I sensed we might have to do that for quite a long time.

THE ARCHITECT'S REACH

In a private room in a top-class restaurant, twelve of us sat round an enormous round table bearing the finest food imaginable. The first bottles of 'baijiu', Chinese rice wine, had already been emptied in toasts. We were celebrating the signing of a new contract.

'Maybe, architecture in Europe is more advanced', someone said.

I qualified this by stating that every simple comparison was speculative. Architecture in China was difficult to compare with architecture in Europe. I mentioned the differences in scale, speed and budget.

My argument was well received and was a reason for the client to propose another toast. He then smilingly asked that if that were the case, how could I guarantee that a concept would be implemented the way I had envisioned it.

The question was a rhetorical one. The client knew better than I did that much of the influence on a project was beyond the architect's reach.

'By being patient and by visiting building sites as often as possible', I responded.

The answer was rewarded by proposing a new 'ganbei', another bottoms up.

'He likes building sites?' the project manager opposite me remarked in surprise to no one in particular. He then said that at his former employer's they had once worked with an Italian architect whom they referred to among themselves as a 'strange guy'. The project manager laughed as he recalled that the architect was always complaining. He imitated an Italian–English accent as best he could: 'My Italian shoes get dirty on Chinese construction sites!' I laughed too, but without really sharing the humour.

In my view, building sites were magical places because ideas were put into practice there. I enjoyed visiting them, in the first place to keep as much control as possible over the construction but also because they offered outstanding opportunities to learn.

Pretty soon after my arrival in China, I realized that 'less is more' had a different significance there from what I had learned as a student. Chinese low-tech was the fitting answer to what Chinese colleagues described as 'over-engineering'. Thinking in complex terms and advancing complex design proposals were, I think, the first pitfalls that Western architects encountered in China.

For instance, at one building site I had once stared for a full fifteen minutes in fascination at a staircase being installed. Construction workers were manoeuvring a landing upwards with a lever. Someone shouted 'xia!', which can be roughly translated as 'now!', and a welder who was squatting nearby sprang into action in an attempt to fix the landing into position.

Another time, I watched in astonishment as holes for foundation piles were dug by hand. Those digging literally dug themselves in, while others winched up the baskets of earth.

Once I was witness on a building site to a play of forces normally hidden from view. It was my only experience of an angry Chinese client, and the limits of the architect's reach became crystal clear as a result.

Ms Qin and I had turned up unannounced at the building site of the five towers project. To our great annoyance, the first signs that the façade design had been adjusted soon began to manifest themselves. The planned transition in four stages from stone below to glass in the towers had been reduced to two. We also began to doubt whether the designed elevation detail would be implemented.

'Can I see the drawings?' I asked the project manager, via Ms Qin.

'Perhaps the drawings are not here right now,' she translated the response.

'We're at the construction site, how can the drawings not be here?' I replied in Chinese, irritated. Ms Qin appeared to appraise the situation differently and gave me an uncomfortable look.

Back at the office I showed photos of the addition to our project manager. He confirmed my suspicions: 'You know, the client asked us to change the drawings'. Almost immediately, he tried to change the subject: 'About the elevation detail – now we have two designs, an *up-market* one and a *more economical* design.' He probably didn't know that I wasn't even aware of the existence of a *more economical* detail.

'So many – too many – projects are falling victim to *more economical* variations!' I responded loudly.

I received no answer to my question as to why this change had not been communicated to me, but I could easily guess it. I had not been informed 'in order to protect me from bad news'.

I printed the photos and the original details and wrote a memo to Mrs Hu, who was not at the office at that moment. I left everything with her assistant, with the announcement that it was urgent. The next day she confirmed, through the assistant, that the changes had been made at the client's wishes.

At my request, the project manager sent a fax to the client. It emphasized that two crucial changes were on the point of being carried out and these would substantially influence the design. There was no reaction from the client.

Some time later, I visited the building site again in connection with a previously arranged appointment, this time in the company of the client. We made our way amongst hundreds of construction workers to a number of mock-ups of façade material. I asked, en passant, if he had read our fax. He looked at me and then at his project manager in a questioning way.

While our project manager spontaneously explained the content of the fax, the client appeared to become furious at his own project manager. 'Why haven't I seen that fax?' he hissed. Our project manager gave him a copy.

As if struck by lightning, the client's project manager began to explain that the planning schedule was very tight. If they wished to meet the deadline for completion, it was necessary, according to the foreman, to 'simplify' some parts of the project. So the foreman had put forward a number of proposals and the project manager had no other choice than to agree to them. 'The deadline was very important', was his conclusion.

During the project manager's explanation the client seemed to become even angrier. Waving the fax in his clenched fist, he repeated the question: 'Why haven't I seen this fax?'

The project manager was silent, let his head fall on his chest and stared at the ground. Dozens of construction workers had stopped work and were gaping at the spectacle.

The client read the fax once more and then asked his project manager just how far things could still be adjusted. 'The contractor... the deadline...', the project manager stammered, avoiding the client's gaze as much as possible.

We crossed the building site in silence, while I became increasingly annoyed with the client's project manager. He had fallen seriously short in his responsibilities, with the result that a project of 200,000 square metres had acquired a completely different look than had been anticipated.

On our way back to the office, I asked our project manager how it was possible that a client could be internally sidetracked in this way. 'Two reasons', was the answer. I could guess the first: 'To protect him from bad news.'

The second left me speechless. 'The foreman is our client's elder brother.'

I immediately felt sympathy for the client's project manager. His powerlessness made me feel powerless too.

ONE STEP AT A TIME

'You are experiencing China, but do you have the idea that you are understood in China?' The question was put by Peter de Winter of 010 Publishers, and was the reaction to my draft manuscript entitled 'How to Build in China?'. Previously, during a dinner in Amsterdam, I had responded to a similar question by remarking: 'One step at a time is good walking.' The same reply could be given to the converse question: whether or not I understood China. The answer was not exactly clear-cut in either case.

It was during the lunch with Mr Chen, when I had sketched the forum staircases again on a serviette, that I was made aware once and for all of a common intention. Until then, I had struggled relentlessly within Huanyang to get design ambition onto the joint agenda. It was a struggle against internal and external hierarchy.

An example of this was the 'Big One' project with the five high-rise blocks, for which the façade had to be designed in less than an hour. After the first discussion with the client I wished to adjust the façade of the central tower, the hotel. There had been simply too little time to produce a good initial proposal. But no one had understood this at Huanyang, in view of the fact that the client had not requested any adjustment. Even worse, perhaps I would be changing a design that the client actually found 'very good'. In the end Huanyang was convinced and we made a new proposal, which we presented as 'another option'. The client was surprised by this initiative and accepted the new proposal. Although Huanyang never did understand the necessity to create a new façade design, I regarded it in retrospect as a small joint architectural triumph.

I regarded my struggle to place design ambition on the joint agenda as an 'unconscious internal struggle' because I only became aware of it after the lunch with Mr Chen. I considered the outcome as an 'absolute awareness of each other's intentions' because Mr Chen after seeing the sketch on the napkin had resolutely said: 'Let's try it one more time!'

On his initiative, we therefore opted for a common architectural goal. And if I were NEXT, and Mr Chen were Huanyang, NEXT and Huanyang had never understood one another as well as they did then.

Was Mr Chen an exception? No, was my firm conclusion.

Mr Jiang had told me a year earlier that he had known me a long time. I didn't understand what he was referring to. He grinned and mentioned the lecture on 'The Image of Metropolis' at Tsinghua University in 2002. 'I was there and I listened to your story.'

I was surprised. 'What did you think about it?' I quickly asked.

'Years ago I thought: who gave these architects all that money to travel the world and take all these pictures?' 'And what do you think now?' I responded. 'The same thing!' he grinned.

I grinned back, not having expected any other answer.

Was there such as thing as being aware of one another's intentions at the very highest level?

I thought about another discussion I had had recently with Mr Yang. He had again emphasized his view of things: 'In China there is only one way, the way of development. Stagnation is decline!' Armed with this ambition, Huanyang had outgrown NEXT in giant leaps in the period of our collaboration. And not only outgrown us in terms of size but also in the nature of that ambition. Totally self-confident, Mr Yang talked about his dream: 'A position among the top ten greatest architectural offices in the world.'

He looked at me in an attempt to discover whether we shared a common agenda here. He saw the doubt on my face. That too was an awareness of one another's intentions.

NEXT and Huanyang: 'Sleeping in one bed, dreaming two dreams'? We had articulated our two dreams. NEXT dreamt about '*How* to build in China?' Huanyang dreamt about 'How to build *more* in China?'

> 1,000,000 M²

China was celebrating a national holiday, a 'golden week', and I was in Vietnam, on a bus heading to Cambodia. The journey would take the whole day. An e-mail from Amsterdam came in on my phone:

Hello John,
Property magazine is issuing a top 25 of the most productive architectural practices. This year's winner saw 97,500 square metres onto site. Interesting to see how this relates to 'our production'. Could you give me an overview of square metres per project and the year of delivery?
Regards, Marijn

I compared 'our production' to that of 'the most productive practice in the Netherlands'. Since our arrival in China we had been involved to a greater or lesser extent with more than a million square metres of work in progress. I wondered what our 'production' meant in reality.

As the bus drove through the Vietnamese landscape, I tried to order my thoughts. The five years in China had unconsciously made me a numbers fetishist and I now shared my Chinese colleagues' interest in quantities, sizes, heights, lengths, depths and volumes. In Amsterdam, in appreciating any new project, the *type* of commission was decisive for the degree of enthusiasm at a new project. In China, I had added a new motive for enthusiasm: size.

In my mind's eye I saw the many building boards in Beijing displaying the frequently gold-coloured superlatives: 'The world's tallest atrium', 'Asia's longest building' or 'China's largest glass curtain wall'. In China it seemed as if quantity was enough to guarantee quality: the larger a thing was or the more there was of it, the greater its importance.

This also applied to an architect's status: the more square metres realized, the more respect an architect in China enjoyed. That was why Huanyang invariably began a presentation by mentioning the amount of work it had had built. This way, it was implicitly made clear that it was a 'powerful company' and therefore that the 'possible risks' for clients were minimal. In other words, unlike in the Netherlands, references bore little relationship to architecture per se.

The bus wound its way through small villages and paddy fields. I recalled the New Year's gathering of a few years ago, when the prize for the best project had gone to the largest project.

I remembered my first discussion with the Chinese developer at IBM. The developer presented his portfolio: millions of square metres of building volume here, hundred metre tall towers there, etc etc. The Americans at IBM appeared to be sceptical about the ease with which the developer zapped through the images, while the numbers flew about. I began NEXT's introduction by stating that the task was 'quality' rather than 'quantity'. The Americans seemed immediately put at ease and nodded in approval. The client's Chinese employees looked at me with a smile that I couldn't quite decode at the time.

By now the bus was driving through just paddy fields. The colours here were so much more intense than in Beijing. If 'quality' to us really prevailed above 'quantity', I thought to myself, how should we assess our own 'square metres'? Put another way, was building volume genuinely the most a Western architect could hope to achieve in China?

Resolutely rejecting this notion, I looked back at the mini revolution around the forum staircase. The possible added value this gave far exceeded the temptation of quantitative superlatives. From this point of view, a small project could be much more interesting than any 'Big One'.

I smiled and doubted whether Huanyang had reached the same conclusion. I saw the face of Mr Chen before me, and the excitement with which he always spoke about 'Big Ones'. The difference began right at the start, with the idea of a 'working concept'. To Huanyang, the distinction between 'something that works' and 'something that doesn't work' seemed to be a measure of the client's final choice. In other words, a concept 'worked' if a project was executed. But, from that viewpoint, more concepts 'worked' than I could ever have hoped for.

The bus stopped at traffic lights and dozens of Vietnamese vendors surrounded us. It was a fascinating spectacle: everything a traveller could possibly require was sold through the small bus windows. The lights changed to green. Spluttering and stuttering, the bus got under way again.

What did I think about the quality of the built results? Was I proud? I was surprised at my own questions. In the Netherlands these questions would never arise since they would only ever get a positive answer. I believe the question was only valid because of my increasing experiences with 'blue eyes staring at China'.

I remembered an Italian student of architecture who was visiting the office in Beijing. Since his arrival in China, he had been systematically photographing errors in architectural detailing, and proudly showed me his collection on the screen of his camera.

I also recalled a discussion with a Dutch architect who was on excursion in Shanghai and was annoyed by the quality of building in China: 'I would start a sealant factory here.'

I thought about more Western assessments of architecture in China. And then I thought about the way many of my Chinese colleagues reacted to such assessments.

Essentially, it was about the architect's accountability. In the Netherlands, I shared the Western need for accountability to the discipline itself. But such a need seemed utterly unknown to many Chinese colleagues. For example, any possible discrepancy between the concept and the detailing was much less problematic to Huanyang than it was to me. After all, only a client could take financial decisions and thus was ultimately responsible for final choices as regards materials, details and the quality of the contractors.

When did a critical attitude morph into an opportunistic one? Once again it was a Western question and it soon got a Western response.

Didn't the border between the critical and the opportunistic lie where 'exploiting a situation to the maximum' changed into acceptance of an architectural fate, into 'surrendering to the almost unavoidable encroachment on quality in the Western sense of the word'?

And again I thought of Mr Chen. After we had prematurely left the crucial meeting to discuss Xidan, he said out of the blue that architectural decisions should only be taken through us 'and not in meetings where we don't take any part in.' To my great surprise, a few days later he added something that would have been inconceivable in the past: 'The architect's most important task is not saving money but finding value.' We had gone a long way together, and his remark was diametrically opposed to the one he had made a few years previously: 'The architect's most important task is to save the client money!'

The sheer number of stalls along the road indicated that we were approaching the Cambodian border. The bus driver called out something in Vietnamese and people in the bus began to gather up their luggage.

Our projects that had been or were being implemented – our 'production' – were the first in a quest for an architecture created *because of* rather than *in spite of* Chinese conditions. This quest was consciously conducted as a collaborative effort, from the inside, and was nurtured by the added value of acknowledging as many perspectives, similarities and differences as possible.

The bus stopped and everyone got ready to alight.

In the queue at customs I replied to Amsterdam with an update of our list of Chinese projects.

The customs official gave me a stern look while I handed over my passport.

'Profession please?' he asked gruffly.

'Architect!' I answered with pride.

THE FILM, NOT THE PICTURE

Weeks later, in an old warehouse in New York, at a meeting to discuss a Chinese project for an American client, I received a telephone call.

'What were your motives for becoming active in China?'

The question was posed by a journalist who wanted a preliminary interview before she came to Beijing. Looking out over the Hudson, I considered a possible answer. My original reason for *becoming* active in China was less interesting than my current reasons for *being* active. I was in doubt.

Chinese colleagues were becoming increasingly critical of 'foreign architectural offices' in China. According to them, many of the foreigners were there 'only to earn money'. When I articulated my surprise that they shared their criticism with me, I received the response: 'You're different because you are *investing* in China.'

I was taken off guard: 'Why do you think I'm *investing* in China?'

I interpreted the answer as a compliment: 'You're investing because you've been living a long time in China and you're trying to understand Chinese culture and Chinese people better. You're a friend!'

If I were investing in China, then it was exceptionally profitable: my world increasingly seemed to be transcending all its original limits.

With these thoughts at the back of my mind, I told the journalist the story of an architectural office driven by a constant search for boundaries. This search was fed by current developments, other disciplines and, more concretely, the context of projects. The findings gained in this search had been embedded in the concepts that our architecture wished to represent: conditions for added value, in both use and perception, for the user and for the surroundings. Our presence in China was a direct consequence of this search.

A few weeks later, the journalist and I were walking across a building site in Beijing. While she laboriously avoided the many scaffolding tubes lying around, she looked in fascination at the hundreds of construction workers at work there. All at once she asked: 'To what extent do you feel responsible for the construction workers here?'

I felt a confrontational discussion looming.

I told her that there were an estimated 700 million peasants in China. Around 200 million of them had moved to the cities because there was no work in rural areas. It was the largest population shift in the history of humanity. A large share of these migrant workers were employed in factories, in 'the workplace of the world'. Another part worked in the untold number of building sites in the metropolises. These former peasants were the engine of the economic miracle that was now happening in China.

Because I realized that she was probably aware of all this, I ended with the question: 'In what respect do you mean "responsible"? And in what respect, seen from the perspective of an architect?'

'Social responsibility, for example', she replied.

I referred to a brief discussion we had had with a construction worker a little earlier. He told us proudly where he came from: the Province of Shaanxi. With a smile he went on to say that he had been working in Beijing for years and was very contented. In his village, there were simply no opportunities to earn a living. And by working in Beijing he could offer his family a future. In two years, his son would do his 'gaokao', China's entrance exam for higher education.

The journalist waited to hear what was coming next.

I continued: Of course, many things were invisible to foreigners in China, but people such as this construction worker from Shaanxi were a large part of my reality.

It irritated me that I had automatically opted to go on the defensive. 'So you are proud of the unemployment relief work?' was the question. Unemployment relief work at what cost?, I immediately thought.

The question touched upon my previous dilemmas regarding 'nail houses'. I thought of Mr Guo, who had once resolutely dismissed such dilemmas by declaring that Westerners systematically underestimated the Chinese capacity to adapt. And of Lao Qing, who typified Westerners as 'ignorant' when it came to such Chinese subjects as nail houses. If I were to believe them, there were golden opportunities to turn an eviction into a 'golden day'. It was trade and, in negotiation processes, strategic thinking reigned supreme. Even foreign media attention could be deployed for this purpose, said Mr Guo much to my surprise.

In the meantime, Huan had gained his Ph.D. by completing his research on alternative models for expropriation. I was most curious about his findings, but he regretted that he couldn't share them with me. His research was in Chinese and not meant for foreign eyes. The subject was an internal Chinese matter and was about improving the situation from a number of perspectives – politics, the academic world and the market. End of story.

Families had once lived on our building sites too. Thousands of construction workers were now at work on these sites. Did this mean I could now accept what was still fundamentally unacceptable to a Westerner, despite what Mr Guo and Lao Qing said about it? Was unemployment relief work an argument?

I replied: 'It is unemployment relief work for thousands of people who previously had to survive on less than a dollar a day. Our presence in China is contributing to the opportunities for them and their families to change their future. Yes, I am proud of the unemployment relief work, but not of the relief work alone. Proud of enabling the opportunities for change would be more accurate.'

A little later I continued: 'To the fixed gaze of a Westerner it is difficult to predict what will happen in China. For that reason it is important to look beyond the picture and at the film depicting China's transformation. Sometimes you can see change in it, sometimes you can't and sometimes almost but not quite.'

One aspect at least had changed for good at the office since our arrival here: the world-view of my Chinese colleagues. It had irrevocably transcended the borders of China. And, I realized then, my worldview had irrevocably transcended the borders of Western reality.

I looked at the journalist. Instead of a response, I was asked if I would translate a brief interview with another construction worker.

MY WAY BACK TO CHINA

'Would you be willing to give a lecture on your experiences in China?' I had someone from the Netherlands Architecture Institute in Rotterdam on the telephone, following up an unanswered e-mail. 'At the office in Amsterdam they said that you're not in Beijing. And that you were probably pretty busy?! I'd still like to know whether you're interested...'

I was with Michel Schreinemachers, a partner from Amsterdam, in Shenyang, a metropolis in North-east China. We were to spend two weeks 'on site' collaborating with the Local Design Institute on a competition for an international exhibition centre of 600,000 square metres. We had been there for just one week and were faced with an almost impossible task. Other offices had been allocated four weeks, whereas we had been invited to take part two weeks before the deadline. Fatigued by a serious shortage of sleep and at the mercy of utterly chaotic processes, I wondered what new insights into China this experience could possibly bring.

Of course I was interested, was my reply.

A few weeks later I landed at Schiphol Amsterdam airport. Exiting the terminal toward Schiphol Plaza, I stopped for a moment at the site of my graduation project. My thoughts took me back ten years to the process of graduating and my quest for ways to begin a design. A design began with finding space, space to create, I now concluded.

The next day I was on my way to Rotterdam, to the Netherlands Architecture Institute. I entered the hall where 'The Image of the Metropolis' had been exhibited a few years ago. I continued on to the auditorium where a member of the NAi staff was waiting for me. While my laptop was connected, I looked around the still empty hall.

My eyes paused at the spot where I had sat at the conference on China, more than five years ago. It was there I had said to a former colleague at NEXT: 'That's where we have to be.' Now I occupied the place where the keynote speakers had stood, communicating their experiences and their ideas on China.

I left the auditorium, looking for coffee as a remedy for the jetlag. Just outside the auditorium I remembered a moment just after the lecture at the opening of 'The Image of Metropolis'. Professor Carel Weeber had critically remarked that we had allowed ourselves to be too surprised by what we had encountered during the world trip. I hadn't known how to react at the time, but now, while walking to the bar to order coffee, I reasoned that it was just that surprise that had given me energy all those years. Looking was not the same as seeing. For this reason, surprise was a great virtue; it enabled you to see more sharply.

The auditorium filled up slowly. While I was announced I looked around the hall once again. Victoria, the brilliant Chinese girl who had gone off to study in Delft, had said she would attend the lecture, but I couldn't identify her in the half-lit hall.

There was applause, which meant I could start. The first slide I presented was of a Chinese building site. I was standing with Ms Jia amidst the chaos. We were talking to the contractor's project manager. 'This has been my life for the past five years', I began. 'In this world I have tried to discover structure and direction. In this world I have tried to find and enable mutual understanding.'

One of the following slides was a group photo with Huanyang. Almost 200 people were posing for the photo. Even on the large projection screen, the faces were almost too small to distinguish. But I recognized them; every face had a story and was a part of the continuous dialogue I had been seeking in China.

I directed my laser pen to the group and pointed out Mr Chen. I explained that Mr Chen had defined my 'first China' – the stepping-off point of my first interpretations. Then I indicated Mr Guo and, with a smile, talked about his unshakeable pride in Chinese culture. Then I spoke about Mr Jiang who, in my view, represented the idea that nothing was impossible in China, regardless of how small the chance appeared to be.

Then I proceeded in leaps and bounds through our Chinese projects. It was a journey through the experience called 'China', a journey through risks and uncertainties but also through opportunities and ambitions.

After forty minutes I finished my lecture by inviting the audience to put any questions they had. And there were enough of these, particularly questions expressing surprise. I had not expected such questions, and being confronted with these transported me back to eight years earlier, when I had held a lecture on 'The Image of Metropolis' at Tsinghua University in Beijing. The questions I had received there made me realize that I had completely misjudged my audience and offered me an insight into a world entirely different from my own. The questions I now fielded had a similar effect, the difference being that this 'entirely different world' was my own world of five years ago.

My reality seemed to split in two, and all at once I realized that I was wholly immersed in another world.

A few days later at Schiphol, I still couldn't fully qualify this feeling. After a quick glance at my graduation site, I vanished into the anonymous world of aviation, back to China.

YOU CAN'T CHANGE CHINA, CHINA CHANGES YOU

Back in China, my world moved into the fast lane. We acquired new projects throughout China, in such places as Hainan, Sichuan, Fujian, Hebei, Henan and Inner Mongolia. I had the feeling that I was permanently on board a plane flying to ever new meetings and presentations.

Successes and disappointments succeeded one another at a rapid rate.

For example, I received a phone call about 'Xidan'. The new client had been working on a new proposal with an American architectural office for almost a year. The design was due to be presented to the local authorities and I was invited as an 'external specialist'. It was a crucial presentation; the mock-ups were already installed on the façade.

The atmosphere in the meeting room was electric. Mr Chen translated the client's advice to the Chinese–American architect who was due to hold the presentation: 'First, always take the response of the government leader into account. Second, keep him satisfied at all times. Third, if you see he doesn't like what you're saying, always change the subject.' I broke into a broad smile and waited patiently.

The design process was the theme of the presentation. Dozens of proposals pieced together what it was that the client wanted. Then came the harshest condemnation that I had heard in China until then: 'The government leader thinks the design is very ugly!' All the designs were rejected and a year's work went up in smoke. The issue of who determined what was 'dust and mosquitoes' in architecture seemed to have been decided at a stroke: this privilege lay with the government to an even greater extent than with a regular client.

What an opportunity, was the thought that reverberated in my mind. A little later, I was asked whether it would be possible to make three new designs in the coming week. A week later we presented four designs to the government: three new ones and – the highest stakes of all – our own original design from years before. The original design was chosen without a moment's hesitation. 'We wait patiently', Mr Chen had said a year ago. And that patience had now been rewarded.

But euphoria soon made way for an entirely different feeling.

We had been working non-stop on a project of some 400,000 square metres in Shijiazhuang, a metropolis to the south-west of Beijing. For the first presentation the client had had us picked up and dropped at an impressive building that unmistakably bore the label of 'government'. When we entered it I was informed that 'something had changed': I would hold the presentation for the Head of the Shijiazhuang Urban Planning Bureau.

We were shown into a large meeting room where a range of specialists and the client's general manager were waiting for us. The A0 panels with renderings were placed against the walls and, when everyone was seated, a distinguished-looking woman entered. She was the head of the Urban Planning Bureau. The client's general manager requested us to start the presentation. The client himself arrived in the room halfway through the presentation. I was struck by a dilemma: this confirmed that the presentation was important but also that I was unaware of the client's preference and agenda.

After the presentation, he asked the head of the Urban Planning Bureau for her opinion.

'How tall will this tower be?' she asked.
'A hundred metres', I replied in Chinese.
'A hundred metres', she repeated, while studying the renderings concentratedly. She looked at the client and said: 'We have so many towers that are a hundred metres tall, can't this one be much taller? And the location is so very good, can't this project become very, very special?'
I noticed that I was now sitting bolt upright in my chair. 'Very, very special', echoed through my mind.
A week later I presented a new proposal to the client.
Back in Beijing, it turned out that an e-mail had been sent to the office that had not been intended for us. The e-mail referred to projects we knew nothing about and announced a 'new' project. The astonishing fact was that our new design – the design that the client envisioned – had been sent as an attachment. Someone at the client's office had blundered by sending the e-mail to us instead of to a different architectural office altogether.
This, too, was China, I concluded. It was the 'dark side' of China, as one Chinese colleague described the experience. There was nothing more to say on the matter, was my response.

A few weeks later I stated with conviction: 'In China, if you see an opportunity you need to seize it!'
Mr Chen and I were in discussion about an Urban Planning Museum with a surface area of 17,000 square metres in the Chaoyang district of Beijing. Mr Chen was reconsidering his own statement that I had just quoted to him. Huanyang had doubts about entering this competition because our rivals had had far more experience with this type of brief. But it was a dream project: three old factories in the middle of the largest park in Beijing were to be transformed into a museum and a theatre. Huanyang allowed itself to be convinced, and our underlying intention was to preserve as much history as possible: details, materials and even slogans from the Cultural Revolution that had been painted on the walls. We envisaged the space between the factories as a central access zone. This 'T-space' was to be an indeterminate area where, say, temporary exhibitions or banquets could be held. Two independent routes, one for VIPs and one for regular users, ensured maximum flexibility of use.
The crucial moment in the design process came with the design of the programme for placing outside the envelope of the factories. My incli-

nation was to position the programme on top of the factories beneath an undulating roof. The formal language contrasted with the old factories and reinforced the idea of old versus new and history versus future, themes that would be foregrounded in the Urban Planning Museum.

Huanyang immediately suggested the idea of a 'lucky cloud concept'. Mr Chen referred to the Zhou Dynasty and said that clouds had many positive meanings in China. For instance, they represented heaven, happiness and 'never ending fortune'. I reacted with a smile: 'Dutch concepts are about conditions, Chinese concepts about form'. Without waiting for a reply, I continued: 'Let's make a lucky cloud building!'

After the first presentation for the local government, a presentation for 'national masters' followed a week later. One jury member confronted me in fluent English: 'Are you making these shapes just to make spectacular shapes?' His second question was a sharp one: 'If not, then what's the *meaning*?' I talked about the dialogue between old and new. Then I referred to the positive significance of the 'lucky cloud concept'. I stated that the design would be ready once these two underlying premises had been reconciled.

The jury member then repeated in Chinese his questions and my answer to the rest of the jury and the public. To my surprise he concluded that 'this architect was right'.

An hour after all the offices had presented their ideas we were called back to the presentation room. The choice had fallen on us, unanimously. We were given nine months to complete the project. And nine months later the Urban Planning Museum enjoyed a festive opening.

The feeling I had experienced after the lecture at the Netherlands Architecture Institute now dated from more than a year ago.

So what had happened since I arrived back in China?

I had surrendered once and for all. Voluntarily and out of conviction I had softened my original ideas about good and bad. I could now freely combine rational thought with irrational design decisions.

Paradoxical though it may sound, this gave me a firmer footing than ever before on the often ambivalent Chinese soil.

Lao Qing was right: 'You can't change China, China changes you.'

Epilogue

NEXT Architects Amsterdam, 2010

'Are you aware of the risks?'

I responded without really thinking about the question: 'What do you mean, risks?'

'A book is a slow medium, many of your findings are probably already out of date.'

Schreinemachers took a sip of wine. We were in Eindhoven, at the prize-giving ceremony of the Dutch Design Awards 2010. Two NEXT projects had been nominated, including the project with the forum staircases. It was as strange as it was remarkable that a project carried out so far from the Dutch context had been appreciated as 'outstanding Dutch Design'.

'It's a moment frozen in time, so of course much of it will be out of date', I replied. 'But why is that a risk? I haven't spelt out any truths, if anything I may have taken the edge off them', I continued.

As this book acquired more concrete shape, everyone at NEXT began to react in their own particular way. And with that, our joint China experience took on a new dynamic of its own.

Schreinemachers hoped to be able 'to cope with the risks of transience'. Reuser seemed briefly in search of 'a possible new architecture, beyond the Western notion of modernity'. Schenk was seeking 'even more information, even more layers that illustrated the communication between Chinese and Western thinking'.

In the meantime, I myself had the idea that the text gave a balanced picture of the experience of our first five years in China. And I was busy with our future in China, rather than with our past.

Huanyang, 2009

'This next step could symbolize the further cooperation between NEXT and Huanyang.' Mrs Hu looked at me with great concentration while she waited for a response.

'Living apart together?' I replied smiling. This was my way of politely turning down her proposal while leaving scope for dialogue.

Shortly after the completion of the Urban Planning Museum, NEXT was faced with an existential dilemma. From a Chinese point of view, the collaboration between Huanyang and NEXT seemed to have become so effective that Huanyang was all set to incorporate NEXT. This 'next step' would be part of an ongoing greater development whereby Huanyang – by now acquired by an American architectural office – had earned a place in the 'world's top ten largest commercial offices'. Mrs Hu saw only advantages: the future brought the opportunity to build in China *more than ever before*. I on the other hand was more aware than ever before of the unbridgeable discrepancy between our different dreams.

'Living apart together?' she repeated my proposal with a smile. I answered in the affirmative. Then I realized that this was the moment at which we as NEXT Beijing were consciously opting for total freedom. Suitably restrained but full of adrenaline, I left Mrs Hu's office soon after, on my way to everything that had all at once become possible. Some time later, we moved into our own office as NEXT. And, together with a new start, this became the first step in our quest for a more selective collaboration with Huanyang.

NEXT architects Beijing, 2009–

'Independence is "oxygen" for development', I stated resolutely. Mr Jiang looked at me in agreement and responded: 'Let's toast again together with Mr Cheng, let's toast to the new contract!' We were celebrating the signing of one of our first independently acquired contracts.

The driving force behind NEXT Beijing is the search for *how* to build in China. For this purpose, Mr Jiang has joined us as China partner, thereby adding a new, critical component. Besides a greater Chinese reality, it has undeniably brought more possible answers within our reach. NEXT Beijing believes it will be able to build *better* as a result.

How and *better* are only two of the many motivations NEXT Beijing and NEXT Amsterdam still share. And it is from these common motivations that NEXT Beijing is evolving both parallel to and independently of NEXT Amsterdam.

This seemingly paradoxical development issues from the difference in dynamics between the Netherlands and China. In short: when I moved from Amsterdam to China, various projects were in the process of being developed in the Netherlands that are now, eight years later, being implemented. In China, our first projects have already been demolished (the Waterstone Sales Center, the first office interior). Other projects have already undergone wholesale modifications (the project with the five towers, the office block on the factory foundations, the 'demo center' for ABB, and 'Xidan'). The difference in dynamics between the Netherlands and China not only results in an essentially different need to design, but also in essentially different designs.

The designs foregrounded in this book ought to be understood from this perspective. They are key projects in the development of the first five years of NEXT Beijing, and represent extremes of the framework within which our work and thought have developed in China. And continue to develop: a number of new projects have been realized in the meantime, dozens of new projects are at the point of being implemented and even more are in preparation.

What they have in common is that they are all, without exception, projects for China, from China. And, borrowing loosely from Confucius: the inherent process of learning, re-learning and un-learning has shaped and is shaping NEXT. Every possible result is an integral part of our character.

And what has happened to the others in the past few years? Three years is a long time in China:
HUAN is now a professor at Tsinghua University
MR CHEN has begun his own architectural office in Beijing
MR ZHEN has also begun his own office
MR GUO has become vice general manager at a large Chinese architectural office
MRS YUAN, VICTORIA has graduated from Delft and works at a Chinese architectural office in Beijing
MR HONG is currently working at an architecture management company
MS JIA has become business development manager at a design office for exhibitions
MS WANG has returned from Dubai to China, and is currently making preparations to emigrate to Canada

MS QIN has become personal assistant to a general manager of a large hotel chain in Beijing

MS WANG lives and works as a Chinese teacher in Perth, Australia

LAO QING continues his tireless quest for differences between the West and China

AND ME? I am still on my way to the world that lies ahead of me.

Acknowledgements

This book is a personal reflection on NEXT Architects' first five years in China, from 2004 to 2009. The fertile ground on which we developed consists of so many meetings and situations. I wish to express my thanks to all those who have contributed to them. There are a number of people I would like to mention by name.

Those beyond the immediate reach of architecture: First of all Patricia: you are one of the foundations on which my China rests. And China is one of our shared foundations. And then my parents, whom I thank for their unremitting trust and support. Beppie Langerak, do you remember advising me more than twenty years ago to study architecture? JJ – I know, gratitude is inappropriate, but still ... thanks for your always unconventional vistas. Lot van Schaik, former Head of the Cultural and Press Section of the Netherlands Embassy in Beijing: thank you for organizing that one dinner in 1999, to which the entire China experience can be traced back. And Lao Qing, my thanks to you for consistently showing me China's richness.

Those within the immediate reach of architecture: A particular debt of thanks goes to the partners of NEXT Amsterdam: Marijn Schenk, Bart Reuser and Michel Schreinemachers. Quite simply, without you there would have been no China for NEXT. China partner Jiang Xiaofei: thank you for your acute mind and for the added value that our differing insights always seem to produce. I thank my colleagues at NEXT Beijing: Huang Ming Xing, Wang Bo, Gao He Song, Wopke Tjipke Schaafstal, Ma Yun Feng, Yu Peng, Chen Long Fei, Sun Yi Meng, Lu Fang, Yin Ya Ling, Jiang Ci Ai, Wei Qi Feng, Wu Ye Long, Liu Xiao Xue, Zhou Hui, Li Xin, Liu Feng Qin, Xu Gang, Yan Bing Liang, Liu Qiao and Ren Shu Guang.

Zhou Huan: my gratitude once more for that first e-mail about the competition for the Olympic Games. And more gratitude still for its impact which you couldn't possibly have foreseen. Hu Rong, we met through coincidence and intuition. Thank you for your trust, which has coloured all those years of collaboration between us. And thanks to you, Yang Hong Wei; you taught me many aspects of life in China, but above all the strength of Chinese pragmatism. Chen Song – I don't know where my thanks should begin, so thank you for everything.

My deep appreciation also goes to my (former) colleagues at Huanyang: Yuan Duo, Jia Yuan, Zhang Rui, Qin Qin, Hu Qin, Wang Xuan, Tong Lin Fang, Guo Zhi Fang, Song Wen Yu, Wang Ling Fang, Wang Bo, Li Gui Feng, Yang Bin, Duo Jing Jing, Yao Peng, Xin Hong, Yang Zhong Hui, Wang Lei, Wang Xuan, Ling Lang, Zhen Zhao Ying, Ma Qin, Cai Xin, Li Jia, Su Yue, Wu Yun, Zhang Yu Hua, Lu Ming, Jiang Nan, Mo Li Sheng, Ye Wei, Shi Mo, Wang Yuan, Xue Hong Lei, Yao Jing Rong, Hong Feng, Yang Bao Li, Qi Geng, Yu Qiang, Xie Bo, Wang Yun and Zhang Zheng.

And a debt of gratitude to you, my friends in China: Bob de Graaf, Michel van Tilborg, Thijs Klinkhamer, Laz Çilinger, Eric Lekahn, Bauke Albada, Henk Schulte Nordholt, Frenk van Eeden, Thijs Cox, Ruud van Winden, Bert Treffers, Martijn Schilte, Willem van de Nes, Daan Roggeveen, Victor Leung, Xia Yuan and Xu An.

And I thank those who held up critical mirrors in front of me when getting this book into production: Peter de Winter, Anne Hoogewoning and, last but certainly not least, Piet Vollaard.

谢谢大家!

John van de Water, Beijing, February 2012

This publication has been made possible by contributions from the Netherlands Foundation for Visual Arts, Design and Architecture, Amsterdam, and the Netherlands Architecture Fund, Rotterdam

When reconstructing the history of China in the chapter two and elsewhere, the author has made use of the following sources: Henk Schulte Nordholt, *De Chinacode ontcijferd*, Amsterdam, 2007; Jonathan D. Spence, *The Search for Modern China*, New York, 1999; Duncan Hewitt, *China: Getting Rich First: A Modern Social History*, 2009; and a variety of internet sources

TEXT EDITING:
Piet Vollaard

TRANSLATION:
George Hall

ENGLISH TEXT EDITING:
John Kirkpatrick

GRAPHIC DESIGN:
Studio Joost Grootens (Joost Grootens and Tine van Wel)

PRINTER:
Lecturis, Eindhoven

© 2012 John van de Water, 010 Publishers, Rotterdam

ISBN 978-90-6450-762-5

www.nextarchitects-china.com
www.nextarchitects.com
www.010.nl

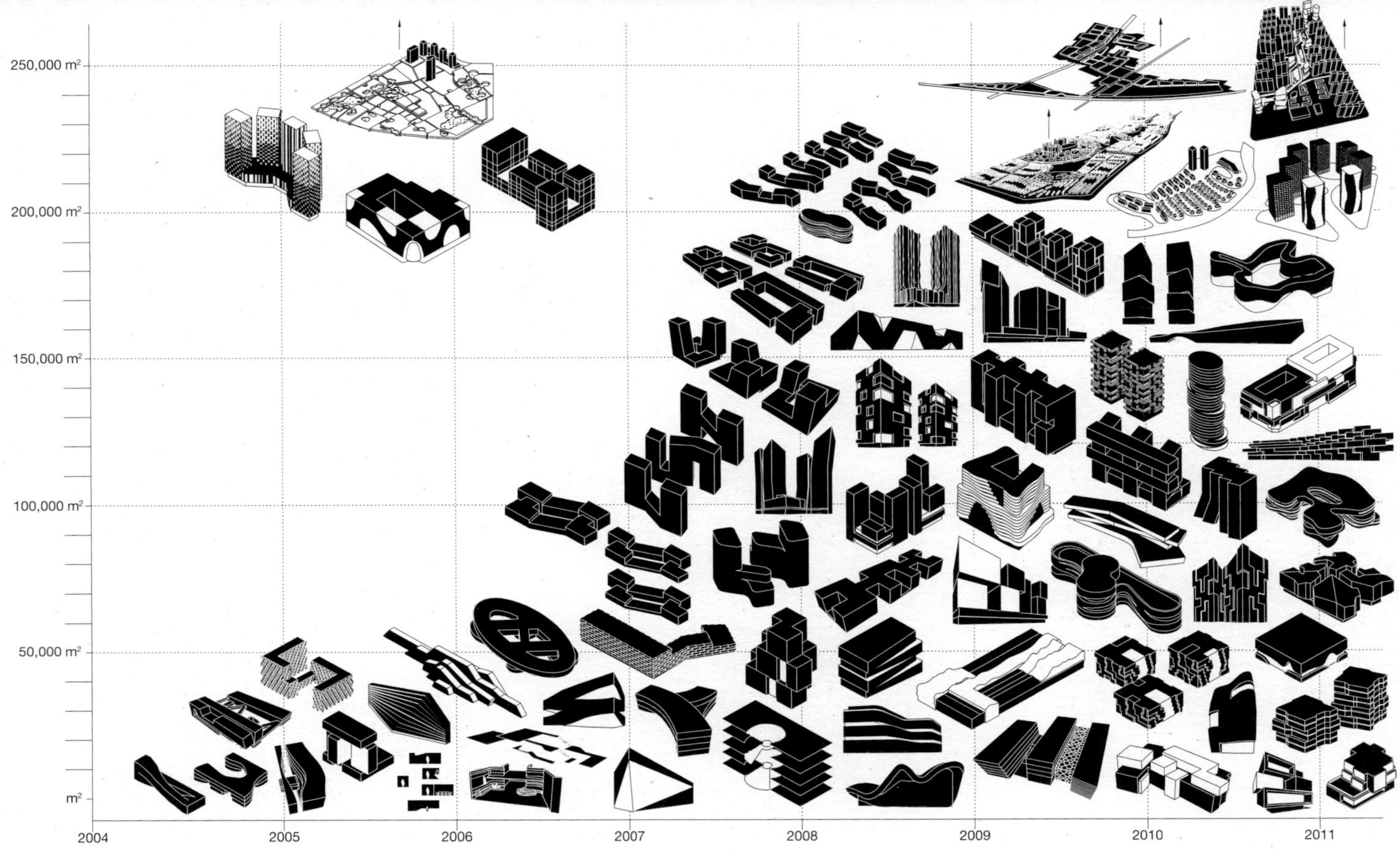
250,000 m²
200,000 m²
150,000 m²
100,000 m²
50,000 m²
m²
2004
2005
2006
2007
2008
2009
2010
2011

Liuming sales centre, Beijing, 2004 p 61

Watchdata head office, Beijing, 2004 p 80

Xintiandi child day care centre, Beijing, 2005 p 84

Beijing Tobacco head office, Beijing, 2006 p 115

Ceiling at Huanyang, Beijing, 2005 p 67

Yanqing Mountain Range Hotel, Beijing, 2006 p 147

Student accommodation, Beijing Normal University, Beijing, 2006 p 120

Shangdi International Plaza, Beijing, 2005–2007 p 157

Shoutinanlu office, Beijing, 2005 p 144

Kelejia live-work complex, Beijing, 2007–2009 p 179

Huan Yang Mansion, Beijing, 2007 p 208

IBM China R&D head office, Beijing, 2007–2009 p 225

Waterstone Sales Center, Beijing, 2007 p 174

ABB Demo Center, Beijing, 2007 p 181

Longcham apartments, Beijing, 2007 p 151

Xidan 110, Beijing, 2006– p 231

Huazheng Plaza, Beijing, 2008 p 227

M13 offices, Beijing, 2007 p 162

Huanyang headquarters, Beijing, 2008 p 200

Chaoyang Urban Planning Museum, Beijing, 2009 p 249

Ordos 20+10 sustainable offices, Ordos, under construction

Tiandi Plaza, multi-use retail and hotel, Jinan, under construction

Egret Hotel, Fujian, under construction

Urban Exhibition Museum, Xianghe, 2010, under development

Shunfeng head office, Ningde, under construction

HAYA retail office, Beijing, 2009

Jingdalu apartments, Fuzhou, under construction

Creative Design District (CDD), Beijing, under construction

Lianjiang villas, Fujian, under construction

Ordos 20+10 sustainable offices, Ordos, under construction

IMAX, Shijiazhuang, 2011, under development

Master plan for Xiasha, Hangzhou, 2011, under development